Backpacking into Darkness

Darcie Silver

I have tried to recreate events, locales and conversations
from my memories of them. In order to maintain their
anonymity in some instances I have changed the names of
individuals and places, so I don't get shot. I may have changed
some identifying characteristics and details such as physical
properties, occupations and places of residence

Edited by Maggy Whitehouse & Becky Mistovski
Front cover image by Luke Sargent

A CIP catalogue record for this book is available from the
British Library.

ISBN: 978-1-9164056-0-8 (paperback)

Visit: www.darciesilver.com
           Twitter: @DarcieSilver

Dedication

This book is dedicated to my darling wife Natalie. You are the bravest, strongest most beautiful person I have ever met and I adore you. Thanks for putting up with me.

Prologue

"It's bad news I'm afraid. There's no easy way to say this but there's nothing else we can do for your eyesight. It could last six months to a year, maybe a little longer. We don't know when exactly it will go. There is no current treatment. I'm so sorry."

We could hear the words but they weren't going in. A feeling of nausea washed over us and tunnel vision set in. No, this can't be. Why? How? Please let this be a nightmare we will wake up from.

So there we were, sat in the doctor's surgery with tears streaming down our faces as we both sobbed in each other's arms, and it was at that point, that very moment, that we decided to leave our jobs, our flat and the world we knew; to pack our bags and see the world whilst Natalie still had vision.

Most people go backpacking when they're students or wait for 50 years and do it when they retire. Natalie was in her 20s and on the corporate ladder working as a purchasing officer and I was in my 30s working in marketing. We had all the stresses of being young adults; money, jobs, money, deadlines, money, a new car engine because I forgot to put oil in the car for a year, money, money, money. This was not a good time to stop everything and go on an indefinite holiday but what was the alternative? Sit and wait for her to go blind? That was not an option.

So, we would see as much of the world as we could because suddenly nothing else mattered. And what could possibly go wrong? My wife Natalie, a beautiful woman with rapidly diminishing eyesight and me her transgender wife? I was born a man externally but have lived as the woman I am for more than eight years.

It would turn out that everything that could go wrong, would. Mostly in hilarious ways. So this is our adventure. It's not depressing, don't worry.

*

Chapter One

27.06.17. Tuesday. London.

I started the day of departure by wrestling Natalie's ridiculously over packed bag down the stairs and out of the house. Saying she over packs doesn't do it justice. Never mind the kitchen sink, she'd bring the whole kitchen, the house it's attached to, the street and just about anything not glued to bedrock. In fact if it wasn't for my endless whining about how needless all the shit she packs is, I reckon she'd take the garden with her and possibly half of next door's because they have got a particularly pretty tree. Get this gem of a fact for an example, she brought with her backpacking 37 pairs of knickers. Why? What possible reason is there for that? She's not incontinent unless she's hidden it very well for 12 years. Thirty-seven pairs of knickers? And high heels? Yes, I love high heels. I would gladly buy every pair on the planet to wear, hug and generally drool over but they are about as useful to a backpacker as a lawnmower. Leave them at home where they are safe. Other gems she took with her included a medicine bag containing the cure for every single ailment on Earth. Should we have caught trench foot, the bubonic plague, leprosy or anal warts she'd have the cure. The medicine bag weighed three kilos. I tried to explain that most of the places we were going also had pharmacies but it was useless and only reminded her of more medicine to buy.

Me: Make sure you've got cowpox medicine.
Natalie: Wait we don't have cowpox medicine?
Me: Natalie, please, this is ridiculous. Does cowpox

even exist?

Natalie: I'm going to the chemist to find out.

We closed the door on our flat and the world as we knew it and started our round the world trip. We made it as far as the end of the drive and that's when the trouble started because the taxi driver who we estimated to have been over two thousand years old was old-fashioned and wouldn't let us put the bags in his boot ourselves but unfortunately he couldn't actually do it himself so we had to watch him struggle.

Me: Can I help?
Ancient taxi man: No, no. I'll do it.
Me: But this bag weighs about 89 kilos because it's full of her, um, everything, including, Mr. Taxi man, get this, 37 pairs of knickers.
Natalie: Darcie, shut up.
Ancient taxi man: I'm doing it.
Me: Please let me help.
Ancient taxi man: No, no. I've got it.
Me: I have a car jack you can borrow if you want. A winch perhaps? Maybe we could call in a chopper?

We eventually arrived at the airport and checked in with minimum fuss, which made a nice change. Normally airports are somewhere that involve hideous amounts of cringing and embarrassment for me due to the fact that I'm transgender and it's a whole load more obvious in certain lights than I'd like. Check in staff and security look at me, my passport, me, my passport at least five times before building up the courage to ask why it says I'm male when I'm dressed as a woman, with a dress, three centimetres of makeup on and to top it off, fake boobs.

Me: Well you see it's not that easy to change that part of the passport so how about you just wave me on through because this is fucking killing me.

Security: Look Mr, Mrs. Darcie or whatever you are.... I'm going to have to ask you to stand on this counter in front of everyone and show us all your genitals. Hold on a second... "This is a tannoy announcement, Gender checking being carried out on a questionable tranny at gate number 22"

But all the dread and fear of the airport had been in vain. We checked in and passed through security, easily boarded the plane and before we knew it we were in Sri Lanka.

*

Chapter Two

We collected our bags and were just about to leave the airport when the worst thing possible happened: Natalie spotted a candle shop. Now I don't mind the odd candle if it's dark, there's no electricity and no other source of light, but what I do object to is nine million of them all around the house. Everywhere you look there's a fucking candle. I have enough troubles in my life without having to compete for oxygen with my wife's collection of 28 billion fucking candles. It's an obsession and right before we set off on a round the world trip with bags already bulging with medicine, knickers and high bloody heels, buying lumps of useless bloody candle wax seemed to me to be exceptionally daft.

Natalie: Oooh, look candles! Wow, that one's beautiful isn't it?
Me: To be quite honest darling, I have seen prettier looking turds.
Natalie: You're just saying that.
Me: Well yes, but we have approximately 30 billion too many of the pointless waxy bastards already. We can't have anymore. No. Where are you going to put them? In the bed? In the shared bathrooms? We are backpacking round the world, the last thing we need apart from high heels, a fully stocked pharmacy and 37 pairs of knickers are bloody candles.

Obviously she couldn't hear me. No, the essence of candle wax had seeped into her brain and blocked out all her senses and she was powerless to stop herself being drawn into the shop. Thinking quickly I grabbed her by the bra strap to control her movement like some sort of massive puppet. This was pretty effective until she retaliated and did the same to me. And so there we were having been in Sri Lanka for four minutes, stood in the main arrivals hall having a massive bra strap war. This was greatly amusing to just about everyone who got a free fucked up lesbian show.

A couple of hours later and with a bag full of bloody candles we got to the guesthouse delirious with tiredness. I'd like to say the guesthouse was merely a shit hole. We were on a budget and didn't expect luxury but this was in the realm of being uninhabitable. For a start it stank. We discovered why when we opened the bedside draw and discovered a pile of semi decomposed French fries. You know when you do a double take because you can't quite believe what you're seeing? Well I did about four of them.

"They look like French fries, they are French fries. Natalie, why are there rotting French fries in the drawer?" Fuck knows how long they'd been there but I could tell they were really old because they tasted terrible. Maybe it was a thing in Sri Lanka? European hotels have a Bible in the bedside drawer and Sri Lankan ones have French fries? The rotting potato in the drawer was not our biggest concern however, no, that would be the bathroom which would have been fine if you didn't mind washing in a filthy box that stank like an open sewer and had most of the planet's mosquitoes residing in it. On the positive side, the bathroom did have lots of hot water. On the negative side however there was no cold water. So turning the shower on released a deluge of water and steam so fucking hot you instantly poached your face off. As amazing as poaching yourself in a mosquito-filled room that stank of sewage sounds, it was not on our bucket list.

*

28.06. Wednesday. Colombo, Sri Lanka.

After what an optimist might call a shit night's sleep we got up, blanched ourselves in the volcano shower and made our way to the local hospital to get the upcoming eye treatment we had booked before leaving the UK.

Natalie's eyesight is declining fast and she's on a whole heap of drugs to try and slow it down. It was one of the biggest hospitals in the country but it was old and in the process of being renovated and was dirty, chaotic and full of mosquitoes. The staff however were excellent, friendly and super helpful. The consultant was lovely and told us that we could have the treatment there in a few weeks' time and she would organise everything. The rest of the day was spent walking through Colombo drinking mango juice and eating curry. The city had high-rise buildings like you'd see is any major city but next to them old red-tiled colonial-era houses. In between there were street markets with people haggling over exotic fruits, vegetables and spices, the scents mixing with the traffic fumes, telling even someone with limited sight that we were somewhere oriental and exciting.

Buddhist and Hindu temples stand shoulder-to-shoulder with mosques and churches each with their own pilgrims and total social cohesion. There is no segregation in society everyone just gels, which is how it should be. We wandered here and there inhaling the strange scents and enjoying the bustle of buyers and sellers and then marvelled at the beauty of Viharamahadevi Park with its abundant trees and slightly-tired greenery before pottering through Pettah, a maze of streets and alleyways stuffed with colourful silks and cottons, gold and silver, and colonial-era antiquities, reeking stalls of dried fish that made me gag, electrical stuff, clothes and footwear. Luckily for me, Natalie did not spot any candles though, to be fair, a few scented ones might have alleviated the grossness of the room where we slept.

*

29.06. Thursday. Colombo, Sri Lanka.

Even though we'd only been in Colombo a day, we made our way to the train station to catch our train to Kandy. We planned to stay in Colombo for longer when Natalie had her eye treatment in the coming weeks but for the moment we wanted to go and see this Sri Lanka place and also find somewhere that had a shower that didn't melt our faces off.

The train was clean and habitable apart from the ride itself which was about as smooth as a badger's ring piece. I can only assume the track was so old it was last re-laid by dinosaurs. We never thought we'd experience turbulence in a train. We bounced in our sweltering seats for four long torturous hours before we arrived in Kandy, which is Sri Lanka's second city. Now, normally when we travel, it's Natalie who picks the hotels and hostels because she's got style and taste and

I always pick shit places. But this time I had done it because Natalie couldn't see the options on the screen and although she normally manages I didn't want to stress her so early in the trip. (We bought an iPad shortly after which when zoomed in means she can use it almost normally.) True to form the place I chose was even worse than the home of the mouldy French fries. Calling it shit would be too nice. No, this place was condensed shit wrapped up in the carcass of a rotting pig and placed inside a cow's rectum for a year.

For a start the cack-fest was in the middle of the fucking jungle and I distinctly remember it *not* saying it was in the middle of the fucking jungle on the webpage when I booked it. The problem with the fucking jungle is, well, everything. I know it's full of mystery, magnificence, jaw-dropping beauty and all that but it's also full of mosquitoes, creepy crawlies and worst of all, spiders. Spiders are the worst things on Earth ever and I absolutely hate them. The room we were shown had one such eight-legged bastard in the corner of the room and, I'm not kidding; it was the size of my fucking hand. I promptly had a complete fit in which I'm told I actually briefly levitated before running outside whilst flapping like a chicken and going berserk. This was greatly amusing for everyone including Natalie who thinks it's cute that I'm scared of spiders. She on the other hand has no such fear of them and said calmly said that we could make do. Yes, we can make do if you have some fucking petrol and a lighter. That's the only way to make a spider-filled room habitable, burn the fucking bloody thing down and build a new one. After practically crying, we were offered a family room instead. This was only fractionally better.

There were no eight-legged monsters in the corner but instead it was dirty on a scale not seen since the Great International Dirt Exhibition of 1812, which according to historical accounts was so dirty there was only one survivor who didn't instantly die from bacterial infections. Also, something else I hated about the place, and I don't want to sound too weird, but the walls were painted a livid lime green colour and I have wholly irrational issues with bright green walls. I'm pretty easy going with all other wall colours with the exception of bright green because green is a shit colour and will be banned when I'm **Ruler** of the World. What's the thought process behind painting your guesthouse bright green though?

Moron: Oh hello, Mr. Hardware Store Man, perhaps you can help? I need to paint some walls in my guesthouse. What colour should we choose?
Hardware store: Okay how about a nice magnolia?
Moron: No, no. I don't think so.
Hardware store: Okay, perhaps a shade of white?
Moron: Are you mentally sound? White?
Hardware store: Um, peach colour?
Moron: No. God no! What's wrong with you? Were you dropped on your head as a child? What I want is green, bright fucking green.
Hardware store: Okay then, good choice sir. Out of interest, can I interest you in any poo-coloured wallpaper?
Moron: Oooh, yes please. Now you're talking.
Hardware store: And some piss yellow carpet perhaps?
Moron: Yes, yes, yes. You are a man of amazing taste if I may say so?
Hardware store: Um thanks? (shouting to back of

shop) Oi, Barry! Remember how you said I would never sell any snot green paint, piss yellow carpet or poo coloured wallpaper? Well you owe me ... hold on let me try to remember the bet ... ah yes, 8000 pints of beer.

Let me continue to describe the epic shitness of this place. There were cigarette butts under the bed, the bathroom stank of piss and there were more mosquitoes than anywhere else on the fucking planet. There was a mosquito net over the bed, which had a massive hole, cut in it, seemingly on purpose I should point out. The bed was harder than a slab of granite and there was a pane of glass missing in the window so that any of the planet's remaining mosquitoes that hadn't already made their way into the room could pop in for a snack. It was just cack.

Annoyingly however, the owner of the place happened to be the nicest guy in the world and he made us laugh so that made it a bit better.

In the evening we went for a little walk in the jungle which, apart from the mosquitoes, bugs, spiders and spike covered plants was lovely... right up until we walked past a sign warning of the danger of big cats, as in the type as in the type that eat people. Oh great! I've always wanted to be eaten by a fucking leopard. In fact it's on my Christmas list every year. Please Santa, I've been such a good girl this year, please get me a giant fucking cat, which will eat me.

No! What one is supposed to do with this big cat warning was a bit of a mystery to us. "Oh look a warning sign for man-eating cats, Well, I do have pockets full of catnip but now after seeing this sign for man-eating cats I will empty them out" There's fuck all anyone can do and now we're both scared shitless. We really didn't want to be eaten so we ran back to the now welcoming shitfest of a guesthouse where we sat and drank tea.

At this point I think I'll tell you why this room was especially bad. You see two weeks previously I'd decided to come off hard-core antidepressants as I was on an insanely high dose, supposed to be enough to make a suicidal elephant dance around in an ecstatic delirium of pure joy. But I'm only little and they were doing more bad than good so I decided to try coming off them. To start with, all was going strangely well and I wasn't depressed but I had the unexpected problem that I was constantly horny which let me tell you was really annoying. Yes, we love each other but neither of is normally very highly sexed but for the two weeks I had been off the antidepressants I had been the horny-eyed sex monster. Luckily, Natalie was liking it and we had lived our lives in one long sex-athon which was mostly fun apart from the side effect of us both hobbling round with sore wrecked genitals. I have no doubt everybody was wondering if we've been in some sort of accident. So having a green revoltingly filthy room with a hard dirty bed was not exactly conducive to the pursuit of sex because Natalie was having none of it. So I hated the room even more.

With Natalie out of action and my horniness only getting stronger everything was starting to look attractive, stray dogs, table legs, cars, the guesthouse itself, the ground. Frankly any man-eating leopards would have had to contend with me having sex with them before they got chance to eat me. Even the spiders were nervous.

We stayed in for the rest of the day and chatted to three Indian tourists, one of whom kept burping in our faces which was gross. In the evening we went into the bug-filled shower. Now we weren't expecting much and we were not disappointed because despite the jungle being a billion degrees this guesthouse had somehow found a way to pump water directly from the Arctic. So we'd gone from a hotel which burnt us alive to one that froze us rigid. It was just awesome.

*

30.06. Friday. Kandy, Sri Lanka.

I woke up stupidly early at 5.30am which is another withdrawal symptom from antidepressants. I thought I'd be proactive though and was as annoying as possible hoping Natalie would wake up to keep me company. This did not succeed so I blocked my number and called her. This did the trick really well and she woke up. Unfortunately I'd forgotten I'd already done this trick before and had been caught out. She instantly woke up and told me off for being "a completely insensitive stupid selfish little bitch." Still, she was awake which was the important thing.

I sat in the communal room drinking tea waiting for the angry Natalie to emerge. Eventually she did and I did my best, cutest most innocent smile hoping she wouldn't beat me to death. I quickly asked her if she'd heard the annoying bird that squawked outside our window all day and night and we spent half an hour bitching about the annoying feathery gimp instead of me selfishly waking her up. Honestly, although I'm an animal loving vegan, I would have slapped that bird in the beak. It was so annoying. It never even moved. It just sat there and squawked 24 hours a day for the entire duration of our stay. I even went out to try and make it move but it didn't care.

Then came breakfast, which we were told, was $4 a day. Now for a bright green painted, insect filled dirty shit hole with no hot water in a cheap as fuck country, a $4 breakfast is mega-expensive let me tell you. It's approximately $3.85c too expensive but like I said the owner of the hostel was super nice so we thought, oh well, let's have it just the once. I was asked what I'd like and said just some toast please. Natalie asked for an omelette.

Now what turned up was either hilarious or insulting I can't decide which. Natalie was given a wafer-thin omelette smaller than her perfect, dainty hand. I on the other hand got handed a plate, which had, no exaggeration, 36 pieces of toast piled up in a fucking tower. I don't know what he was trying to tell me but experience suggests it was along the lines of, "eat a loaf of bread and you will be cured of freaky girl disease and be a proper man" or more likely "you are fat." On principle I ate the lot. At least I can laugh at it now. I have a history of bulimia and anorexia and being given a loaf of bread just for myself would have totally messed with my head until not that long ago.

Shortly after breakfast Natalie plucked up the courage to have an ice shower. I on the other hand had decided smelling was a much better option. I was sat alone in the common room happily drinking tea when of the Indian guests came over to tell me that I must have brought great shame to my family and if I was in India I could be killed. Then he told me that Natalie was beautiful and could do better. So many people in the world are mean to transgender people. I just don't get it.

Well fuck, if we had a choice about being like this believe me we wouldn't pick this, no one would pick this. It's a horrible thing being transgender and anyone that says otherwise is a fucking liar. I've hated it my entire life. I'd much prefer either to be a boy in a boy's body or a girl in a girl's body or just plain gay. But no, I'm some monstrous fucked-up mix with the wrong brain-body-mix, which has led to a life of hell, stress, bullying and a mountain of mental problems. In my case I'm a woman who also likes other women so I am a lesbian. But I'm cursed with having the body of a man including a massive hideous penis stuck to my body, which I should point out, my wife and soul mate is rather fond of. But people always ask why I don't just live with her like a man because "it's the same thing." Well I just can't, that's why. I just can't. It makes my skin itch. It's like living your entire life as a lie. Like spending your life in a costume putting on an act. It's tiring being a fraud and being in a false character all the time; it's intolerable. I did it for long enough to know that once I came out I was never going back.

Yes I am lucky to have found my beautiful wife but I don't need to feel any shittier about my existence than I already do. She has a hard time being with me and people wonder how she copes, whether she even finds me attractive but we are soul mates. I would love her regardless of how she looked and she feels the same about me. Life has given us a shit hand but we have love and when the times get hard and we get abuse, threats of violence, actual violence, stares, insults and knowing that just about everyone is talking about us behind our backs, we do, at least, have that to hold onto.

If you're straight and reading this, imagine being forced to wear the clothes of the opposite sex all your life? It's like wearing the football shirt of your rivals' team your entire life. It makes your skin crawl; it hurts you, it's just wrong and you just can't ignore it; being labelled something you're not; having to act in a never-ending pantomime. You hide it and pretend it's not there until one day the burden gets too much and you either come out or die. It's that simple really.

Of course I didn't say any of this to him. I froze like I always do, then went to tell Natalie who wanted to kill him. We decided to calm down and talk to them later in the day. We got ready and asked the guesthouse owner for a lift through the jungle into town where we hired a tuk tuk for the day to see the town's sights. Beautiful old Buddhist temples perched on top of rocky ancient hills, stunning waterfalls, wild rivers and rice paddies as far as the eye could see. It was entrancing. Along the way we stopped every few metres to be shown a new jungle plant by the driver, which we would have found interesting had he told us in a language we actually spoke.

In the evening when we got back to the guesthouse we saw our bedroom door open and everything had been moved to the side. We politely asked the owner what the actual fuck was going on and were told, "Very busy day many local people." Unbelievably, our shit room had been sublet to some locals to have sex in — the primary function of our guesthouse was as a local sex pad. We couldn't believe it. We were so pissed off. You know a place is shit when they rent your room out for a few hours for locals to use for sex. We were so shocked we didn't know how to respond. We had already paid for the shitfest and apart from that, we were in the middle of a man-eating cat-filled jungle and this really didn't really give us too many options to stay anywhere else that didn't involve certain death by being eaten.

Whilst we sat there seething with anger at the thought at sleeping in a brothel bed, I thought it would be a good idea to write them a nice online review.

Trip Advisor Reviews.

XXXXXX Guesthouse, Kandy... AKA Shithole Jungle Fuck Pad, Spider-Fest Mosquito-Ville Local Brothel Fuck Hole.

What did you like most about XXXXXX Shithole?
Well I particularly liked the mosquitoes. I've always felt that people give them a hard time. Just because they cause the deaths of millions of people and are the biggest cause of disease worldwide doesn't mean they don't have feelings too. XXXXX Shithole Guesthouse helped look after these persecuted poor little souls by opening their hearts and windows to them giving them a safe place to live. It was an honour to share a room with so many of them. The hole cut in the mosquito

net let us get up close and personal with these beautiful little understood tiny things where we got a chance to feed them with the use of our own blood... what an honour.

We also liked the fact our room was sublet by the hour for local people to have sex in. According to popular belief people like sex. It not only keeps you warm but some people say it makes babies. I don't know about that, it seems a bit far-fetched to me but still doing the sex can be fun and giving local people the opportunity to do the sex on the bed we'd paid for was nice and we felt good knowing that we may have helped make a baby.

What did you like least about XXXXXX Shithole?
Nothing. It was absolute Nirvana. All I want to do in life is be able to return and live out my days in this glorious slice of heaven.

What did you think about the location of XXXXXX Shithole?
It's amazing ... if you are a mosquito, spider or fucking leopard. Also it is great for locals looking for a bright green room to have sex in and then having a freezing shower to cool your smoking genitals.

Did you enjoy the food?
Well my wife said the omelette was delicious, all the single mouthful of it. My 36 pieces of toast piled into an impossible tower was lovely and didn't freak me out at all. At $4 it was at least 400% too much but it was nice to pay for such quality toast. Forcing myself to eat it all definitely didn't cause me to have constipation for two days afterwards.

Would you return to XXXXXX Shithole?
We'd rather die.

Rate XXXXXX Shithole from 1 to 10?
Minus twenty five billion.

*

01.07. Saturday. Kandy, Sri Lanka.

We spent the day in and around Kandy. In the centre of town there is a lake, which is full of fish, I don't know what type, but they weren't goldfish or tuna fish and that's the extent of my fish knowledge. Around the lake lots of people sold special fish food to feed the slimy little bastards. I say special, it was popcorn, so we bought some and fed them for a while. After leaving a lot of fish very happy we walked around the main temple of Kandy, the imposing Temple of the Tooth, so called because it is the home of the relic tooth of the Buddha. I do hope when I'm dead people take my various body parts and keep them as relics. Well not my genitals that would be a huge insult if in hundreds of years people are praying to my severed decomposed penis. Although on the other hand, at least it would be finally off my body. We sat on a rock outside and watched the world go by. The whole day then took a wet turn because it started raining so hard that when it hit the ground it bounced back off again. We were drenched.

*

02.07. Sunday. Kandy & Trinco, Sri Lanka.

In the morning we got the tuk tuk to the bus station for our trip to Trinco. The bus station was mayhem. Imagine a small car park big enough for three buses, now ram 12 in there, a billion people, a thousand rickshaws, 40-degree heat, dust, noise, dirt and some random cows and you're close. It was the worst place on Earth. Somehow we found the right bus got on and went straight to the middle seats because lots of buses crash and although I love being rear-ended by huge lumps of fast moving metal and occasionally getting my front smashed in, the middle seats offer more chance of survival (I have absolutely no idea why I just wrote this).

The journey was pretty horrific. The bus was hotter than Satan's asshole and we struggled not to vaporise and die. I resorted to pouring water on tissue and dabbing it on us. Poor Natalie struggled more than me. She's Scandinavian and as such finds temperatures over minus 20 degrees Celsius too hot. It was not a good situation, especially as our only tissue started to dissolve and left us looking like we had some kind of weird fucked up skin disease. The locals were looking at us like we were lepers.

Five hours of hell later, covered in dissolved tissue and with my tits literally sweated down to my waist, we arrived in Trinco or to give its full name Trincomalee. Trinco is a beach town on the East coast. It is a lovely and pretty town but that's not the commendable thing, no the commendable thing would be that it's hotter than the inside of a volcano. In fact I'd go as far as to say there are penguins that have been force-fed chilli peppers, been basted in goose fat, wrapped in loft insulation and thrown in erupting volcanoes that would be less hot.

The guesthouse was really nice. It was directly on the beach and had the huge advantage over the previous place of not being a filthy spider-filled brothel. It had air conditioning which was so lovely we both wanted sex with it. It didn't have green walls which was another bonus. Instead it had white walls with various splats and splodges, which looked disturbingly like they came out of people's bodies. Oh and once again we still didn't have hot water. This time we just a tepid sprinkling of mist from a shower head so high off the ground most of the mist blew away or evaporated before it hit us. The shower would have been totally unusable had it not been for the Sri Lankan toilets because, interestingly, the toilets have a hosepipe attached so one can clean ones anus hole. This hosepipe did have lots of pressure so we washed ourselves using that. This probably explained why we both quickly became super ill.

In the evening we walked down the beach path to find a local restaurant called the Crab Shack, which weirdly reminded me of an old girlfriend. I ordered vegetarian curry, which was so spicy I lost the ability to talk, and could only croak. Natalie ordered ice cream, which I ate, for her to put out the flames.

Quotes from the last few days:

Me: I think the question on everybody's lips is, in Holland is Winnie the Pooh called Vincent von Shit?

Me: I wouldn't want to work in a cockpit. It sounds terrible. A pit of cocks.

Natalie: All I can taste is the sweat that's poured down my face into my mouth.
Me: That's the most disgusting thing I've ever heard.

Me: I can smell egg.
Natalie: I can smell kebab but I'm pretty sure that's you.
Me: Is that why you go out with me?
Natalie: Yes, I love a girl that smells like kebab.

Me: You need to get out of the sun you're going red like a mushroom.
Natalie: Mushrooms aren't red.
Me: They are when you dip them in paint.

Natalie: I'm freezing do you have a hat?
Me: No, but you can put my knickers on your head.

*

03.07. Monday. Trinco, Sri Lanka.

The only problem with staying on the beach was what to wear. You see my tits aren't real and I have a penis, which I absolutely hate. Yeah having a huge thing is the dream of most blokes and the desire of their partners but I'm not a bloke. It's just stuck to me like some kind of huge parasitic cucumber. I'd cut the bastard off if it weren't for Natalie who is rather fond of the thing. Well you just make do with life don't you?

So hitting the beach or pool anywhere with the

likelihood of exposing the contents of my underwear is avoided at all costs which is why I generally sit on the beach in a full suit of armour. Unfortunately due to the airline's ridiculous weight restrictions I couldn't bring my suit of armour so I spent the day hiding in the shadows where I made friends with a puppy and tried not to die from heatstroke.

*

04.07. Tuesday. Trinco, Sri Lanka.

We decided to go diving because it's an amazing thing to do. It's a bit like flying in an alien world but fuck me, it's expensive. Thirty pounds per person! For that money I want to meet The Little Mermaid and ask her a thing or two about her vagina or lack of it that I think a lot of us would like to know. Maybe speak my mind to that Sebastian crab prick. "Oh, I'm just Ariel's friend." No you're not, you exoskeletoned knob, we all know your game.

You don't want to hear about how I hid my bits because you'd probably be sick, but it's a damn sight easier to hide them than wearing a swimming costume. So we all wet suited up and got onto a boat and before you could say, "Ariel, where's your vagina?" We were 25 metres unda da sea, unda da sea. Diving is pretty much the same every time. "Look a fish, look a fish, is that The Little Mermaid? Aghh a shark." It was pretty good until halfway through when Natalie suddenly became the most buoyant thing on the fucking Earth and kept rocketing to the top dragging me with her. It's not good to shoot up to the surface without a safety stop. We have enough medical woes without getting the fucking bends. The diving instructor we were with was about as useful as an underwater hairdryer and helped by doing absolutely nothing. We tried everything to make her sink but she had clearly turned into polystyrene. It was a bit of a let down. My theory, which she disputes, is that her breakfast consisting of pancake and curry had created an abundance of gas, which is rather buoyant.

In the evening we went to the Crab Shack again. We ate curry so spicy we were both reasonably sure of imminent death. I doubt eating hot coals would have been any more painful. We think the staff made it insanely spicy on purpose for a laugh. "Let's watch the fucked up lesbians die." They thought it was hilarious as we gasped for air, choked then both got the hiccups. There's no way anyone could have eaten it. It was like eating pure pain. We downed glass after glass of water but were in agony. Then they brought us of all things, pineapple juice, which they insisted, would work better at extinguishing the flames. We have no idea what the substance was but I estimate contained approximately zero pineapple. We don't know what it contained, but if I found out it came out an animal's anus I wouldn't be surprised.

As we were sat there trying not to spontaneously combust the strangest thing happened. Inside Natalie's handbag we randomly found a packet of seven huge hair combs. We literally have no idea where they came from. We don't even use combs and if we did we wouldn't have seven of them in our bag. It was, and still is a complete mystery. We kept checking for more magic objects like for example, gold. Yeah if something was going to magic itself into our bags why did it have

to be bloody combs? We want gold goddamnit.
GOLD!

Quotes of the last few days:

Natalie: If our landlord put a kitchen like that in here
I'd have sex with the oven.

Natalie: After your shower can you bring the axe to
open the coconut?
Me: I'm not sure that's such a good idea. The only
thing scarier for these people than a tranny is a semi
naked tranny carrying an axe.

Me: You're a stupid head.
Natalie: No I'm a good girl head.

Natalie: Don't worry little fellow we won't eat you
(Natalie talking to an orange).

Me: I'm going to weapon you with my sharp nail.
Natalie: Um, weapon isn't a verb. Ow, that hurts.
Me: Yeah, if you're naughty I'm going to weapon you.
Natalie: Fine I'm going to tickle you with my tickle
weapon.
Me: Agh no I don't like the tickle weapon. Ceasefire,
ceasefire.

*

05.07. Wednesday. Trinco & Jaffna Sri Lanka.

In the morning we got a tuk tuk to the bus station
for our journey to Jaffna. The buses in Sri Lanka are

really good apart from the heat, the dust, the seats, the lack of air-conditioning, the buses themselves, the standard of driving and above all else the Bhangra music played at a volume so goddamn loud it begins to actually cause physical pain. Apart from all these things we had the other pressing issue in that the 13 inches of makeup I plaster to my face began to melt and I started to look like some kind of diseased leper. I looked a bit like if someone took a Ken doll, covered its head in cheese slices and meringue and microwaved it for an hour. Natalie tried to reassure me but I was sure I looked like a monster. I hate to think what the locals thought — "Oh wow, look, foreigners ... arghh, arghh. What the fuck is it? What happened to its face? Arghh, arghh hit it with the stick. Arghh, kill it."

There are very few tourists in Sri Lanka outside the main resorts so you are quite a novelty. Added to this the fact that the Sri Lankans are the friendliest people on the planet who are practically all fluent in English and it makes it a lovely experience. Still at some point every time we leave the comfort of our room this happens:

Oh my god look, white people! Giggle, giggle.
Oh my god I think they're lesbians. Giggle, giggle, giggle.
Oh my god is she...? No this is too much (head explodes).

So it makes being on a packed bus pretty interesting. We do try to tone it down here so we blend into the background a bit more. I know the more radical elements of the LGBTQ community would probably disagree and say we should be having sex on restaurant tables and fisting each other senseless to show our gay pride but they are wrong. People don't even hold hands in Sri Lanka for example. There is no public display of affection. It's very conservative, so two lezzas holding hands would be a big no-no, let alone if one of them was born with the wrong bits between their otherwise girly legs. We are proud but don't want to be disrespectful or be lynched.

Still I reckon two clearly in love women was entertaining enough for them.

On one of our change-over buses there were no seats and no less than five separate people got up and insisted we sat down. What do you when old people stand up for you on the bus and refuse to take no for an answer?

Lovely old Local: Please sit down. Where you from, Miss?
Me: I'm from the UK but please I'm happy to stand.

Lovely old Local: No, sit down. Is okay.
Me: No please, I like standing. At home I just stand all day.
Lovely old local: No, no. Please take seat.
Me: Sit down before you fall down, Dr. Jones.
Lovely old Local: Who's Dr. Jones?
Me: Fine, we'll sit down. Thank you so much. Oh god, the rest of the bus are looking at us like we just forced two old people to stand up so the young white people could sit down.

Seven hours later we arrived in Jaffna, which is right at the top of Sri Lanka. It's where the baddies in the civil war lived and for 30 years it was totally off limits to tourists and Sri Lankans alike. We got a tuk tuk to the guesthouse and were delighted with it. It was clean, it had clean bed sheets and best of all unlike all the other hovels the walls weren't covered in body juices. We went for a curry and went to sleep.

*

06.07. Thursday. Jaffna, Sri Lanka.

Here's a tip for all the budding travellers out there: don't travel halfway around the world to a place where the temperature makes doing anything impossible. Jaffna was 48 degrees with humidity of such hideousness it effectively made it 65 degrees and pretty much impossible to do anything. It was the most inhospitable environment since Kermit the Frog accidentally got locked in the house of a Frenchman.

So that you too at home can experience the hideousness of Jaffna weather for yourself I have created this handy guide.

Step 1. Turn your oven to 200c.
Step 2. Climb in oven.
Step 3. Cook until dead.
Step 4. Welcome to Jaffna.

We got up and had breakfast of ... curry. Who wouldn't want to eat something so spicy your ass actually twitches? We loved it although our stomachs were rather less impressed and spent the rest of the day making it known that 8am spicy curry was a bad idea.

After breakfast we went to see the local Hindu temple, which can only be described as simply breathtaking. Hindu temples are truly a feast for the eyes. Every single space is filled with detail, colour and statues of animal's and deities. All Hindu temples are remarkably different which is unusual in other religions buildings which although beautiful in their own right, tend to follow a similar format. When you walk in a Hindu temple your jaw literally drops because it's so much for your eyes to take in. After sitting on the floor for an hour taking in the beauty of the place we realised there was nothing else to do in Jaffna and it was too fucking hot even if there was. So we tried to find the market to buy some fruit but that didn't go to plan because we were dangerously overheating. So we came up with a plan, we could walk round town and every few minutes' walk into an air conditioned shop and pretend to be interested in stuff.

Me: Okay, so how much is this tractor? Wow, okay, and does it come with sun visors? Okay, cool and can you paint it pink? Great, and um, combine harvesters? I have brand new combine harvester and I'll show you the key. No? You don't know the song. Well that was a joke. You're right, It wasn't very funny… well maybe if you knew the song, no, okay then. Right well we'd better be leaving.
Man: You take tractor?
Me: Maybe later.

We went to a few such air conditioned shops before realising that this was shit. I honestly have no idea how people in this part of the world procreate. Even me in my still perpetually horny state could barely be bothered. Although I did try.

Me: You're so beautiful, I love your body.
Natalie: Don't even think about it. I won't have sex with you unless you cover me and the bed in ice.
Me: Um, okay, give me half an hour.
Natalie: No, fuck off it's too hot.
Me: But the ice?
Natalie: I said fuck off.

In the afternoon we went for coffee which we are pretty sure had never seen a coffee bean in its life and judging by the fact it tasted like curry I can only imagine he realised he was all out of coffee so decided to invent his own out of curry spices.

Waiter: Well this looks brown they'll never know.
Me: PHPHPHPH!! What is this shit? Arghh, my mouth's on fire.
Waiter: It's coffee, Miss.
Me: No actually it's about as far from coffee as I can imagine. The only similarity is that it's brown and in a cup, and to be honest I've seen some horrific stuff involving a cup, brown liquid and two girls.

Maybe they thought it was funny, which it would have been if it had been someone that wasn't us.

In the afternoon we went for more curry because we like eating and shitting fire. The Sri Lankans eat sloppy curry with their hands instead of using cutlery, which is something we endlessly tried to emulate. This is hugely amusing for all the locals in the restaurants who gawp in amusement as we get food in every place but our actual mouths. Mainly on our clothes, faces and in our hair. So we were the typical foreigners who asked for cutlery so we could actually shovel the food into our mouths. This in turn was like the second part of the joke for the locals who thought it was hilarious. This happened about 15 times over the weeks before we gave up and decided that eating sloppy curry with hands was too difficult so we should just ask for spoons.

*

07.07. Friday. Jaffna, Sri Lanka.

We went sightseeing. It's not so interesting to write about because, well, no one gives a fuck. Okay fine I'll tell you because Natalie reckons you'll want to know. So firstly we went to a famous library, which was handily closed, then as we stood across the road we got told off for talking pictures it. Why? What are we going to do with these pictures of a library exactly? Are there secret books? Shhh, don't mention the library it's a secret, it's not there - you imagined it. We then made our way to an old church, which was closed. Following this fantastic sight we went to a memorial which wasn't closed but was shit and then we walked twenty minutes in 45.c heat to find a temple and nearly died from heatstroke. See I told you.

Quotes of the last few days:

Natalie: I like strawberry marmalade.
Me: Um, you mean jam?

Natalie: I'd love to shit on my boss's desk and leave.

Me: These grapes are weirdos. They are lumpy

weirdos.

Natalie: I know loads of people In the UK that make mouth trumpet noise.
Me: I have literally no idea what you're on about?
Natalie: Mouth trumpet noise.
Me: What the fuck are you on about?
Natalie: You're stupid.

Natalie: Wash my boobies. I don't want mushroom fungus boobies. (She had a fucked up heat induced fungal rash on her boobs)

Me: My toes feel stupid.

Natalie: So, it's okay to spit in a tissue and wipe your child's face but if I spit in a kids face and wipe it off I'll get arrested?
Me: Um, yes.

*

08.07. Saturday. Jaffna & Nuarelia, Sri Lanka.

At 5am we woke up to the sound of the stupid alarm. We rushed to the train station and jumped on our train for our 11-hour trip to Nuarelia in the mountains. The train would have been fine had it not been horrendous in every single way. For a start the seats were facing the wrong way so we were going backwards. This, for someone who gets motion sickness whilst thinking about motion sickness is decidedly not good. I believe my words were, "Oh fuck, prepare to be covered in vomit"

The carriage did at least have fans on the ceiling to blow boiling hot air into our sweaty revolting bodies. This would have been somewhat helpful had they not cleverly installed all the fan switches three seats behind where you were sat. So if we pressed our fan switch, the fan some three rows in front of us would turn on. I don't think it was normal because it confused the fuck out of everyone. Literally a hundred people on our carriage scratching their heads trying to work out what the fuck was going on.

The train journey was split in two halves, six hours to a village in the middle of nowhere called Polgahawela where we needed to switch to a different one to get to Nuarelia. Unfortunately for us we are shit at planning and there were no connecting trains that day ... or the next day but there would be one in three days' time and even this one was a slow train and would take 14 hours to get there. So we sat under a tree feeling sorry for ourselves wondering what the fuck we were going to do. At that point a friendly local guy came over to tell us our research was terrible and what had we been thinking? Yeah thanks for that Mr. Man. He also happened to tell us the only way of getting there the same day would be to take a bus for three hours then change to another bus and catch a further two buses, oh, and it was probably fully booked and would take minimum of 15 hours.

We were upset and didn't know what to do but then Natalie had the most amazing idea ever ... we'd take a rickshaw. This was pretty ridiculous because they are made for the city, they are dangerous, they have no seatbelts, doors, airbags, decent brakes, acceleration or anything you'd actually want when travelling halfway across a huge fucking country. Everybody even including the rickshaw driver thought we were insane but with a charge of £30 (about a week's wage), he still jumped at the chance to take us. We love a good insane adventure and driving through the heart of Sri Lanka in a flimsy rickshaw was a kind of insanity we thought would be hilarious, should we actually survive it.

Our first stop was the tuk tuk drivers house so he could tell his wife that two weird and insane Westerners including one he suspected to be a man wanted to be driven for seven hours across the country. She looked at us like the freaks we are as we smiled back coyly. After initial scepticism of our mental state she decided she liked us and invited us in for coffee, which was delicious. Then Raj, the driver, asked if we wanted some star fruit and we said yes so he came outside climbed a huge tree we didn't even realise was there and started throwing star fruit to us.

"Catch, catch!"
"Arghh, that's my head"
"Too slow. Catch Mrs Natalie, catch."
It was one of the funniest memories in a while having wild star fruit launched at us from a man in a tree.

With three bags of star fruit, a mango and half a bag of tea leaves, we set off. The countryside was gorgeous. Lush forests and jungle with cute villages every so often. After about an hour Raj pulled over, pointed to a fruit and told me to go and pick it; it turned out to be wild chocolate.

Should anyone want to know what the chocolate fruit tastes like, it tastes like shit! Absolute shit! It has a hard shell and needs some serious hacking with a knife to get in it, then once inside you are presented with yellow and white flesh with some the cocoa beans in the middle. All of these things tasted utterly terrible.

A short while later he stopped again and he pointed to a bush and told us to pick the fruit. Whilst I was picking them he'd told Natalie that they were coffee beans that taste vile but let's try and make her eat it anyway because it'll be funny. So as I got back they both tried to make me eat them. I however already knew it was coffee so when they told me to eat it I pretended I did and that they were really good. The look on their faces was amazing. Total shock. Then I set about throwing the remaining beans at their heads for trying to trick me.

After three hours of bumpy roads our bodies were beginning to revolt. Thankfully the most stunning waterfall on Earth was close by so we went to gawp at it. If Disney made waterfalls this thing would be it. It was out of this world. And even better because I got to practice some live comedy (I'm an aspiring comedian… come and see me!) This moment of comic genius happened when Raj pointed out a monkey in the tree I was next to and I absolutely shit myself. I leapt three feet off the ground then in a desperate bid to get away proceeded to trip over a rock and land face first in a muddy puddle.

This was without doubt the funniest thing the locals had ever seen and around 50 people laughed hysterically at me. Strangely instead of feeling embarrassed I thought it was hilarious too and laughed like a psychopath for about thirty minutes whilst still lying in the mud because getting up hadn't occurred to me. In fact I only stopped laughing when someone pointed out the monkey again and I screamed. I hate monkeys. Not just a slight dislike of the mother fuckers but I'd happily shoot every last one of them in the face. I've been attacked three times including by one who we have on video eating the poo directly out of his friend's ass hole before climbing on me, sitting on my shoulder and attacking my face with his poo-covered hands. Yeah that shit will scar you. Another time 12 Macaques ganged up on me and stole my bag, which had Pringles in. So yeah I'd shoot them all in the face if I had a choice. I even prefer spiders to monkeys such is the level of hatred and fear I have for them.

Another four hours later and we started to climb into the hills. The scenery was beautiful but it was cold and we'd cleverly only dressed ourselves in summer dresses. The logical thing an intelligent person would have done would be to ask the driver to stop so we could retrieve more clothes from our bags which were behind us in an open boot but we cleverly decided to sit there and freeze instead. We had a Pashmina scarf thing so huddled together and tried not to turn to ice.

Eventually we arrived in Nuarelia and ran into the guesthouse to try and get warm. Only the place was a fucking dump and more importantly than that it was absolutely fucking freezing which is just what you want when it's five degrees. So we asked for an electric fan heater knowing deep down that there was more chance of Jesus carrying in an industrial heater through the door whilst riding a unicorn. Unsurprisingly they didn't have one. So we went through the list of heat sources that they should have had.

Natalie: Please can you turn the heating on it's freezing?

Guesthouse Man: No heating.

Natalie: No heating? Well how do you expect us to stay here? Do we look like bloody snowman?

Guesthouse Man: Sorry, Miss.

Natalie: Sorry? You're sorry? We get hypothermia and you're sorry? Do you have a hot water bottle at least?

Guesthouse Man: No sorry miss no have. Jug hot water have?

Natalie: Um what exactly shall we do with this jug of water? Hug it? Pour it on our heads? Pour it on the bed to warm it up? I'll tell you what, why don't we go to bed and you spend the whole night pouring jugs of hot water on us to keep us warm. I'm sure it'll be more comfortable than this freezing fucking dump of a room with a damp bed, walls, floor and general fucking shitness.

Guesthouse Man: No can, sorry.

Natalie: You are a turd.

Me: Bloody hell Natalie, he just works here probably.

Natalie: Fine, whatever. We'll just freeze then.

Guesthouse Man: Thank you. You can pay now?

Me: Oh do fuck off you turd.

The room was supposed to have a hot shower which we'd been looking forward to as our first hot water in a few weeks, but it produced that little water it may as well not be there, you just stood there freezing cold as boiling hot water dripped slowly on your head.

We went to bed and froze. The bed was damp and we couldn't get warm no matter what we did. It was awful. At 3am we decided to wear all of our clothes to see if that helped but dampness has a way to get through anything and before long we were shivering again.

*

09.07. Sunday. Nuarelia, Sri Lanka.

After a night so cold a fucking snowman would have been like, "Fuck this shit I'm off to sit in the oven," we woke up trembling and huddled together like two lesbian penguins. We had a freezing "hot" shower then went into town. Our first stop was to buy me a jumper because I had no warm clothes. We found a little stall selling fake shit and thought yeah okay then. I wouldn't have minded so much had he not tried to tell us it was real when they were the most obvious shit fakes in the world with quality was so bad we could have made better tops out of twigs and elastic bands.

Jumper Man: Best quality, real brand. How many you want?
Me: Real brand? I don't think so.
Jumper Man: No, no. Is real brand, Miss.
Me: No it's not. North Face is spelled wrong.
Jumper Man: No, this is correct spelling.
Me: Um, no it's not. Nortp Face is not how it's spelt.
Jumper Man: Yes it is.
Me: Fine, you win, the whole world are wrong. It is called Nortp Face. Sorry I questioned you and your incredible knowledge of clothing brands. So anyway how much is this $2 lump of turd?
Jumper Man: Ten dollars Miss.
Me: Ten dollars? For that price I'd want 10 of them and a free cash-back gift of $20.
Jumper Man: No deal.

Me: Yeah you're telling me. I'd prefer to wear a sack than this.

Jumper Man: You want sack? Real Prada sack.

ME: No

So we left with nothing and went for a walk around town. Nuarelia is an old British hill village where all the Brits went to escape the heat of the plains during the summer. Once there they set about planting tea everywhere, which was really jolly good of them because we are rather partial to a cup of tea.

We walked around the quaint old English town, admiring it and wondering what life must have been like. Foreign rule over any people is stupid and wrong but the British knocked up some nice buildings around the world, which was pretty decent of them and definitely compensates for stealing their countries and stripping them of assets whilst subjugating their entire populations.... The post office, church, town hall and shops looked like they'd been taken out of an English village. It was weird.

In the town we spotted Natalie heaven, the only thing better than candles. A stationery shop. She's obsessed! If it wasn't for me reigning in her insane wild ways I have no doubt she'd currently be sat in a flat somewhere surrounded by candles and bloody stationery. I didn't even try and point out how much we don't need more bloody stationery because she obviously wouldn't listen and would buy a few new items for the ridiculous collection anyway.

With four new highlighters, three of which were the same colour, a pen and for some inexplicable reason a ruler, we set off for the train station to pre book our next journey back to Colombo. It's tragic to think that when she loses her sight they are products that will be almost useless to her so I even helped and pointed out a lovely eraser I thought she'd like to which she shouted at me "why would I need that?" "Yes but your highlighter pens are the same ... oh never mind, sorry."

We got a local bus through the twisting hills and old tea plantations and arrived at the train station which beautiful, old and weirdly English. Natalie asked for the tickets and then tried to explain that if possible we didn't want to be sat backwards because I'd vomit everywhere. Her demonstration of not going backwards was comedy gold. Shuffling her feet backwards whilst making wooo-wooo train noises and the 'no' sign. It was so funny, I wish I had it on video. The guy thought she was insane but eventually understood and told us it was not possible to pick the direction the seat faced.

Instead of taking the bus back through the hills we decided to walk the 20 kilometres. You know like you do when you're wearing dresses, have no warm clothing and it's about five degrees. It was so beautiful though, rolling fields of tea bushes, beautiful smiling people everywhere and everyone saying hello to us and inviting us in for tea. It was just heaven.

Right at the top of a top of a hill we found a tiny little tea shop and decided that it would be wrong not to have 12 cups each. There was a lovely local woman who worked on the tea plantation and we got chatting to her. She told us she had previously lived in the UK working in accounts. She decided that money wasn't important as we all die anyway and that the rushed, busy, money obsessed life of people in the UK have is not actually worth it so she decided to move back to Sri Lanka and now has a great happy life as a farm labourer. We loved her instantly because they are our views too. Most people in the Western world believe that money and happiness are intertwined and live their whole lives in the rat race unable to see the bigger picture that in fact this belief is nothing but a mirage, a fake and a fraud. The pursuit of money does not equal the pursuit of happiness. She told us all we need to be happy is family and friends and nothing else mattered. We agreed.

Sri Lankans are so, so friendly. It's beautiful. Everyone waves at you and says hello. Most invite you in for a drink and something to eat and they want to know about you. I used to think that Australians were the friendliest people in the world but now they have lost the top spot. Sorry Aussies you had your time at the top so skip along and catch Chlamydia from a Koala Bear because Sri Lankans are the new number one.

*

10.07. Monday. Nuarelia, Sri Lanka.

The night was spent unable to sleep because it was absolutely freezing. At about 3am Natalie had the great idea that we should just have lots of sex to stay warm. So despite neither of us really being in the mood for sex (my libido had returned to zero again) we did it four-and-a-half times. It was literally the only way to stay warm.

In the morning we got up, had a freezing shower and went out. We went for traditional breakfast where they bring you a tray with lots and lots of different fried spicy things on them then you just pay for what you eat. It's nice provided you like insanely spicy things first thing in the morning.

The town's only downside as far as I could tell was that there was a huge horse racing track in the middle of town and the locals had cottoned on to the fact that tourists like horses, so they ride around everywhere trying to get you to go horse riding. This would be fine apart from the fact that much like monkeys and spiders I am utterly terrified of horses. I have also been attacked by them twice including once nearly being killed by The Horse of Death. As such, when confronted by a horse I panic, shit myself and quickly hide behind Natalie so she can protect me/get eaten first. I'm nice like that. This has always amused people who seem to think it's funny I'm so scared of them. I've been known to have panic attacks and cry when confronted by the big stupid hairy bastards. Once in my early teens, years before I came out and during a bout of denial I was with some male friends when a policeman on a horse came over to us. I panicked and cried thus denting my image of being a tough bloke. I was mocked mercilessly for it for years. This time was much, much more terrifying though. We had our backs against a brick wall so I couldn't even run away when a man on horseback came riding over to us.

Scary Horse Riding Man: Miss, you want horse ride?
Me: Arghh. No, no, no. (Push Natalie in front of me as a barrier).

Scary Horse Riding Man: Only cheap, you come.

Me: Arghh, help me Jesus.

Scary Horse Riding Man: You scared, Miss?

Me: Yes, I'm bloody scared. Please go away.

Scary Horse Riding Man: No, this friendly horse.

Me: No, there's no such thing. Please go away.

Scary Horse Riding Man: Is Okay. Nice horse. You stroke.

Me: No, I'd prefer to head butt a spike thanks.

Scary Horse Riding Man: His name is Kamil.

Me: I don't give a fuck what his name is. Please go away or I'm going to cry. Natalie stop laughing and help me.

Natalie: You're too funny.

Me: I've told you before this isn't funny. Please help me.

Natalie: Sorry, she's scared.

Scary Horse Riding Man: Okay, just you want to ride?

Natalie: Hmm ... well, I would like to. Out of interest, why did you name your horse Camel? Did he get the hump? Hahaha?

Me: Oh, let's just stand around and joke.

Scary Horse Riding Man: No his name Kamil not camel. Haha. So, you come ride for one hour, okay. Scared girl-boy-thing stay here. Okay? Hahaha.

Me: You treacherous wench.

Natalie: No, sorry I can't. She'll be angry.

Me: Angry? I'm thinking more like divorce, you traitor. Look will you and your beast go away if she pays you to go away?

Scary Horse Riding Man: Yes okay.

So he rode away and Natalie laughed and told me how cute it was that I'm scared of them.

"Yes so cute. Haha... No, it's terrifying. When the British supermarkets were found to be selling horsemeat in their hamburgers, I was happy about it. One less horse."

I didn't say any of this because I was too busy crying and being angry at Natalie for not respecting my acute phobia of the bastards. To summarise: Fuck Horses!

Why do we say horseback riding anyway? Is there another part of the horse you can ride? It's like saying I got here by car seat. Oh, I went to Sri Lanka by plane seat. I guess some people don't use the horse's back, they sit on its face. Horse-face riding, have you heard of it?

About two hours later and my heart rate had just about returned to normal so we went for some noodles. Sri Lanka is not famous for noodles, but Natalie decided that noodles were vital to her immediate survival, so we found a noodle shack thing. Now let me try and explain the shit fest we were presented with. Okay, imagine someone pulled a handful of noodles out of their anus, well it would have smelled and tasted better than this. I don't know what they did to them but my guess is that it involved anal fluids. We couldn't even eat it. This was apart from the fact that the shack was full of most of the planet's flies. We don't mind a bit of dirt and actively avoid fancy places but this was just horrific. So we left and got a salad, which, we assumed, couldn't be that bad. Apart from tasting like curry, it was nice.

In the afternoon I got pointed at and called a fucking faggot bastard by a lovely foreign tourist. Why do people feel the need to insult me? I just don't get it. I'm not asking you to live like this. It's just so stupid. It's a bit like pointing to a child and saying, "Fuck you, you, child bastard." They can't do anything about being a child and I can't do anything about being like this. It's just pointless commenting.

At night, we sat in bed freezing our real and fake tits off even though we were wearing every item of clothing we had with us. We comforted ourselves by eating two kilos of passion fruit we'd bought and a weird blob fruit thing. We had no idea what it was but looked like Slimer from Ghostbusters. It was green, squidgy and full of green slime. It was nice as long as you didn't look at the gunge you were shovelling into your face.

As we sat there shivering I thought it was only right I leave them a nice review on Trip Advisor:

Trip Advisor Reviews.

XXXXXX Guesthouse, Nuarelia.

What did you like most about XXXXXX Guesthouse, Nuarelia?
The thing we liked the most was the fact that there was no heating whatsoever and the temperature was cold enough to give a snowman hypothermia. We had to sleep whilst wearing every item of clothing we owned which, due to the bed being damp, strangely ironed out all the creases meaning we didn't need to iron, and seeing as there was no iron presumably because that would be a heat source it was quite handy. The best thing about sleeping in a room colder than a penguin's

penis was that in order to keep warm and thus alive we had to have sex 10 times without the ability to shower. I mean the shower was amazing, who doesn't want to stand in a freezing room with slightly warm water slowly dripping on your head like some kind of torture device? It was lovely. Finally we are happy that we are almost certainly expecting a child due to having so much sex.

What did you like least about XXXXXX Guesthouse, Nuarelia?
It wasn't cold enough.

Would you return to XXXXXX Guesthouse, Nuarelia?
I have since bought a large home freezer so when I feel the need to sleep in sub-zero temperatures I simply sleep in it.

Rate XXXXXX Guesthouse, Nuarelia?
Minus 30 - The same temperature as the fucking room

*

11.07. Tuesday. Nuarelia, Sri Lanka.

For the three days we'd been in Nuarelia, Natalie had been pointing to a huge mountain and saying we should climb it. I was less excited about climbing up a ridiculously dangerous jungle covered mountain with no paths. But then I figured, who was I to stop her from doing incredibly stupid stuff whilst she can still see? So we got dressed and headed towards the thing. There were no paths, signs or any sign of human activity. I don't think anyone else would have been dumb enough to climb the fucker but here were, two pasty, white lesbians dressed like they were going to a summer party heading up the bastard. It all started off quite well and we dragged each other up the thing getting increasingly covered in mud. After an hour we were in thick jungle, and couldn't see anything but vegetation but upwards we climbed.

After another 30 minutes we walked around a huge tree and there was a weird shrine covered in red paint or blood. Fuck knows what it was. It freaked the fuck out of us because there were no paths, this was thick jungle and it was ridiculously steep and muddy. If someone would have jumped out of a tree and sacrificed us, we wouldn't have been surprised because it was that creepy.

After three hours we finally reached the top — only it wasn't the top, it was a false peak, but we agreed we'd lie to everyone about it being the top for the rest of our lives. At that point we took some carefully crafted pictures that obscured the huge mountain above us and made it look like we were at the top. Then we set about returning to civilisation. This is when we discovered that going uphill is significantly easier than going downhill, especially because I'm not good at going downhill. It's like I'm top heavy or something. I claim I need my special downhill shoes but unfortunately they don't exist. I just don't like going downhill, my legs get shaky and go stupid.

Three hours later, we were still stuck in the fucking hill trying not to fall over cliffs and sheer drops to certain death and that's when two kids appeared out of literally nowhere to tell us to be careful of leopards. Firstly, where the fuck did you come from? And secondly, this is the second time in a fortnight we're scared about being eaten by fucking cats. The kids unfortunately couldn't tell us anything else because the only words they knew appeared to be "leopard" and "careful." We tried to follow them so at least they would be eaten first, being small and easier prey than us, but they were kids and kids don't need downhill shoes or to be careful. No they just ran straight down the fucking vertical hill leaving us there to be eaten by a fucking cat.

To say we were scared would be an understatement. Particularly Natalie who rather objects to the thought of being eaten alive. I tried to act tough and wind her up as revenge for teasing me about the horse but I was secretly scared too.

A few hours later we were extremely lost. Somehow going up a hill and down a hill had become confusing. The jungle was so thick you couldn't see out and had we had no idea where we were. We were covered head to toe in mud and it was starting to go dark which is when leopards hunt, so I made my peace with the world and was ready to be eaten. An hour later and with Natalie in tears we crossed a ridge and found ourselves in a small field of tea bushes. In the middle of it was a wooden shack. We practically cried with joy.

We ran over and tried to find someone but no one was home so we sat on the porch playing with a dog trying to work out what to do. It was cold and we discussed having to break in to the building if no one arrived because it would be better than hypothermia. Half an hour later a man showed up and looked pretty bloody surprised to see two white women sat in his porch hugging to keep warm. We somehow explained we were lost and wanted our guesthouse and no, we weren't a lesbian gift from the gods for him. He was so nice and invited us in for tea and curry. He loaded us up with tea leaves and a bag of spring onions he'd grown and we gave him a little picture of Natalie, which is all we had with us, but he loved it. I'd have given him a picture of me too but we didn't have one and he'd have probably either have seen it as an insult or a joke. He told us which direction to go and we set off. A good few hours later in the cold and dark we made it back.

We had a freezing shower to remove the layers of mud we had on us, put on all of our clothes and got into the damp bed. The only highlight of the night was the fact it was so bloody cold we needed to keep each other warm and so we beat our personal sex record. Still sex only kept us warm for a short time (10 seconds) then we froze again. So all throughout the night one of us would wake up shivering and demand a spooning. What the other guests must have thought to us shouting "I need spooning! Spoon me!" we will never know. "Spoon me, please spoon me". It has to be the most sexually sounding non-sexual term in the world.

Quotes of the last few days:

Me: You teddybeared me all night.
Natalie: Teddybeared isn't a verb. I think you mean hugged.
Me: No, it's teddybeared. I'm English and therefore I'm right.

Natalie: Our house in the middle of our house our house.

Me: They're not the lyrics. Why are you incapable of ever getting lyrics right? That doesn't even make sense.

Natalie: Shut up.

Natalie: Girl with no name wants to snuggle other girl with no name.

Me: Girl with no name says fuck off. I know you're after my warm spot.

Natalie: Is it like dinosaurus.

Me: A what?

Natalie: A dinoceros.

Me: A what? Like a rhinoceros but a dinoceros?

Natalie: Shut up. What's the animal called? Shut up. What's wrong with me? What the fuck's the animal called? A dinosaurus? No it's dinoceros. Wait, what the fuck's wrong with me? Shut up Arghh!

Me: I'm not telling you I like dinoceros too much. (My family still call them dinoceros).

Natalie: I made you a sandwich but it jumped into my mouth and ate itself. Sorry.

*

12.07. Wednesday. Nuarelia & Colombo, Sri Lanka.

In the morning we took the bags to town and ate a ridiculously big meal in preparation for our seven hour train journey to Colombo. At the train station things went wrong instantly because the train was delayed due to a bridge falling down or something. It was a five hour delay, which was shit but still better that going over a bridge that's wasn't there. I have seen enough films and cartoons to know that doesn't end well. Well unless you're Sandra Bullock, of course.

We spent the time in the old cafe drinking tea. The train station was weirdly British and would soon prove to be in more ways than one ...bus bloody replacement services. Yep after half an hour on the train we had to jump on a bus to go around the broken bridge and then get back on a different one. The only problem with this was the fact there were at least a billion people there so trying to coordinate it wasn't easy for the authorities. They did brilliantly to be honest. We made it onto the train and didn't move for nine goddamn hours.

We got to the Colombo guesthouse at 11pm and it was so nice we almost cried. It was clean, nice and best of all it had hot water, which was quite honestly better than sex. We practically orgasmed. We couldn't even wait for the other to finish in there so we were both stood in the water fighting for the water all while making loud euphoric sex noises that we couldn't have stopped even if we tried.

The only downside to the place was a French girl who perpetually sat in the common room all day. She was lovely apart from the fact she was learning the ukulele and played the same three chords all day every day, which drove us and everyone else with eardrums insane.

The other point of interest about the guesthouse were the beds. They were luxurious and huge but they were easily one-and-a-half metres off the ground. Even

I had to climb onto it so Natalie who is best described as an unusually small dwarf hobbit had to pretty much scramble up the thing. Falling out of it would have been like skydiving. It would have taken four minutes to hit the deck, at which point you'd splatter all over the room's lovely floor. Still it was the best night's sleep we'd had since the trip began.

*

13.07. Thursday. Colombo, Sri Lanka.

It was Natalie's hospital day. Do you want to hear about her eye disease? Okay, so get this for a horror story. Aged 16, just as she was about to sit her exams, she went to school one day and thought someone had played a prank on her because all the pages in her textbooks were completely blank. She couldn't see any text whatsoever in her textbooks, phone, whiteboard, computer or pretty much anything. A week later she was diagnosed with Uveitis and Macular Oedema, which are two utterly, shit diseases. Uveitis causes inflammation of the eye — in her case the goo in the middle of her eye becomes inflamed and cloudy and this damages her eye causing terrible vision and retinal scarring. The other terrible thing about Uveitis is the secondary disease that it causes — Macular Oedema. This is basically leaking of the tiny capillaries in the eye which dump loads of liquid behind the retina killing retinal cells and forever risking a liquid-filled bulge behind which can burst leaving a retinal hole, in essence a huge permanent hole in the vision, or total retinal detachment — darkness forever. This is not in any way good.

Sometimes the cause for Uveitis is known: it can be

bacterial or viral and can be treated. Unfortunately though, there is a third type, — mystery cause. No one knows what causes it and it is untreatable. Over the years she's had every treatment under the sun and nothing has worked.

She's had over 20 injections directly into each eyeball (yeah, I know). Each time the eye is injected it carries the risk of cataracts, eye pressure, infection and a host of other nasty things. Still nothing worked and she did develop cataracts, which clouded what remaining vision she had. It is almost as if nature and the world is conspiring to rob her of her sight. The new drug she was trying was an arthritis treatment, which isn't even licensed for the eye disease, but it just may slow the fucker down. You never know. It was experimental to say the least and she is always on trials that don't work so we didn't get our hopes up again only for them to be dashed. All these years of treatments and inflammation has scared the retina beyond repair, which is so sad.

To give you an idea of her vision, Natalie can barely see the first big letter on the eye chart. She is registered blind and yet surprisingly the little sight she has is still enough to live an almost normal life. You wouldn't believe how much you can do with very limited vision. Throughout her countless eye injections, drips, scans, blood tests, spinal taps and other horrific treatments she has never once complained. She just deals with it whilst smiling and joking the whole time. She is a truly amazing woman. I on the other hand am generally sat in the waiting room trying so hard not to cry I almost shit myself. Then she'll waltz out with eye patches unable to walk properly with a giant smile on her face, which pushes me over the edge, and she's there comforting me telling me everything will be okay. She is without doubt the greatest person I have ever met.

Right, that wasn't that nice was it? I hope you're all

suitably depressed? We don't normally like to talk about her eyes because it upsets people, which upsets her. Unless it's brought up it's just normality for us, like having a bad leg, asthma or being a woman with a penis. You just deal with it. I'll try to keep things positive now because they are positive and we are an annoyingly happy couple. The eye thing almost never affects us, we just make do. I'm her eyes and she's the GPS.

She might not be able to see well but amazingly she has an unbelievable sense of direction, which is handy because I have none. I can spin around 360 degrees and not know where I am. Together we are one. When her sight does go we will deal with it and she will live life to the full, I have no doubt. All that mattered to us was to see as much as we could in the limited time she still had vision.

The treatment went well. The drug was administered through an IV drip and she lay there making jokes with all the doctors and nurses who were all more concerned with the tragedy of her sight than she was. I spent my time between holding her hand and crying in the toilets.

After the hospital, we went for coffee and breakfast. Sri Lanka sure knows how to do breakfast. We had these things called string hoppers, which is one hell of a name. They are like tiny patties of thin cold noodles, on top of which you put daal (a type of lentil curry) and on top of this you put something called sambol, AKA napalm, AKA arghh my mouth, AKA fuck my ass hole, AKA I can't feel my face, AKA I think I just shit myself, AKA I've got food poisoning and am dying, AKA don't eat this when you are a pussy. It was delicious.

Patties is a bad word isn't it? When I'm Overlord of the Universe that word will be banned. Patties, patties, patties. Ugh, gross. Worst word ever.

In the afternoon we went to buy local clothes. I have always adored Indian/Sri Lankan clothes because they're simply beautiful. I bought a red green and black Salwar Kameez dress. Needless to say I was rather happy. I can't remember what we did in the evening so I'm just going to make something up. Okay so in the evening we were walking by our hotel when Meatloaf turned up and told us what he meant by "but I won't do that" He meant dolphin sex. Understandable I suppose.

*

14.07. Friday. Colombo, Sri Lanka.

In the morning, we rushed to the Chinese Embassy to try and get a visa for China, which is the country we'd decided to go to literally one day earlier. It all went pretty well apart from the fact that the room was like a greenhouse and the air conditioning was broken. There were four guys hanging out of the ceiling trying to fix it but it wasn't bloody quick enough and we were sweating like Pinocchio in a mulch factory.

Following the embassy we had a massive argument which was totally all Natalie's fault and not my fault whatsoever because I never do wrong and am an angel.

In the evening we decided we rather liked each other and didn't like fighting so we made up. We went out for dinner and amazingly found a Pizza Hut but for some incomprehensible reason we didn't eat there. No, we walked passed it and went to the tiny shack next door where we had a mountain of fried rice for the massive sum of 25 pence.

Quotes of the last few days:

Natalie: Fuck! This bench has given me a hole in my tights. Look.
Me: Natalie, were sat in a church courtyard and you're lifting your skirt and pointing to your vagina. Jesus is going to strike you down.
Natalie: But look there's a hole.
Me: Seriously Natalie shut up. You're going to
Get us lynched.

Natalie: I know how to solve the Greek crisis. Tell them to stop smashing plates. That's where all their money's going.
Me: You should be an economist.
Natalie: I know.

Me: Why do people in choirs look like they're trying to shit a cabbage when they're singing?

Natalie: Hey try this, it tastes like ass poo.
Me: Um, no.

*

15.07. Saturday. Colombo, **Sri Lanka.**

We sat around all morning listening to the hideous sound of three repetitive ukulele chords.

It was our last night in Sri Lanka and in the evening the owner of the guesthouse made us a traditional meal, which was really nice of her. It would have been nicer had she not presumably dropped a whole tub of salt in it because it was literally inedible. We were sat at the dining room table as she looked on approvingly. It was painful. We tried to force it down until it was coming out of our noses. "Wow," I said. "Sri Lankans really like salt," hinting that the meal was ninety percent pure salt and totally inedible. She said that this dish wasn't salty. "What? Yes it is, the Dead Sea contains less salt than this. Just admit you ruined it so my kidneys don't have to blow up." There is only so much polite eating you can do before the very real fear of kidney damage sets in so we made some excuses and ran upstairs to hide.

So that was Sri Lanka. It is without doubt the friendliest country in the world. Just wonderful and great people. The land is varied and beautiful. If there is paradise anywhere on Earth this is it.

*

Chapter Three

16.07 Sunday. Hong Kong, China.

The flight to Hong Kong was pretty straightforward unlike the Hong Kong underground system, which is the most confusing thing on Earth. It took us four fucking hours to finally find our hostel. Now, as you know, I never complain about rooms and am fine with anything but this room was something special. It was a two metre by two metre box with only enough room for one person to actually stand, so someone had to be on the bed or in the toilet at all times. Directly next to the bed was the smallest toilet-shower-box-thing ever created. Nobody who wasn't skinny would have got in it. Here was the deal breaker though, the wall separating the toilet from the bed was made of glass ... clear glass. Clear glass — you know, the sort that could be seen through. Now I love my wife dearly but watching her poop is not something I ever want to do for fear I will actually love her a little bit less. No one wants to see that. And likewise I'd rather have my bowels blow up than have to take a dump in front of her.

"So how did Darcie die?"
"Well, her only toilet was directly next to the head of her wife and she didn't poop for a week and her bowels blew up."

The only positive thing was that the toilet had a shower directly above it so the only way to shower was by sitting on the toilet. I am totally okay with this. I am exceptionally lazy and the idea of showering, pooping and brushing my teeth all at the same time actually sounds good to me. Not really. Yes really.

All in all, though, it was a shithole. The entire building was a dump, full of graffiti, smoke, prostitutes and filth. It had one lift for 25 floors and the stairwells were all blocked with rubbish and massive cockroaches. If there were a fire no one would have survived. Normally I'm not overly concerned about fire safety but this scared the bejesus out of us.

Prostitutes freak me out, I find it really hard not to stare at them just trying to work out if they're prostitutes or not. The giveaway is normally when they shout. "Fuck off tranny" at me as if I'd actually be interested in paying for some rancid sex with a guaranteed STD. The other problem with being in a building full of prostitutes is that everyone, and I mean literally everyone, assumes I am one. No, I'm not one. Go away. Yes I'm serious. Do I look like a bloody prostitute? Okay, don't answer that. Look just fuck off, okay? I'm sorry, how much are you offering? Bloody Hell! Hold on let me ask my wife...

We got an early night in which I was forced to listen to music whilst covering my eyes in a dress so I couldn't hear or see Natalie empty herself. I decided to use this time to write a review for the absolute shithole.

Trip Advisor Reviews.

XXXXXX Towers, Hong Kong. Mosquito-ville local brothel fuck hole.
What did you like most about XXXXXX Towers Hong Kong?

I liked being able to pee, poop, brush my teeth and shower at the same time. In this modern rushed world we have to save time wherever we can and this amazing system allowed me to do everything at once, which was simply stupendous. When get home I'm going to convert our bathroom into a bedroom and use a small kitchen cupboard as our bathroom just like this place. It'll be awesome.

The other things I liked were certain death if there was a fire and most of all being looked at like I was a prostitute by everyone. It got to the point where I had to buy some non-feminine clothes so people stopped winking at me and speaking gibberish languages to me which I assumed was asking how much it would cost to do the sex with me. Oh, I also disliked the argument and awkward questions I had with my wife on asking if she'd agree to let me be pimped out if the money was good enough.

What did you like least about XXXXXX Towers Hong Kong?
The thing I liked least was the bed because it was located centimetres from the toilet and no one wants to be that close to another pooping human.

Was the location good for XXXXXX Towers Hong Kong?
It was in Hong Kong, so no.

Did you enjoy the food?
Define food. Hahahahaha — No!

Would you return to XXXXXX Towers Hong Kong?

I'd rather dress up in an American flag and go through a walk through Afghanistan.

Rate XXXXXX Towers Hong Kong out of 10?
Minus 10.

*

17.07. Monday. Hong Kong, China.

We wandered round for a few hours among Hong Kong's huge skyscrapers shops and people. There's far too many people in Hong Kong. It's depressing. No one wants to feel like an ant. Well apart from an actual ant, or Adam Ant or Ant from Ant and Dec. I always thought flying ants must have really bad superiority complexes.

Ant: Hi.
Flying Ant: Fuck Off.
Ant: Well that's not very friendly.
Flying Ant: I can fly and I don't want to associate with you lower class non-flying scum.
Ant: But I'm an army ant.
Flying Ant: I'm sorry do you fly?
Ant: No.
Flying Ant: So fuck off then.

Feeling peckish, we went in search of something to eat. The streets of Hong Kong are lined with thousands of restaurants so picking one should have been easy. However, and this is a big however, we are vegetarian, more or less vegan in fact. We are fussy to the point of insanity. Neither of us actually likes eating and I've struggled with anorexia and bulimia for longer than I can remember. We are the worst dinner guests ever. There's no one we don't annoy including ourselves and all the restaurants in the whole of Hong Kong have dead animals cooking in the windows, most of them still with their heads attached. It's bad enough to see a headless chicken but seeing one with its head and eyes staring at you as it's being spit roasted is just gross. I gagged and nearly vomited. But we're not like those fanatical vegetarians you meet. You know the ones, they struggle to say a sentence without mentioning the fact they're vegetarian.

Brian: Hi I'm Brian, vegetarian Brian, did I mention I'm vegetarian? I only eat vegetarian food as a vegetarian, because that me, a vegetarian.
Me: Oh fuck off Brian, you absolute twat.

No, we don't mind other people eating meat. I mean yes it's bad for the environment and being eaten is not very good for the animals themselves but I don't expect the world to stop eating meat but personally, since the age of four, it has repulsed me. Natalie has a similar story. By the way did I mention that I, me, Darcie Silver, am a vegetarian? Because I am you know, a vegetarian.

We eventually found a place that looked like it made things that didn't contain animals so we wandered in. I ordered a bread bun thing and Natalie ordered noodle soup. My bread which was described to me as, "Yes Miss, vegetarian no meat" unbelievably had chicken in it and Natalie's soup had pork. When we politely asked the waitress what the fuck was going on and she insisted these were vegetarian ingredients. Great. And this was Hong Kong a former British outpost. What

the fuck would China hold for us? Still if we didn't die from hunger we'd be thin which was somewhat comforting. We left feeling green with nausea and we both wanted to purge ourselves so, to take our mind off it, we found a
cake shop.

Me: So is this cake vegetarian then?
Woman: Yes is.
Me: So, no hidden chicken like last time?
Woman: No chicken.
Me: Any pig, cow, horse, goat, fish, dog, cat, hamster, goldfish, unicorn, griffin, panda?
Woman: No only vegetarian flour.
Me: It tastes funny. What's this?
Woman: Oh, that's duck vagina.

There was no actual duck vagina but it definitely tasted decidedly non-vegetarian. Feeling sick to the core we walked down to Temple Street where there is a night market. It was mainly tourist shit but the highlight was when Natalie picked up a vibrator and said what the hell is this? Um that's a vibrator Natalie. It goes in your vagina. "Arghh, arghh, no, no. Oh god," she said. I laughed solidly for about 30 minutes as did the shopkeeper and 20 other shoppers. So funny. And now I know what she's getting for Christmas. I don't know what this says about me? I'm clearly so amazingly good at the old sex that she has never even considered a sex toy. Score for me.

We then stumbled across a bag shop. We have our big backpacks and also two smaller rucksacks, which we keep on us. These contain computers chargers and cameras etc. These were pretty old and shit so we'd decided to get new ones that had both backpack straps and also wheels because dragging is better than carrying especially when you're lazy like us. We found the perfect ones and asked the price which the shop man said were £200 which must have been about a hundred times too much. We told him we could pay 20, which was still more than they were worth. Then the oddest thing happened, he completely lost his temper.

Crazy Bag Man: Why you bad people?
Me: I'm sorry, what?
Crazy Bag Man: Why you ask price if you don't pay?
Me: Because that's what people do. Um, welcome to Earth. Oh and it's about a hundred times more than it should be.
Crazy Bag Man: No you pay 200 that is the price.
Me: Um, no.
Crazy Bag Man: Yes, you pay.
Me: No.
Crazy Bag Man: You get out of my shop you very bad people.
Me: And you sir are a knob head with psychopathic tendencies but you are the first person to lose their temper at me and not resort to mentioning me having a penis so well done. Can we hug?
Crazy Bag Ban: You no make no sense, stupid girl pussy boy.
Me: Ah there you go. And I do hope you fall into a vat of piss and drown. Bye bye now.

We left feeling a bit strange. In a shop down the street I bought some absolute tat including a fridge magnet in which China was spelt wrong and a weird puzzle thing I don't understand. I bought it thinking,

Ooh, I like puzzles, I bet this one's really fun. 3 weeks later I had discovered I hate puzzles and am shit at them. We then set off back to the fire hazard shit hotel when around five minutes away from it I got a sudden stabbing pain in my stomach and instantly shit myself. The whole thing happened so quickly even if I'd been next to a toilet I'd have still pooped my pants. It was not a good moment. I was so shocked at what just happened I didn't know what to say or do so I stood there with a stunned look on my face for a full minute whilst Natalie asked me what was wrong and if I was having a stroke.

Me: I just shit myself.
Natalie: Haha, no you didn't.
Me: No, really I did.
Natalie: You didn't.
Me: I can assure you I bloody did. Oh god what are we going to do? Oh god oh god.
Natalie: Um, hahaha.
Me: Don't laugh you bitch, I just shit my pants.
Natalie: Hahaha.
Me: Fuck you I want a divorce. Help me.
Natalie: Okay, okay is it leaking out?
Me: That's disgusting. No.
Natalie: Okay, I'm going to find the nearest toilet stay here.
Me: Okay please hurry I think I'm going to cry.

And so my main memory of Hong Kong was waddling down the street to a gross squat toilet to sort myself out. I'll spare you the details because I think you have heard enough about poo for a while but needless to say I was in there 30 minutes, covered just about every surface of my body and the room in shit juice and left with a thousand yard stare like I'd just witnessed a massacre in a war zone.

A while later we got to the hotel where I showered and scrubbed for an hour whilst Natalie laughed at me and called her family to tell them about the incident as if that was a nice and normal thing to do.

Natalie: So Darcie shit her pants…
Natalie's Mum: What? So he's transgender and now can't control his, her, its, bowels?
Me: I can hear your Mum Natalie! Tell her I said fuck you, you bitch and I'm not an "it" any more than she's not a fat lump of hideous lard. *(I love her really, best mother in law ever! Please don't sit on me you hippo)

The only other highlights of Hong Kong were seeing a business sign for a company called 'Excellent Brilliant Limited' which I came to the conclusion must have been shit. Also two hours before we left I unbelievably pooped myself for the second time. I will spare you the details but it was significantly more hideous than the previous time. This time involved being spotted by just about everyone. I was so traumatised that I made myself a solemn promise to never eat anything ever again and to learn how to photosynthesise instead. It didn't work.

So to summarise Hong Kong: It would be easier to eat a diet solely consisting of unicorns than being a vegetarian in Hong Kong! Oh and if you don't like publicly shitting yourself, it's a country that should probably be avoided.

*

18.07. Tuesday. Hong Kong China

We boarded the Hong Kong Metro, which is like many Metro train systems around the world in that it has trains. Unfortunately that's where the similarities end because in Hong Kong they have developed a system so fucking complicated Einstein would be, like, fuck this shit, I'm walking. As such, we got lost four times in the warren's den of underground tunnels. On a side note, what the actual fuck is a warren? Has anyone ever seen one? Do they even exist?

Thankfully the staff were on hand to help direct us, but being fucking rude asshole pricks they just said, "Not here, that way" And that way, my friends, involved pointing to a solid wall. It was like a Monty Python sketch.

Unhelpful Metro Prick: Station that way
Me: That way?
Unhelpful Metro Prick: Yes Miss.
Me: That's a solid wall.
Unhelpful Metro Prick: That way yes.
Me: That way no.
Unhelpful Metro Prick: Yes.
Me: No.

We chose not to try walking directly through a wall like David bloody Copperfield and instead went to try and find someone less idiotic. We found a lovely Hong Kong woman. What are they called? Hong Kongouns? Hongkongites? Nobody knows. Let's just call them Hongs for now.

Anyway the lovely Hong lady pointed us the right direction, which thankfully wasn't through a solid wall.

*

Chapter Four

We crossed the border into China, which was super easy, and for the next few hours we took China's super high speed bullet train, trying to get to Guilin. It was all going well until we got stuck in Shenzhen because the trains were fully booked. So slightly dejected we set about finding a local hotel.

The room we found was all really beautiful faded grandeur. It was a massive room with a high ceiling. In the middle of the room was bizarrely a big professional poker table. Old paintings were hanging on the tattered old wallpaper; there were beautiful old cabinets, a huge 1980s TV and the hardest bed in the known universe. To give you an idea of how uncomfortable the bed was, if you smashed bottles and set them in concrete it would still be more comfortable than that bloody bed. They say diamonds are the hardest substance known to man — well they clearly haven't seen this bed. It was not nice. Thankfully we found a local fruit shop so consoled ourselves by sitting at the poker table and eating lots of fruit.

The night was spent on the rock hard bed with Natalie thinking it was hilarious to attack me with her hideous feet. She's a very pretty woman but her feet are utterly monstrous, and no I'm not being mean, that's the nicest thing you could say about them. They are a biohazard. They would scare ogres away. You could use them as a punishment to make children behave. I would put a picture of them here but I fear being sued for psychological damage. After my threats of pinching her nipples failed to stop her from the foot attack, I pinched her nipples really hard. This normally stops her attacks but this time she retaliated with tickling. I'm unbelievably ticklish and unluckily for me, she is not. I turn to mush and practically poop myself in fits of laughter and I can't get her back.

Well that was until this night when on the verge of being tickled to death I picked up the nearest weapon I could find, a 30 year old TV remote and started jabbing her in her ass with it. She very promptly stopped tickling me and, get this, she was in a mood with me. She was wearing knickers for fuck's sake it wasn't exactly like it went in. Why am I writing this? Oh god I'm going to be in so much trouble. Still this was the day I realised how I can stop tickle attacks. I simply jab things in her ass. It's not fair being married to someone who's not ticklish when you're so ticklish the word ticklish makes you laugh. What can I do? Punch her? I can't do anything apart from nipple pinching. This was a ridiculous thing to do and I hated doing it but I didn't have anything else, well, until discovered poking her anus with random objects.

Quotes from the last few days:

Me: What kind of plant is that?
Natalie: A tree.

Me: I'm so full. Don't mention food.
Natalie: Potato.
Me: Noo! I'm serious. I'm actually going to spew.

Me: I'm a mermaid.
Natalie: You're a mersquid.

Me: You're a merlion.
Natalie: You're a merpansee.
Me: You're a merpotimus.
Natalie: You're a mertiupus.
Me: That sounds like a disease.
Natalie: If we have a cat can we call it mertiupus.
Me: Yes.

Natalie: They make really nice sausage soup.
Me: That can't be a real thing.
Natalie: It's really nice.
Me: It sounds like a dirty phrase. Is it salty?
Natalie: You've just ruined sausage soup for me you disgusting pig.

Natalie: I need the toilet.
Me: What do you need from the toilet?
Natalie: The toilet.

*

19.07. Wednesday. Shenzhen & Guilin, China

In the morning whilst waiting for a taxi to the railway station, there was an absolute monsoon and we got completely drenched. Well, I did, Natalie had an umbrella, which she was using on herself and keeping her bag dry. Thanks Natalie, how very considerate of you. I knew I married you for a reason.

Dripping wet, well not Natalie, we got a taxi and got on the high speed train where we were whisked away at warp nine to Guilin.

Here's an interesting fact for you, China has more

high speed trains than the rest of the world combined. They are so advanced it's unbelievable. There are no delays, because of leaves on the line, the wrong type of snow, signal failure or because of lazy inept bastard striking bastard tube driving bastards. No these trains just work like they do in most of the world outside the UK, yet still, being a train, it's compulsory that they have to have disgusting toilets. That is the law of the train as was written in the commandments handed down to Moses. This one didn't disappoint. It stank worse than a bag full of cat shit and was covered floor to ceiling in disgustingness. Natalie being a toilet snob, outright refused to go despite desperately needing the toilet, so instead chose to just sit there shaking trying not to piss and shit her knickers simultaneously.

When we arrived at our station Natalie ran about like a mad woman trying to find a toilet but somehow couldn't find one. She insisted she could wait and we should go straight to the guesthouse. At that point seeing her beautiful sweaty distressed face I thought she looked so beautiful so thought it would be a good idea to hug her whilst telling her how much I love her. Her response was to scream, "don't hug me you idiot unless you want to see stuff oozing out of all my holes." I did not want to see this so we went to the taxi rank.

The hostel was lovely. We had a big room, a soft bed and a separate bathroom. We particularly liked the total lack of prostitutes or guaranteed death if there was a fire. Guilin was so dreamlike and beautiful it was almost as if Disney built it. The centre of the city was around three beautiful interconnected lakes. These had walkways round them with parks, traditional Chinese buildings, sculptures and art everywhere. It's easily one of the most beautiful cities we have ever been to.

After dumping all three tons of Natalie's knickers and several other needless bags of her luggage we went for a little walk around town and all the quaint little shops. Practically all the shops in Guilin are dress shops and Chinese women really know how to dress. The only slight problem is that the Chinese are petite, thin and beautiful and I am effectively a Western-sized man in a dress. Nothing in the entire country will fit me, which is particularly upsetting. Natalie on the other hand is significantly more Hobbit-like than me and bought about six of them for a grand total of £60. Totally unfair.

With bags in hand we went to find something to eat. Guilin is famous for its noodles so we found a noodle restaurant. We carefully translated what we wanted on our phones. 'Vegetable noodles without meat, duck, cow, pig, goat, sheep, cat, dog, unicorn, hamster of giraffe please.' We figured this way we'd be able to guarantee we wouldn't get any dead animals in our food. And success! There were no dead animals. Instead what turned up was an enormous cauldron of plain noodles in boiling water. There must have been enough to feed 20 people. It was ridiculous. Obviously Google translate fucked up and now we were faced with a hideous amount of noodles to eat. I don't even like noodles, I mean I'm no culinary expert but it's just spaghetti isn't it? Spaghetti but with a stupid taste and generally more stupidity. I should really be a food critic.

"Hmm the foie gras was stupid, the potatoes were stupid and the fish tasted like the stupidest thing in the world." I don't like Chinese food anyway to be honest, because I object to drinking a pint of oil with everything I eat, but now we had the waitresses and the chef looking at us to see if we were enjoying it. So we tucked in. It was a bit like eating four kilos of soggy tasteless hay.

*

20.07. Thursday. Guilin, China

We started the day with a huge panic because our one functioning bank card wasn't working and the ATM kept giving us the message "insufficient balance" which scared the living poop out of us. Cleverly we had set about a round the world adventure with one single bank card which, should it not work, would lead to a whole heap of trouble. As such, we absolutely filled our pants. We went from bank to bank becoming increasingly stressed until we were almost crying. At this point we needed to get on the internet to check our online banking but our phone internet had randomly stopped working a few hours earlier so we stood in the middle of the town flapping like deranged chickens until Natalie devised a clever plan. Firstly, stop panicking, secondly find a cafe with Wi-Fi and log into online banking to see what the fuck was going on. The plan worked well and we soon enough discovered the problem with the money, I hadn't loaded any money on the card. Honestly, sometimes I scare myself with my own stupidity. After we loaded the card we went to the bank, the phone shop and the railway station. All in all it was a shit and very stressful morning.

In the evening we wandered around the lakes. It's common across the country for parks to be full of people dancing in the evening and the little plazas around the lake were full to the sound of Chinese music with people practicing different types of dancing. It's very romantic and reminds me a lot of the parks in the UK where if you go at night you get to experience the beautiful sights of drugs, violence and in my case a high chance of rape, assault and death.

*

21.07 Friday. Guilin, China

Over a breakfast of mystery brown substance which was supposed to be vegetarian but we suspected to be actual poo we met three lovely Italians and decided to take a day trip to see the Longji rice terraces which were a three hour drive away. So, at 7am, we all jumped in a car and were driven into the hills where we set about climbing a fuck off fucking mountain in the ridiculously hot weather. Some 600 years ago the local tribe had found a mountain and decided to make the entire thing one huge rice farm so they cut huge terraces into it and diverted streams to make the whole mountainside into lots of small rice filled pools that cascaded down the mountain. It looked unreal. Even now in modern China the local people in their traditional dress were working away in them. Well, the men were. The women had cottoned on to the thousands of rich tourists traipsing up and down their hill and were selling tourists water, huge chunks of wild cucumber, wild honey and other bits and bobs.

What always strikes us about Asian tribes is how

happy they all seem to be. They lead a simple existence with no offices, no money, rat race, mortgage or any of the modern stressful shit we have all been convinced is normal. They live how humans are supposed to live and I think they're happier for it.

The walking was tough though because it was steep and the temperature was at least forty degrees Celsius. Natalie's poor little pasty, Scandinavian body didn't know what to do so it just started spouting water. She was dripping with sweat, which I found somewhat arousing.

Hilariously, for the entire walk up the hill, the Italians were talking about pizza, pasta and ice cream. It was like they were performing stereotypical impressions of Italians. Our other Italian friends don't do this. It was funny. I don't know what the English equivalent of this would be? Fish and chips, pies and football probably. The French talking about snails and frogs legs. The Germans talking about sausages, beer and evil world takeovers.

At the top of the mountain, at the point where you'd expect to see, um, the top of a mountain, there were about 20 restaurants and tat shops. Everyone apart from me wanted to eat there so we sat down at the gross dirty tables and were given our appalling food. Thankfully to wash down the oily terrible food were given free fruit juice. I say fruit juice, it was a type of mushroom the area was famous for. It was absolutely vile. Imagine buying a bag of frozen mushrooms and putting it in the tumble dryer for two days then burying in the garden for a year, digging it up, mixing it with water and dog shit then drinking it. That's what it tasted like. Like essence of mushroom mixed with rotting shit.

We left feeling sick so Natalie had the amazing idea to get some ice cream to take the taste away.

Natalie: Here you go Darcie. (Giant grin on her face)
Me: What the actual fuck is this?
Natalie: Hahaha, it's a pea lolly.
Me: I hate peas at the best of times, but frozen pea juice? Really? Why would this exist? What's wrong with the Chinese? You know I hate them.
Natalie: Haha, I know.
Me: I'm going to get you a mushroom ice lolly let's see how you like that.
Wife: I'd be sick on your face.
Me: Oh god it's got bits of peas in it. I'm going to spew. What kind of a monster would like this? How many times do you have to be dropped on your head as a child to think pea ice lollies are anything but perverse?
Italians: Mmm, Mamma mia, these pea lollies are buenisimo.
Me: What's wrong with you all?

Here's a gem of advice for you reading this out there. Pea juice ice lollies are revolting. What other frozen gems they like in China I don't know because we didn't have anything else, but I presume they have turnip ice cream and perhaps Brussels sprout ice lollies? Fucking gross.

We spent the evening completely lost and not being able to find our way back because I have no sense of direction and, due to it being dark, Natalie could barely see anything. We would have used Google maps like you can in every other country in the world but you can't because China very cleverly blocked it, you know in case someone accidentally Googled something like cute kittens, talking dogs or Tiananmen Square. We asked for directions but no one spoke English and responded to our polite request by staring at us like we were aliens. It took us three hours to find our way back. The annoying thing about Google being blocked is that you can't get your emails or get on Facebook and I need Facebook to live. If I remember correctly it's number two in Maslow's Hierarchy of Needs. 1, Food. 2, Facebook. Access to Facebook is a basic human right, surely? If I remember my religion lessons properly it's one of the commandments: Thou shalt be able to post pictures of thy dinner and thy cat's reaction to a cucumber on social media. The block was driving us mad until a few days later when we downloaded a VPN and got round it. Darcie & Natalie 1 Chinese System 0.

Quotes from the last few days:

Me: Have you farted?
Natalie: No.
Me: Yes you have you smelly animal.
Natalie: I swear I haven't, you can smell my ass.
Me: That has to be the least attractive proposition you've ever said.

Me. Shit, I nearly fell off the cliff.
Natalie: Yeah, your last words would've been, Whoop Gangnam style, which are not good last words.

Natalie: Oh, Mrs. Cucumber Pants.
Me: Please don't call me that.

Me: Let's start a chocolate brand called Ass Chocolate.

Natalie: Do you know what all the piano pedals do?
Me: Yes, brake, accelerator and ejector seat.

*

22.07 to 29.07. China.

I have literally no idea what we did on these days because I somehow accidentally deleted the notes off my phone and can't actually remember, but for continuity's sake I'm going to use the notes that weren't deleted during this time.

24.07. 'Buy **diarrhoea medicine and shampoo.**' From this note I think we can deduce that we both had diarrhoea of such severity … it went in our hair. Yep that's what happened, I'm sure.

25.07. **'Go to tailors, call Mum & call brother.'** Okay, what I assume happened was I went to Tailor's as in Taylor Swift's house where I called my Mum and brother. Can't think of what else this could mean.

26.07. '**New joke to polish.**' I watched the Formula One. The only excitement was when they announced the safety car was coming out. Well good for you safety car. To be honest I think we all had our suspicions.

27.07. **'Buy fruit & apples for train.'** I've no idea what this means but my guess is that the train was hungry and wanted some fruit and apples. Maybe it meant buy some gay people some Apple Mac products? We shall never know.

28.07. 'Write **up joke**.' They say the early bird catches the worm. That's a bit bloody optimistic. I prefer to think of it as the early worm dies!

29.07. **'Buy train tickets.'** I can't think of anything stupid to make up about this so I guess it's just as simple as us buying a train and some raffle tickets to raffle it away with.

Okay, so seeing as I can't remember anything from these few days let me tell you more about Natalie. Okay, so prepare to cover everything in vomit because this is going to get cringe worthy. Natalie is the kindest, purest, most loving and caring person in the world who would do anything for anyone. She is entirely selfless. She is also happiest person you'll ever meet. She never stops smiling. She even smiles in her sleep. Sometimes she'll wake up in the middle of the night smile at me and go back to sleep. She brightens up everywhere she goes and everyone loves her. She doesn't get in moods. She's just unbelievably stable in a euphoric mood 24/7. I'd change shoes with her in a heartbeat. She's an angel.

She was born in Sweden but was schooled internationally as her father worked abroad. She sounds American and speaks English as a first language except annoyingly when she sleep talks, which is in Swedish, and I don't understand it.

I am the luckiest girl alive to be with her and I know it. Okay, now wipe to vomit off your book because I have some more complaining to do.

*

30.07. Sunday, Guilin, China.

It was 9am and we were lying in bed eating Pringles because they are the only Chinese food that don't make us want to pull our stomachs out and wash them in soap to remove the grossness. Out of the blue, Natalie piped up that we should rent bikes from the hostel and go on a bike ride. This was despite the fact that it was a billion degrees, neither of us had ridden a bike in around eight years and the last time we did ride them Natalie rode straight into a bollard and sprained her face — oh, and not to mention the most important point that Natalie's vision at this point was so bad that she was registered blind. So sensibly ignoring all these irrelevant boring factors we rented bikes and went on a six hour ride.

The bikes were pretty decent. They had approximately two wheels, some handlebars and a seat. Well I say seat, bike seats are more closely aligned with implements of torture than seats. In fact I'd go as far as to say given the choice between sitting on a bike seat or a spike I'd sit on the spike. It'd be comfier. Joining us on the bike ride was an Italian girl named Nicole who we'd met in the hostel. She was a student and rather pleasant looking to say the least. Now Natalie and I aren't normally flirts but this woman was something else. We both found it hard to act normally around her, she was that beautiful. There's something about Italians that makes them extra sexy. Maybe it's their sophistication, their fashion sense or the fact they smell of pizza. I don't know, but this woman was jaw-droppingly beautiful.

We genuinely witnessed a Chinese man walk into a tree staring at her. I know I sound a bit chauvinistic but you haven't seen her so you can't comment. I'd give my left arm to look like that.

To be honest I'd give my left arm for anything, it's completely useless to me. I can barely hold a pencil with it. I just drag it round with like some kind of huge parasitic lump of turd. I don't have a disease or anything just an exceptionally shit left arm. If I had to defend myself, my best form of attack would be to rip my left arm off and use it like a bat in my right hand. Failing that, I'd throw it at them. So yeah she was nice. We both flirted outrageously with her.

It was good thinking to ask Nicole to come with us, firstly because she had cycled on Chinese roads once before and survived which was a feat in itself, and secondly she was in charge of the map because I have a natural inability to read maps and Natalie can't see. Thankfully, being practically perfect in every way she took it in her stride and led the way led the way through the insane traffic. We followed and tried not to die.

The roads in China are like nowhere else. If you are in front of a moving car it will hit you. In all other countries the car will stop or go around you. In China it is your prerogative not to be in front of them. It's not that they drive badly because they don't, it's that the rules are completely different. In the rest of the world, cars will always try and avoid hitting people. In China you must always avoid being in front of a car. We learned this trying to cross a road when a car didn't stop and we had to leap out of the way. He then got out screaming and we guessed he wasn't saying, "My bad, sorry." No, he was screaming, "Stupid white people, you are not invincible, get the fuck off the roads next time I make road kill stew out of you."

It took about 10 seconds of bike riding for me to remember why we don't do it because it was at this point my ass began to hurt. About 20 seconds after that my "man vagina-bits" started to ache. Half an hour after that I was in agony. Natalie had it slightly better because she has a nice proper woman's bottom, not just bones and skin like my bony stupid ass. Still after three hours her undercarriage was wrecked too.

The ride was so unbelievably dangerous, particularly because of the traffic and the fact that people were so shocked to see Nicole - a ridiculously beautiful foreign woman wearing almost nothing, Natalie, a gorgeous blonde woman, and me the freak-show riding down the road, they nearly drove into us. We had an entire convoy of people in cars and bikes following us round recording us on their phones, all the while not looking where they were going and nearly crashing into each other. Also to contend with was the temperature, which was so, fucking hot it was like being sat in an oven. It was 40 degrees Celsius and so humid the air may as well have been water. You'd be better off with gills or a snorkel. If you hung out dry clothes they'd be soaking wet.

By the third hour Natalie and my undercarriages were

throbbing and we had to stop frequently just to avoid crying. Nicole, the beautiful, had no such problems. Her ass was no doubt made of gold and was so beautiful it could feel no pain. She thought it was hugely amusing that we were both shouting about our assholes and vaginas.

Natalie: Oh god, my vagina, it's broken. ...Aghh, my vagina.
Me: Fuck my ball-vagina. Arghh, fuck. I don't think I'm going to need that sex change after all Natalie, these things are going to rub off in a few minutes.

After four hours we followed Nicole onto a highway, which was somewhat safer in that we had more room to swerve out of the way if one of the camera-toting locals swerved into us. It was not long though before Natalie and I reached our breaking point. Nicole the Beautiful could probably have ridden to Italy without so much as a slight ache but we were ruined. We pulled off the highway and went to find somewhere to rest. The countryside was amazing. Huge limestone hills with blue winding rivers and lakes. If you imagine a place where you'd expect to find dinosaurs to be walking around, this was it. We found a little ancient looking village so stopped off for a drink. The look on the faces of the villagers is something I'll remember forever. Their jaws were actually open in shock. I doubt any foreign people had been there before let alone little Miss Most Beautiful Thing In The Universe Ever, Miss Blonde and Beautiful ... and a hideous monster. In fact within minutes someone came over and through a translate app told Nicole she was very beautiful, Natalie she was beautiful — and said, "Hello" to me.

We sat down at a table overlooking the river and drank tea whilst admiring the stunning beauty ... of Nicole. The lovely young waitress kept bringing us gifts of fruit, cakes and biscuits whilst refusing payment for them. She then spent an hour translating facts from the area. She was lovely. It would have been more lovely had her mother not come over as we were about to leave to scream at her, hit her violently on her arm then demand we actually pay for the things we never asked for. The daughter was absolutely distraught, crying and trembling. We had assumed she was relatively high on the autism scale when we met her and were really angry with the mother for destroying her like this. Natalie and Nicole did a really good job of reassuring her and making her okay again. I told her it didn't matter and not to worry and we were thankful for her information on the area. Then I hid round the corner because I (probably wrongly) feel that my looks make me more of a burden at times like this. Then I felt guilty for not having the courage to just be me. The young woman was okay and Natalie and Nicole gave her a huge tip and reassured her.

Now given the choice of riding back to the hostel or hacking my legs off with a rusty butter knife and walking on hot coals, I would have taken the hot coals. I really wanted to hitchhike but the others didn't think hitchhiking with bikes was a good idea so off we set on the bloody bikes again. Along the way we all got dangerously hot and had to stop in a petrol station to stop ourselves literally dying of heatstroke. The face of the guy at the till said it all. "Wow! Oh my god, well hello and who might you be? Wow, another one, you're blonde, beautiful and you came from um...heaven I'm guessing? Then I walked in. "Ugh, arghh! What are you? Quick get the broom this one's broken."

After another hour of riding, our asses and undercarriages were wrecked, red raw and in agony. I honestly don't know whether it was just these particular bike seats because when I was young I could ride around without crying. An hour later, our complaining and whimpering had got to new levels, every bump and every stone: "Aghh my vagina," "Fuck my vag," "Aghh, aghh my asshole's ruined." I guess we thought humour might help or we were doing it subconsciously but what Nicole the gorgeous must have thought we'll never know, probably, "He doesn't have one … there's no way he's got a vagina … I wish he would stop saying that."

Me: Natalie my love, our chance of conceiving a child has gone to approximately zero. Can I have them cut off now?
Nicole: I fucking knew it.
Natalie: Yes, yes, cut them off. I can't have babies either. If my vagina hurts this much from a bike ride imagine having a fucking baby? No, I'm joining a convent and becoming a nun. My vagina using days are over.
Me: Me too.

Three hours later, dripping in sweat and absolutely broken we got back. I didn't even put my bike away. I physically didn't have it in me. I saw the reception woman and dropped it causing it to fall into the road. I didn't care, I went upstairs to sit in the shower. A few seconds later Natalie was there and we sat on the gross shower floor with cold water spraying on us. We didn't move for 45 minutes. It was quite romantic actually, we washed each other's hair and checked each other's anuses and genitals for blisters, bruising and signs of permanent damage.

In the evening we ate pizza in the hostel. It may have been bad pizza but it wasn't Chinese food and that's what mattered. It was divine.

Quotes from the last few days:

Natalie: Come and watch Naked and Afraid on TV with me.
Me: I was just naked and afraid in the bathtub.
Natalie: Yeah ok.
Me: Yeah I was afraid of the bath shark.
Natalie: Was there a bath shark?
Me: No thankfully there wasn't one but it was still scary though.

Natalie: I've eaten that much sugar that if I sit I sit in the sun too long I'm going to caramelise.

Me: You don't like fake almonds? Do they even make fake almonds?
Natalie: I said I don't like Phil Collins.

Natalie: Do you reckon instead of buying tents you can rent a tent?
Me: I don't know but rent a tent might just be the best sentence in the entire world.

Me: "So Darcie who performed your sex change surgery?"

"I rubbed them off on a six hour bike ride in China."

*

31.07. Monday, Guilin, China. I'm going to entitle this day 'exercise is shit and nobody should do it.'

We are normally early risers. If left to our own devices, I'll wake up at seven and if I'm not a "selfish annoying little bitch," who wakes Natalie up too, she will naturally wake up at around nine. We woke up at 2pm. Even before we even got out of bed Natalie was complaining, "Oh god it's 2pm what did we do? I can't feel my legs, oh god I can't move them". I didn't feel anything so stood up, at which point I very quickly realised my legs were no longer a functioning part of my body. I fell sideways into the wall causing me to bang my head and ricochet off it and fall back down onto the bed onto my bruised wrecked ass. "Aghh, nooo! What did we do? I'm broken, the fucking pain, why would anyone cycle? Do they not have genitals or bottoms?"

We literally couldn't walk. Has anyone tried going down stairs without the ability to bend their legs? It took us 25 minutes. Once in the common room downstairs we waddled to get to some chairs then free-fell into them, then both instantly shouted, "Arghh, my ass" to the amusement of Nicole who was sat there looking serene and beautiful. Nicole didn't even ache. We didn't move for the following five hours apart from using the toilet, which interesting in that using toilets involves the use of legs and ours had completely stopped working. The guesthouse normally made a lot of money from renting bikes out, but with us sat in the communal area all day whinging, and recounting how utterly terrible the bike ride was, I'd be surprised if anyone rented a bike there again, ever.

In the evening we had to pack our bags and leave. We called a rickshaw but couldn't get in it due to the fact that you need legs for the task, so we opted for a sideways fall and then clambering onto the seat all whilst screaming in agony and telling the 10 people that were stood laughing at us to fuck off.

We got to the train station ready for our 21-hour trip to Zhangjiajie and got chatting to a German who had the worst cold ever. An hour later I also had the worst cold ever. Well it wasn't a cold it was flu, it had to be and No it's not man flu! Fuck Off! I was so very ill. We found our bunk and I fell unconscious.

*

01.08. Tuesday. On a train in the middle of nowhere & Zhangjiajie, China

At 1am I was awake, aching, freezing cold and sneezing like a mother fucker. Whatever sneezing like a mother fucker actually means? Maybe people who have sexual relations with their mothers sneeze a lot? I wouldn't know because strangely, I've never met a mother fucker before. Well, not that I know of. Maybe I have. It's probably not something people mention straight away. "Hi my names John and I have sexual relations with my mother. You may notice I sneeze a lot. Most mother fuckers do this."

I really needed the toilet so climbed down the ladder from my top bunk, but forgetting my legs didn't work,

I instantly fell down it then smacked my head on a metal bar causing me to shout and fall backwards onto a sleeping woman. If I hadn't have been in such a state I would have found it hilarious but unfortunately I was in agony. I shouted, "Fuck my legs!" and tried to get up but only achieved a slight lift before I fell back and sat on her again this time shouting, "Arghh my ass!" Somehow she didn't wake up, which retrospectively, is a shame because I like the idea of sitting on a sleeping stranger shouting, "Arghh my ass!" Then I couldn't find my own flip flops so in danger of peeing my pants I borrowed someone else's. I was so delirious I don't remember anything else or getting back to bed.

By the morning I was really, really ill with definitely not man flu. My bunk bed was soaked in sweat and nose juice which was dripping out of my fevered disgusting face like a tap, so I thought I'd go and hijack Natalie's bunk which was less wet and revolting. The next thing I remember is waking up and seeing a man searching everywhere. Natalie asked if I'd seen a guy's flip flops as they'd vanished.

"Um, I may have moved them but I don't know where they are though, I'm sorry," I replied. They eventually found them under the next cabin's bed. Fuck knows why I'd put them there. He was not amused. As far as he was concerned, some weird looking foreign tranny beast, who was almost guaranteed to have given him man flu, had gone and hidden his shoes for no reason.

The Chinese are pretty serious when it comes to hygiene and illness. They wear surgical masks when they are ill or someone they know is ill. They really do not want to infect anyone or become ill. And what they really don't do is get the bubonic plague and, when their face is spouting diseased liquid, sleep in a six-bed carriage. They were not at all happy about my existence. I agreed with them. Sick people should be put in a special sick carriage. I was too sick to care and quickly went back to a delirious semi-conscious sleep. When I woke up again the only people in our cabin were a grandmother with her grandson who was really cute. Well he would have been cute but I was too sick to give a fuck and he irritated me with his high pitched squealing. Natalie being nice, fed him chocolate which made him even more hyper which was so annoying.

Me: Natalie why don't you give him a bloody espresso whilst you're at it? Some cocaine perhaps. Please Natalie I'm dying. Please make him quiet, please.
Natalie: Stop being a spoilsport.
Me: He was quiet until you got hold of him. I'm practically dead and I have the loudest happiest squealing directly in my ears.
Natalie: He's so cute though.
Me: No, he's not. He's annoying. I'm just about to die and this will be my last memory.
Natalie: Aww, does someone have man flu?
Me: Oh my god, fuck you. Can you at least make him unhappy? I prefer unhappy children to overly happy ones. Their squealing is less high pitched.
Natalie: What's wrong with you?
Me: I'm fucking dying.

So she pulled out a piece of paper and started drawing with the kid. She started what would eventually become a bird but began by looking suspiciously vagina-like.

Me: Natalie, please don't draw X-rated pictures for a four year old boy. I guarantee it won't be you that gets arrested. They'll take one look at me and lock me up. I can't go to prison, I mean look at me.
Natalie: It's a bird.
Me: Yes, it's part of a bird, the best part, that's the problem — and don't call women birds, this isn't the 1970s.
Natalie: You're sick.
Me: I'm sick? I'm not the one drawing vaginas for four year old boys.
Natalie: It's not a bloody vagina.
Me: Well, the fact it's not menstruating is a huge relief. Well done.
Natalie: You are an idiot and I don't know why I'm with you.
Me: Change the bloody picture.
Natalie Look, it's a bird.
Me: Ah, yes so it is. Please can you get to this point quicker next time I don't want to get beaten to death.

The vagina-like similarities hadn't escaped the grandma who was giving us/me evil looks. It's not me drawing it love, it's her. She's mental.

A couple of hours later another person joined the carriage and said something to us. All we were ever asked in China is where we were from and so we did what we did every time, and showed them, written in Chinese, that we are from England and Sweden. This was unfortunately the one single time they asked something different. It turns out they said, "Please move my grandma needs to sit here," and we'd replied

"We are from England and Sweden."

*
02.08. Wednesday, Zhangjiajie, China.

The hostel wasn't too bad when we eventually found it. Thankfully we had two separate double beds in the room so I could stay in my own without sweating, sneezing and leaking all over Natalie.

At some point I asked Natalie if she could find the chemist and get me something to help me live. She doesn't really go out by herself because crossing roads is a problem. When her sight completely goes, she'll get a stick and a dog etc. but they'd be pretty useless in China because the dog would probably get eaten (joking) and they'd ignore the stick and run her over anyway. This town however was pedestrianised and there were no cars. She wanted to go and who was I to stop her? She left and was bloody ages. I was sick with worry. An hour later she strolled in smiling having made friends with lots of local people who helped her find a pharmacy. She's so friendly, I worry about it. She talks to everyone and can be gone for five minutes and make 20 new friends.

The lozenges she'd bought me tasted exactly like toilet duck and we couldn't work out of they were for disinfecting toilets or sucking on. I have tried toilet duck as well so was pretty convinced they were toilet cleaners. When I was young I was extremely insecure and went through a stage denial about my gender. During this time I went out of my way to prove my masculinity by doing various stupid stunts. Among these, I once drank a shot of Toilet Duck. I have no idea what the logic was that drinking toilet cleaner would make me look manlier in front of my mates? "Look I'm a man, men drink toilet detergent!" Another masculine proving stunt involved punching a hole in a wooden fence. My mates were rather impressed with that one which is more than can be said than our next door neighbour on our quiet residential street who was watching as I punched a hole in his fence, or the hospital who asked how I fractured my hand so badly.

"Punched a hole in the fence innit? Like a proper man." My efforts to show myself as manly knew no bounds, "Nah I don't need a bottle opener I'm not a fucking girl like you, I punch the tops off with my face like a real man".

"Wine? Nah I'm not drinking that girly shit. Get me a pint of tequila. Down in one down in one. Watch this... Oh god I think I'm dying. Call the doctor"

"Razors? Pah, razors are for little girls. I'm so manly I shave with a sword. No, with a chainsaw. A rusty chainsaw that's broken"

"Cow's Milk? Nah, I don't drink that gay shit. I drink lion milk directly from the lioness's tits. Nah I'm lying. I drink lion milk directly from the male lions cock. That's real man's milk."

Mate: What the hell are you wearing, Darcie?
Me: Just my normal clothes.
Mate: You're dressed like a workman.
Me: These are my everyday clothes.
Mate: Are they steel capped shoes and a workman's hat?

Me: Yep. Look I drew a picture of a tractor. A man tractor. Anyone fancy a pint of tequila? Get yer tits out love.

Mate: Um please don't say that to my mum.

Me: Sorry it's just I'm such a man I find it hard not to.

I came out shortly after.

The lozenges did actually help. Whether that was because it was Toilet Duck and it dissolved the infections and my throat or whether it was a proper lozenge we'll never know.

Bodies are stupid when they're sick "Oh I have a fever and am too hot. I know what I'll do I'll make her feel fucking freezing so she has a boiling hot shower and then wraps herself up in two duvets then dies from heatstroke." Great one body, what a clever thing you are.

Whilst I'm on about bodies, did you know ears and noses never stop growing? Well that's me fucked. Of all things to never stop growing, why noses and ears? What's the point in that? If you have to make something grow forever, I think most guys, (obviously not me) would opt for their penises. Actually, on second thoughts, by the time men got to 30 they'd be practically useless. They'd have to start fucking horses or something. Unless of course vaginas didn't stop growing either. Ugh, there's a nice thought. By the time men got to 50 they'd need wheelbarrows to carry their penises round. People would be queuing up outside hospitals to have penis reductions. They'd be 60 year old men with their dicks wrapped all around their bodies. Broken backs crushed under the weight of the things. Imagine pissing? They'd have to unravel it like a hose pipe. You could use them as a lasso. But no, we're stuck with ears and noses growing forever.

Great, my nose is huge and my wife is pretty well endowed in the ear department to say the least. In strong winds she takes off. If we have a child it will be an elephant, we should just call it Dumbo and be done with it. So we are going to look so shit as old people.

The fucking irony of having massive ears is that old people are deaf as fuck.

A: Why Grandpa, what big ears you have.
B: I'm sorry what? You want the tears of a giraffe?"
A: I said you've got big ears.
B: You like to shag queers?
A: I said YOU'VE GOT BIG EARS.
B: Speak English! Honestly you youths speak gibberish.
A: I SAID YOU'RE OLD, SENILE AND STUPID AND I'M PUTTING YOU IN A HOME.
B: Hmm if you're making scones I'll have one too.

Ears and noses never stop growing for no reason whatso-fucking-ever and then we have perfectly healthy milk teeth that fall out aged five for no reason at all. We should really take advantage of that shit. If we knew then how much dental care cost and how painful it was we'd eat more sweets. Fuck, parents know their kids' teeth are being replaced anyway so why did they make us brush our teeth at all?

"I have to do this shit for the rest of my life, I'm

getting a free set of free replacements and you're making me take care of the duds? Why? What's the fucking point?"

When I have kids I'm going to say, "Look here small stuff, you lucky bastard, in about six years your perfectly functioning teeth will fall out and be replaced for no apparent fucking reason whatsoever, so instead of feeding you healthy food and making you brush your teeth for the next six years your diet will consist of sweets and cake. Oh, and you're not allowed to drink water. You may only drink Coke. But hear my words, son, the second you get your adult teeth you're going to polish them daily".

Tummy buttons, they don't serve much purpose either do they. Little toenails ... why? I pulled mine off once. And ate it. Other animals don't have useless features do they? Oh wait, that toe dogs have half way up their legs. Yeah I take it back. Those things are stupid. I'd prefer a little toenail than a toe half way up my arm.

You know what else is stupid, the spare parts list. Women have got a spare ovary and fallopian tube, a spare boob and men have got a spare bollock, you know, just in case one breaks we can use the other one. The only thing is that people don't die from broken bollocks or non-functioning boobs. What most people die from are heart attacks and strokes or when your brain turns into a cabbage. Why not furnish us with spare hearts and heads, the things that actually keep us alive, god damn it. A spare head would be awesome.

"The scar...? Yeah, one of my heads got diseased and

had to be removed so I'm relying on just the one head now, not to worry I can function just fine." A spare liver would be even better.

Doctor: Sir you need to cut down your drinking, your liver is severely damaged.
Patient: Nah mate, got another one innit.

I really don't know how we survived for so long with such stupid traits. How the fuck did we make it through an ice age with noses that leak for absolutely no reason whatsoever every time it gets a bit chilly? What the fuck's the point of that?

"Oooh it's fucking freezing I wish my face would start leaking profusely to keep me warm."

No, it's just pointless. What evolutionary advantage is there to that? Am I supposed to defend myself from wolves with snoticles? If I'm freezing my tits off I'd like my body to produce more heat, not start leaking from the face. Then as if a leaking face wasn't bad enough, hands cease to function in cold weather. I need them! They allow me to live and do things. What the fuck is the point of making them effectively bricks in cold weather? They are much more useful as hands when I can control them and not be limited to swinging them around like mallets because they refuse to do anything else. It's just stupid. How the fuck did we survive the cold in the past with leaking faces and brick hands? I honestly don't know. Is there another creature that leaks from the face when it gets cold? I don't think there is.

Then as soon as it gets slightly warm we start leaking

from the armpits. Yeah that's a good design, well done! Who designed that, somebody without arms? Yeah because every time I'm too hot I wish my arm pits would start spouting fountains of sweat, that's just what I need, thanks. Sweat works by evaporation so why in the name of all fuckery would I sweat the most in pretty much the only place on my body it can't evaporate? May as well make my ass crack sweat whilst you're at it, it would be about as effective.

Then as if it wasn't difficult enough surviving with a leaking face and brick hands, we grow old and morph into bald Hobbits. Why? What the fuck's the point in that? Why take the hair off guys' heads where they need it to keep their fucking heads warm and stick it on their backs and ears instead? How did we evolve such ridiculous things? The only reason I can think of is that for millennia when men reached about 40 they were banished from their houses and had to sit outside with nothing but a hat. That is literally the only reason for going bald but get hairy backs and ears? "Happy 40th birthday now take this hat and fuck off". You're living in the garden from now on.

Have you ever been so cold you actually consider setting yourself on fire? When it's that cold you can't feel your feet and you're pretty sure that if someone bent your toes they'd snap off?

Yeah it's shit. And what does your body to create heat, it makes your jaw convulse.

Yeah good one! Because my jaws well known for creating heat. I sweat my tits off every time I eat. What would really create heat would be involuntary swinging arms. You'd be warm in no time. It wouldn't be any good in a china shop.

A: What the fuck are you doing? You're breaking everything.
B: I can't help it. I'm cold.
A: Put a jacket on you're wrecking the place.
B: I can't get it on. Help me.

Involuntary sprinting that would really warm you up. You'd be heated up in seconds.

A: Where are you going?
B: I don't know. … I'm fucking freezing.
….Mum can you lend me some money for a train. It was really cold and I involuntarily ran to Wales.

*

03.08. Thursday, Zhangjiajie, China

I felt a bit better in the morning so we decided to venture out and go and see the only thing there was to see in the entire area, the world's longest and highest glass bridge. So I took some
painkillers sucked a Toilet Duck lozenge and like a big brave soldier walked with Natalie to the bus stop. The second I got on the bus the driver said something to me and all the 60 other passengers laughed. I like to think he said, "She looks like a comedian and what do you do when you see a comedian? Yes come on everyone... Hahahaha." Unfortunately it was more likely he asked if I'd escaped from the freak show. Bastards.

Before you set off on Chinese buses someone comes on and checks that everyone has their seatbelt on and if you don't they shout at you like a naughty child. Natalie got shouted at and turned purple in embarrassment. It was brilliant. I told the woman that she had indeed been very naughty and suggested a spanking was in order. Natalie did not agree and was in a mood with me because people could hear my perverted thoughts. No one in the entire country of China speaks English and if they did I think they'd agree that a public spanking was in order. Okay, I was out of order but in my defence I'd just been laughed at by everyone on the bus so therefore I was excused from doing any wrong.

We arrived at the bridge and immediately regretted it. There must have been a billion people there. I'd go as far as to say that there were more people queuing to get into the bridge of epic shitness than there are people that actually live in the whole of the UK. It was obscene. There's an interesting thing with Chinese queues, they queue nice and respectfully right up until the point the line moves forward then all order goes out of the window and it's a push-in shit show with people pushing directly in front of you. Being British of course means that it is my God-given duty to "tut" loudly at them and if they don't take heed, change their heathen ways and apologise, I tell them off. They obviously didn't understand a word and just looked at my face with demented confused expressions.

Two hours of queuing later we finally got to the bridge and it was shit, and I mean turd on a stick. The number one problem with the glass bridge was the fact that it wasn't in fact a glass bridge. No it was a steel and concrete bridge like all other bridges, but it had some super thick glass panels glued into it so you could look down at the gorge below. Or that was the idea, but due to there being a squillion tourists you couldn't even see the glass. You couldn't see anything but the head of the person two centimetres in front of you. When eventually we caught a brief glimpse of the glass it was reflecting the cloudy sky meaning we had basically paid and queued to look at a giant shit stupid mirror which had the single use of being able to allow everyone to look up women's dresses which was just fucking awesome. Luckily for me I had worn my chastity belt and was giving nothing away. What a steaming pile of poo. If anyone is planning on visiting this shit-fest please let me save you a lot of time and money with this simple trick: Take little hand mirror to your local bridge. Place it on the ground and marvel at its amazingness. Well done, you have just saved yourself a trip to China and the shittest bridge in the world.

Still you know what they say? When in Rome do as the Romans ... and slaughter anyone who doesn't bow to your commands — or something like that. So we did what everyone else was doing and pushed some people out of the way and a lay on the glass and attempted to take some shit pictures of ourselves. This in turn proved to make such an enormous spectacle for the nine billion Chinese people, they decided we were now the main spectacle of the place and were there purely to be photographed. Such was the commotion that I doubt if Michael Jackson, John Lennon and Elvis came back from the dead and performed together on the bridge it would have caused much more of a fuss. Holy bejesus, they loved us. Let me elaborate ... because it's what I do ... If Elvis, John Lennon and

Michael Jackson performed a new song so amazing everyone instantly orgasmed then a T-Rex jumped out of the trees and performed the Macarena before Jesus appeared and spanked it for being naughty, it wouldn't have caused such a stir. They were practically fighting each other for position to photo us all the while we cringed and wished we were anywhere else.

We are effectively like celebrities in China. I'm a mixture of freak show, clown and strange coloured foreigner and Natalie is a beautiful blonde princess and the most beautiful thing they have ever seen. I think they like me in the way kids love clowns; they like them, but like them more when they're on fire and run into a wall or get eaten by a lion. They have quite different rules about touching as well. They think nothing of coming up to you unannounced and putting their arms around you whilst someone else takes a photo. It happens to me a lot more than Natalie for some reason and even more annoyingly it always seems to happen when I'm dripping with sweat. I bet they will go home and tell their families that they met one of those white he-she beasts you read about. It was really sweaty which is probably a symptom of its disease, I better scrub myself in case I catch gay. Then as soon as one person takes a picture with you everyone else thinks it's bloody open season and they form orderly queues to also have their photos taken. It's so surreal. Women seem to think I'm more of a clown than the men and I usually get groped by at least one of them. Normally boob grabbing. They mean no harm so I let them know this is definitely not okay and move away but don't go cuckoo which is all I really want to do. I normally pretend to grab their boobs to prove the point. Oh god and get this, the Chinese as a nation think it's normal to stuff a baby, a real live baby in your face so you have to hold it then they take pictures of you. Even worse is the fact Chinese babies' clothes don't involve having a bottom to them. Let me repeat... Chinese baby's bottoms are bare, they are cut out of the clothes so they can poo and pee easily — no I'm not making this up. I seriously do not want to hold any baby let anyone one with an exposed bottom! Jesus fucking Christ no. It's disgusting.

After being photographed a million times, we wriggled free and tried to leave to the next "sight." So, together with our legion of fans, we walked over the shit bridge of epic wankness to the other side where it connected to some narrow wooden foot bridges that had been nailed into the side of cliffs. These were supposed to be terrifying and exhilarating but we're not scared of heights so were boring as fuck. Especially being in a crowd of nine billion people who were more concerned with taking pictures of us than walking. For three long hours we all walked together down the gorge, unable to get off. It was so very shit. Just a huge man-made "natural" tourist attraction. They had a huge waterfall which was powered by pumps and even the river which was originally natural had been fucked with and was ruined. All in all, it was the shittest thing we'd seen ever.

In the evening we went for a cup of tea and I saw a girl of about three with a T-shirt that said "Beer and Cigarettes." I burst out laughing in her face, which in turn made her cry. Which made me nervously laugh more thus making me look like the worst human in the world ever. A lot of young children cry when they first see white people for the first time. We think it's hilarious.

Quotes of the last few days:

Natalie: Smell my fingers, what does that smell like? Something brown just went in my hand.
Me: I can't believe you just asked me that.
Natalie: I think it's cake.
Me: There is no way I'm smelling it.

Me: It had a really good cast; it had Dennis Rodman in it.
Natalie: I think you mean Dustin Hoffman.
Me: Yeah him.

Natalie: Can you scratch my leg I have no nails? Oh god, that's so good. Ooh yeah, mmmm, this is like sex. If I had nails like you I'd just scratch myself all day.

*

04.08. Friday, Zhangjiajie & Miluo, China.

A strange thing happens when you backpack. You wake up and have no idea where you are. You lie there trying to work it out. As I was lying there pondering where the fuck we were, Natalie emerged from the bathroom completely naked, ran to my bed jumped on me, farted, then in embarrassment ran back to the bathroom. It was the single funniest thing I have ever witnessed. I couldn't decide what to think. Was I now horny? Grossed out? Or was it the funniest thing ever? Natalie is quite prude about all things fart/poo related which made it all the funnier. I went to the bathroom where she was hiding behind the shower curtain whilst repeatedly stating that it was in fact me that just did that.

Natalie: That was you, it wasn't me it was you.

Me: Okay, Natalie my love it was me, but can you try that again please because that was genuinely the best most kinky way to be woken

up, well up to the point you farted.

Natalie: No.

Me: Aww, please? I'll fart too if it makes you feel better.

Natalie: Ewww, what's wrong with you? You weirdo.

Me: Too late.

Natalie: Ewww, you revolting scrubber.

Me: I was trying to make you feel better.

Natalie: No that's disgusting I can't believe you just did that. You've never farted in front of me in 10 years.

Me: Yeah, but I wanted the naked hug thing again.

Natalie: So you let off a revolting fart in front of me.

Me: I didn't think this through.

The first point of call in the morning was to take our wrecked SLR camera to be fixed. It had somehow become full of dust and crud and had stopped working. Natalie is a huge photography fan, half the time she can barely see what she's pointing the camera at but she still has a natural talent for it. It's absolutely heart-breaking and I cry every time I think about her not being able to do her hobby in the future. I normally avoid all things photography related because it really gets to me. It's just so, so sad. I'd been dreading getting the camera fixed for a while because I can't seem to hold it together thinking about her unable to do something she loves. Even watching her take pictures knowing she won't be able to see them is heart-breaking. Life is cruel. Her strength with it all is just unbelievable and makes me even more upset. She just says she'll find another hobby and that it's fine, it doesn't make her sad she just thinks positively about different things she'll do. She's such an inspiration. So, whilst she was explaining to the technician what was wrong with the camera I made my excuse that I needed to find a toilet and left her to it. It was better than standing there crying.

We met up outside and I tried not to act like I'd been hiding down an alleyway crying my eyes out. Then we went for a coffee which I'm 90% sure was mud. It wasn't coffee whatever it was but it had caffeine or crack in it because we were both tripping afterwards. We are quite a talkative couple and it's been mentioned by more than one person that we shouldn't be allowed coffee because we're go from a slightly annoying couple to, "Just stop talking for a few goddamn minutes will you? For the love of Jesus, just shut the hell up."

In the evening we packed up our shit ran to the train station and got our train to Chengdu but had to spend the bloody night in the middle of butt-fuck nowhere because we still can't plan things properly and once again we messed up. In our defence I'm dyslexic, clueless, a tad ditzy and about as academically talented as a potato and Natalie can't see. So together we are useless. Also to contend with is the Chinese train system which is the envy of the world and super-efficient provided you actually speak Chinese which of course we don't. Nope, if you don't speak Chinese you are pretty much up poo creek without a javelin as the saying goes and may as well just guess what you're doing.

Me: Two tickets to Chengdu, please.
Ticket woman: Wing ping ding fling.
Me: Um, I have no idea what you just said.
Ticket woman: Peng feng weng deng... 400 yuan.
Me: Um what? That's expensive whatever it is.
Ticket woman: Wong pong chong bong.
Me: Fine, fine. I'll pay.
Ticket woman: Fung chung pung dung.
Me: I'm sorry I think. Okay, I'm going now. Bye.
Ticket women: Stupid white she devil didn't know I speak fluent English. Hahaha.

Chinese doesn't even sound like that. I don't know where that stereotype came from. They sound more like, "Con shuur wai fai turr." So next time you want to mimic Chinese try to remember that. Well, no one will know what you're on about so you're best sticking to, "Wang dong wong cheng." No it's not racist. Shut up.

We were stuck somewhere called Miluo, which is a town in the Hunan province. We found a road with lots of hotels and hostels on it and went to each one trying to find the cheapest one. We settled on one that was half the price of others and soon found out why. The bedroom had a huge box of condoms on the bedside table and a selection of cards with pictures of prostitutes to choose from. Yep, somehow we had managed to be sleeping in yet another brothel. There's no way we've not caught some kind of STD from sleeping in those beds.

It wasn't just the horror of sleeping in a whore-stitutes brothel bed, no that was just the half of it. In the room we had the single worst thing I have ever seen in a hotel room, the wall next to the bed was black with human filth. Spit, cum and any other body juice they could squish out. It was the grossest thing we have ever seen and I once saw a seagull rip a pigeon in two and eat it. A lot of Chinese men, how do I delicately put this...are utter fucking pigs. They all seem to constantly clear their throats loudly as fucking possible then spit the contents on walls, as in hotel walls, train walls, any walls. Spitting on the floor in hotels, hospitals, malls, buses, just everywhere. Spitting is something all Chinese men seem to do constantly. It's totally gross. So many hotel walls in China have spit on them and almost all have signs that say no spitting on the walls. What kind of country needs signs for that? What next? Do not shit on the pillows? Don't use towels as toilet paper? Do not fuck the TV? Seriously. Could you imagine that in the West? "No spitting on walls" - well the Ritz has certainly gone downhill.

We only had to spend seven hours in the shit hole and fighting to get our money back wasn't an option because they were bastards. Instead we spend an hour fighting over who slept nearest the filth wall. I lost, had a huge sulk and demanded that I sleep on top of her then. She just laughed leading me to threaten divorce which made her laugh even more.

*

05.08. Saturday, Miluo and a fucking shit train, China.

Around 7am I woke up opened my eyes and saw 10 centimetres from my face the black wall of filth. I screamed and ran into the shower where I scrubbed myself for a while. We were just about to check out when Natalie noticed all the prostitute cards had vanished.

Natalie: You've taken them, haven't you?
Me: What?
Natalie: The prostitute cards. You've got them, haven't you?
Me: No.
Natalie: Darcie!
Me: I was going to make top trumps out of them.
Natalie: Put them back.
Me: I don't want to.
Natalie: Darcie!
Me: Fine.

We had a few hours to kill before the train so decided to try the local speciality because, unbelievably for China, it was a vegetarian dish.

Natalie: Did you know this area is famous for a vegetarian dish?
Me: Woohoo.
Natalie: It's called stinky tofu.
Me: Booo.

Stinky tofu is tofu that's been soaked for days in what is effectively rotting shit. It's described as smelling like rotting corpses and feet. Which, having smelt it, would say is putting it a bit bloody lightly. It smells like your worst nightmares. Like you cooked your granddad in a vat of shit. Like you took the juice of eight particularly dirty tramps and left it to fester in the anus of a celiac pig for a month.

So how does stinky tofu taste Darcie? Well let me tell you dear readers, imagine eating your grandmother's bowels. That's what it would taste like. Decomposing death mixed with a hint of feet, filth and poo. It is the worst thing in the entire world ever. I'd quite honestly prefer to eat a meal of decomposing goat penis with a side order of tramp's toes than eat stinky tofu again. It would smell and taste better. It was so bad we immediately left and went to find something to taste away but obviously couldn't find anything sensible so ate a packet of slimy mystery fruit in syrup. Not only was it so sugary it gave us both instant diabetes but it didn't work and we could still taste stinky tofu for a week afterwards. Do not under any circumstances eat stinky tofu.

We jumped on the train ready for 23 hours of pure train joy. I forced myself asleep quickly to save myself the hideousness of the reality. Our bunk beds were next to the festering toilet and also next to the smoking area. You know how a lot of ex-smokers are bitter and hate smoke? Well I'm not one of them. No I'm much, much worse. I despise smoking. Why can't they just make it illegal? No one likes it. It's stupid. Smoke somewhere else you bastard. No? Okay, how about I take up a cancer-causing activity? Say, asbestos throwing? And start throwing it at your head? Yeah you wouldn't like that would you? No.

Chinese trains that aren't high-speed bullet trains are revolting. Imagine a zoo on wheels then add some filth. They are covered in spit, dirt and are smoky as hell. People ignore the no smoking signs and smoke everywhere, including, get this, next to a new-born baby. It's not my culture or place to comment especially because the mother just seemed to accept it but I very nearly told him to fuck off somewhere else. The beds are six to a cabin and you are literally sleeping with random people. I happened to be sleeping next to a beautiful Chinese woman who had the smelliest feet in the world. It reminded me of the stinky tofu which I could still taste and made me feel sick. Climbing into the top bunk requires you to be part monkey. It takes some skills. You have to climb up a tiny ladder and propel yourself face first into your bunk like a sea lion. It's not glamorous especially when you look down the ladder and see five pairs of eyes staring up your dress inquisitively.

"Ah I thought ahead, dickheads and am wearing shorts. So you're going to have to keep guessing."

I could practically hear the group disappointment. I was half tempted to shout down "yes I am what you suspect now go to sleep" Not that they'd understand.

*

06.08. Sunday. The shittest train on Earth and Chengdu, China.

During the day hours everyone sits on the bottom bunks so we sat there chomping through an entire bag of tangerines. We eat so many tangerines in our day-to-day life, we are noted for continuously smelling of them and have made various work colleagues complain to us and management.

Colleague: Can you please just stop eating those all goddamn day? My wife is complaining I smell oranges

115

because you eat them for eight hours a fucking day.

Me: I've told you I need them for medical reasons. Do you want one?

Colleague: No I can't bloody stand them after meeting you.

As children my brother was so traumatised my relentless tangerine eating that he now hates them and feels sick when he's near them. He really resents me for making him hate citrus fruit so much which amuses me greatly and accounts for one of the biggest achievements of my entire life. I should put it on my CV.

Life Achievements: Successfully scared my brother off citrus fruit by eating 20 of them a day for 15 years.

Strangely when I met Natalie she was also a citrus freak, it was one of the weird things we had in common. Our tangerine munch-athon on the train came to an abrupt end when, while separating one, I squirted the juice into the eyes of a 400 year old Chinese woman sat next to me. No amount of sorrys would calm her down and nothing could stop me from giggling no matter how hard I tried not to laugh. The more she squealed in pain and yapped angrily in Chinese, the more I laughed. It was mostly nervous laughter than anything but I also genuinely thought it was hilarious. Surprisingly, laughing at an injury you have caused to an old woman is not funny in Chinese culture so I looked like an absolute psychopath. Natalie was smacking my arm to make me stop laughing but I was a lost cause. I laughed hysterically for a good 10 minutes with tears streaming down my face. It's safe to say everyone including myself thought I was completely insane.

In the afternoon I was still sat next to the angry old woman who was rubbing her eyes and giving me evils when for no reason I can think of, I randomly had a full on meltdown about how terrible Chinese food was. I hadn't enjoyed eating a single thing in the whole time we'd been in China and just abruptly had a tantrum like a naughty child. As if the people on the train didn't already hate me already enough, they looked at me with open mouths thinking, "Oh god, it's setting off again quick do something, placate it or it'll attack us with tangerines." You go into a shop in China and recognise approximately nothing. Pre-cooked entire duck including its head in a crisp bag. Duck tongues — yes they're a real thing. Packets of chicken feet — I can't even bear to watch people eat them. I think it's safe to say I'd prefer to starve to death than eat chicken feet. Other bits of animal you wouldn't give the dog, probably containing dog, are packaged up and are positioned where the sweets should be. And the biscuits! "Oh, how could they fuck biscuits up Darcie? I mean surely they're nice?" No they fuck them up too. Biscuits in China are dripping in oil and instead of jam or something any normal civilised person would put on a biscuit they have put fucking shrimp paste. FUCKING SHRIMP PASTE! What has to go wrong in life to think biscuits should have shrimp paste in them? No it's not cultural preference and taste! Shut up! The Chinese are completely wrong and there's no more to it than that.

Natalie: Darcie love, I've found biscuits I think you'll like.
Me: Oh you've found some without fucking seafood

in them?

Natalie: Yep.

Me: Are they yummy?

Natalie: I haven't tried them. I think they've got chicken in them.

Me: Fuck ARGHH! Fuck Chinese biscuits. God what's wrong with this country?

There is nothing in the entire country I'd consider edible. I don't even like the fucking Pringles here. I mean who doesn't like Pringles? No one! There isn't a person on the planet who doesn't like Pringles because they're delicious and clearly laced in nicotine or crack cocaine or something because they're addictive as hell. Well Chinese Pringles are dripping in oil and taste like they're killing you. They aren't even addictive due to being repulsively greasy and that's before you even get to their flavour which is a choice of only two things, cucumber or tomato flavour. CUCUMBER FLAVOUR?? Are you mentally insane? Out of all the options to flavour a Pringle you actually chose fucking cucumber! Are you mad? Were you dropped on your head as a child? What kind of hideous trauma do you have to go through to make you invent cucumber flavoured Pringles? Especially in China where you eat marinated dragonfly anus for breakfast. Cucumber? Fucking cucumber? It's not even a fucking taste. It's more like crunchy watery grass.

No one has ever commented on the flavour of a fucking cucumber. "Hmm out of all the millions of flavours what should we make our Pringles taste of?" "Yes cucumber" Fuck off you freaks. The tomato flavour weren't any better because they are not flavoured like ketchup or anything tomato-based you'd consider nice. No, they taste like actual fresh fucking tomato which is fucking horrible in a fucking Pringle. Even instant noodles, the food staple of the whole country, are gross. They all contain fucking lizards bum holes and pigeon teeth and shit. Shelves upon shelves of instant noodles and only one is vegetarian and even that is inedible because the cunts have put half a fucking litre of oil in it. How do they even get oil in a pot noodle? Who has ever tasted instant noodles and thought, "Hmm, it's good but you know what would make it better? Half a fucking litre of fucking oil?" Fucking hell. I'm surprised they haven't found a way to put it in fruit.

Me: Hmm this apple tastes weird.
Chinaman: Yes special Chinese oil apple.
Me: Oil apple?
Chinaman: Yes we take normal apples and inject them with used cooking oil we used to fry shrimp in.
Me: I'm going to be sick.
Chinaman: Okay, please save the sick, we make a very nice cake out of it.

I have a history of anorexia and bulimia that's seen me hospitalised a few times and very nearly dead, I don't need this shit. Why can't somewhere just sell something actually fucking nice?

Funnily a few hours after my train tantrum, we got chatting to the only English speaking Chinese person in the entire fucking country…

Her: If you go to Beijing you will love the food. Very famous food there.
Me: Will this Beijing food be in anyway Chinese?

Her: Yes it's Beijing.
Me: Well I'll hate it then.

Getting to the hostel was fun. We got in a taxi and the meter started talking to us in English which was nice. The second thing to speak English in the country was a taxi meter. "Welcome to Chengdu taxi and to our great city. Please put your seatbelt on."

"Wow, that's nice," I replied ... and that's where the communication ended because the driver couldn't speak a word. He then lied about knowing where the hostel was and looked at our map like it was a crayon drawing by a child.

"Um, it's here in Chengdu; it's written in fucking Chinese. The maps fucking Chinese; just fucking read the fucking map. No, don't shake your head, it's quite easy. What you do is you get your single solitary brain cell to stop thinking about eating cat scrotums and instead think how you will get us to this place."

It took us two hours of driving through utterly soul destroying new tower blocks to get there. At this point we regretted going to China and wished we were somewhere else.

Quotes from the last few days:

Natalie: Aww, look at the baby, that's going to be us when we have our own little fluffhead.
Me: We're not calling our baby Little Fluffhead.
Natalie: Okay, little BooBoo, Fluffy Monster Bottom.
Me: I'd prefer to call it Rasputin Von Poopants to be

quite honest

Natalie: Aww I like it, little Rasputin.

Me: I was joking.

Natalie: Little Raspy.

Me: Oh God.

Natalie: Please can you explain exactly how gherkins are not crocodile penises. Because I'm not convinced that they're not the same thing.

Natalie: I don't want a Bloody Mary, I wanta bloody stay inside.

Me: This tea is so healthy I swear I'll live forever. I think I'm going to name it Invinsibilitea.

Natalie: I spy with my little eye something beginning with green.

Me: Um, that's not how this works.

Natalie: Well you're not getting another clue.

Me: Okay um, snot?

Natalie: Don't be disgusting Darcie.

Me: It's supposed to be a letter not a colour. I spy with my little eye something beginning with P or L for example

Natalie: Shut up, it's my turn. Do you give up?

Me: Is it an apple.

Natalie: There are no apples here. You are shit at this.

Me: Okay I give up.

Natalie: It's grass you idiot.

Me: I'm an idiot? At least I know the rules to I Spy.

*

07.08. Monday. Chengdu, China.

We woke up, as is common among the living. I was in a bad mood so as Natalie showered I went to the hostel lobby to do a bit of writing. Whilst I was sat there minding my own business I witnessed a Frenchman being extremely rude to the hostel staff so felt it my duty to destroy him.

Frenchy: WHAT TIME IS BREAKFAST? Why you no speak English if you work if a hostel? WHAT TIME IS BREAKFAST?
Chinese Woman: Sorry, no English.
Frenchy: YOU ARE USELESS. WHY DO YOU WORK HERE IF YOU SPEAK NO ENGLISH?
Me: Back off her, you fucking idiot she doesn't understand you. Get a translate app on your phone like everyone else you rude fucking moron.
Frenchy: She should speak English.
Me: And you should have manners, compassion, understanding and a brain you moron. You don't shout at people again okay?
Frenchy: Mumbles and walks off.

I was so tempted to say, look Frog Boy, unless you want to add being beaten up by a tranny to your list of failures in life I suggest you fuck off. I'm not a tranny but thought it was more poignant.

I felt instantly better. It's a lot to take being in a strange country where you're unable to communicate, eat and sleep. The stress rises and rises and you have to release it where you can such as destroying rude French people or writing mean things in this book like the Chinese being preoccupied with eating cat scrotums instead of driving for example. It's just a way to cope. I'm quite nice normally.

Ok let me tell you about Chengdu. Chengdu is famous for panda bears. Apart from that, it's boring and shit. So we got ready and went to see the giant furry bastards. I could tell you in detail how it went but I think one sentence will do it. There were a billion tourists and pandas are stupid.

I have never really got the whole panda obsession. They're idiots. They don't do anything but sit there eating bamboo which doesn't even taste nice. And they're are dying out because they don't like sex. Well let them die out then. What are you going to do? Force them to have sex forever? They spend millions of dollars inseminating the furry bastards when the solution is pretty easy as far as I can tell. Panda porn. What better way to get them in the mood with a bit of hard-core panda shagging? All you'd need to do is airlift some TV screens to the bamboo forests and blast panda porn 24/7. Honestly, I can't believe no one else has thought of it.

In the afternoon we went to the hair salon. They were already looking at me like a total weirdo when someone came out of the back, tripped up and dropped a huge box of hair curlers which scattered all across the floor. I laughed hysterically but they didn't think it was funny because that kind of slapstick comedy isn't funny in China. They just thought I was laughing at their misfortune. I looked like a psychopath once again.

As Natalie was getting her roots done I tried to explain through a translating app that she used to be totally blonde but, like many people her country, her hair got a bit darker with age. All their faces dropped and they started tutting and looking at me angrily. Then one of them translated that I should be thankful that she is with me and she is still beautiful. I can only guess what they understood is that when she was young she was beautiful but now she is a hideous monster. I can't think what else it could have meant. It took some serious ass kissing to wriggle out of it. Honestly the shit that happens every day in my life. I should write a book Oh wait…

The bastards did love my hair though, just not the person it was attached to. No they actively hated me. I have a huge mound of curly hair and everyone in China has straight black hair so it's interesting for them. They were mystified by it and desperately wanted to touch it but like many others they were clearly scared of catching tranny gay disease from me.

After they calmed down about me calling my wife not beautiful anymore, and after they were reasonably sure I didn't bite they opened up a little. I thought I'd joke about how bloody hot it is with this mound of fluff stuck to my head so translated on my phone "It's like wearing loft insulation on your head." Fuck knows what that translated as because they went from a little hate to all wanting me dead. I don't even know how that could translate badly.

Me: It's like wearing loft insulation on your head.
Google Translate: I want to smother your grandmother to death with loft insulation and your grandfather has broccoli growing on his penis.

So I sat there being ignored whilst they swooned over Natalie. She is very Barbie like so gets a whole load of attention. I don't mind, really, I don't. I'm not at all a bit jealous of her stunning looks, personality, happiness and rocking body with real life boobs. If I could be half as attractive as her I'd be happy to be honest but I'm still lucky that I mostly pass as female at all.

We chilled in the hostel in the afternoon with almost no calamities and when I say almost I mean I had to fish toilet paper and used sanitary products out of the toilet using nothing but a flip flop. Let me elaborate... No one knows how the Chinese clean their bottoms! It's a mystery of humanity. Some people say they don't have bottoms and don't poop, I don't know. What I do know is that they don't use toilet paper and as such their sewers aren't designed for it and when you try and flush it down you are highly likely to cause a blockage. So everywhere there are likely to be Westerners there are signs absolutely everywhere saying do not flush toilet paper down the toilet but instead to put it in a waste paper bin next to the toilet. However, like most Westerners we find that thought absolutely disgusting and flush it down anyway, (yes we're selfish, sorry).

So when I'd done my business and spotted the toilet paper in the bin I thought that Natalie was a scumbag for obeying the gross rules so I tipped the bin upside down in the toilet and flushed it. The toilet instantly blocked so I thought I'd help by pressing flush again...why do we do that?   What are we expecting to achieve? Needless to say it didn't work and now there was water overflowing. It was then that Natalie came in and pointed out the sanitary products mixed in with the toilet paper and asked me what the fuck I was doing.

Natalie: You can't flush pads down the toilet you idiot.

Every girl knows that. Well... yeah, you, I, you suppose, okay whatever,... Why did you put it in there anyway?

Me: I do know that but I thought it was toilet paper.

Natalie: Yeah it was wrapped in toilet paper.

Me: Wrapped? What like a really shit Christmas present?

Natalie: Would you prefer it wasn't wrapped?

Me: Yeah okay I like the wrapping. I thought you'd put poo paper in the bin like a scumbag

Natalie: Ewww, why would I do that?

Me: Because there's fifty signs everywhere saying to do that.

Natalie: Yeah but we're not doing that. I'd rather die.

Me: Yeah me too. So what are we going to do? Can we call reception?

Natalie: And say what? We ignored all 50 of the signs and thought we'd flush toilet paper and a sanitary pad down the toilet?

Me: Yeah okay we can't do that. We're going to have to fix it ourselves.

Natalie: Okay, well you did this so you fix it.

Me: Me? How?

Natalie: I don't know. Use your hand. How difficult can it be?

Me: What? Are you insane? You might have noticed by the air quality in here and by the state of the toilet that I left a deposit in there as well.

Natalie: That's disgusting. What's wrong with you?

Me: Oh I'm sorry that I poo. I apologise I shall learn to stop ever doing it again.

Natalie: Here use one of the bathroom flip flops and fish it all out.

Me: Ewww, that's disgusting, what's wrong with you... okay, pass me the flip flop.

So I used a flip flop that all the hostels in Asia have for use in the bathrooms and fished out all the floating nastiness. It was gross. Then we had to make a plunger out of an old shampoo bottle and a plastic bag. Thirty minutes later I was covered head to toe in toilet juice and the toilet finally gave in and swallowed the shit. If only the next person to use those flip flops knew it had been covered in poo, period juice and a whole heap of other utterly terrible things.

Once upon a time whilst on a family holiday I blocked the toilet and ran to Natalie in distressed state and said, "I've blocked the toilet, I don't know what to do, please don't tell anyone." She didn't even look at me to respond; she instantly ran into the living room to tell everyone. I nearly died of embarrassment. The whole family gathered around the toilet admiring my work and formulating a plan. God I can't believe I'm writing about this, it has traumatised me for years. Anyway, whilst I was elbow deep in the toilet filth she remembered this story and had a right old laugh to herself. I had been planning to get her back for years and now not only did I have the opportunity but she had just reminded me of the incident. In the evening she was Skyping her family when I appeared from over her shoulder to tell them that she had flushed a sanitary pad down the toilet and blocked it. Apparently this was totally out of order and her 92 year old grandfather was disgusted. Ooops.

*

08.08. Sunday. Hangzhou, China.

Nothing fun happened on the trip to Hangzhou. No

injuring old women with tangerines, no sneezing in people's faces, no stealing people's shoes, no hideous spitting men. We didn't even fall in the squat toilet. We simply got on the train and got off without a single calamity. I was sat there waiting for something fucked up to happen then convinced myself that fate was saving the crazy up for a crash or something. I'd have to wait a few weeks for that though.

So we got up and went for a walk around Hangzhou which it turns out is rather nice. Lots of the streets are pedestrianised and they have a man-made brick stream running through them with lots of flowers, water features and rocks and stuff. I love the way they can build cool stuff like this there. In the UK they couldn't build it in case someone fell in it and broke their face. Health and safety is stupid. Actually on second thought it'd be Natalie that fell in because apart from losing her eyesight she is the clumsiest person in the known world. You could put her in a padded room and she'd break something.

We walked around Hangzhou's famous lake then, slightly tired, we sat on a bench and watched the boats rocking to and fro and I thought to myself what the fuck does 'fro' actually mean, has anyone ever used it without first saying 'to'? I don't even know what 'to' means in that context, does anyone? In the whole world? Come fro, Natalie I need to tell you something, please go to and place this picture fro. Let's all use the word fro as much as possible, with the exception of around black people who might think we're taking the piss.

Along the walk back, a drunk Chinaman thought he'd

bless us with a view of his penis which was awfully nice of him. I had just been thinking, you know what I'd really like right now? To see a drunk Chinese man's tiny revolting penis. We both told him to fuck off at exactly the same time then we laughed at the stereo insult. The twat thought we were laughing at him so proceeded to wave the revolting thing around even more. I've never really understood why some guys are so keen to show women their dicks? Especially online, it's just stupid. What is the possible expected outcome? Wow that's ... a ... penis. I like penis! And you've got one. Can we meet up so I can suck it? No, that has never happened! What are you thinking you thick, fucking morons? Stop sending pictures of your dicks.

With our minds scared with the image of the man's small penis being waved round like a propeller, we decided that we were hungry but China has this amazing ability to make all of the millions of restaurants disappear when you actually want one which is rather annoying. After an hour walking and with Natalie nearly in tears because she was so hungry we found a place where we had noodles and a few vegetarian-looking things. Trying to explain to Chinese people that you don't eat meat is not easy. They give you the same look of "Why? Are you a bit special in the head?" that you'd give someone, if you walked in and found them having sexual relations with a chicken. They just don't get it. To them it's a bit like saying, "I don't drink water I only swallow ice cubes." It's beyond comprehension to them and simply idiotic. You actually start to feel bad telling people that you don't eat animals because the look of, "What the fuck's wrong with you?" is actually quite insulting. "What? So you're man dressed like woman and now you don't eat meat? What the fuck is wrong with you?"

We spent most of the day walking round and looking at stuff. Outside several shops there were men with mallets whacking a kind of hot biscuit/nut mix whilst shouting, "Wah poh wah poh," which was nice, as was their utterly crushed snack. We also spent a lot of time looking at chopsticks to buy. It's so long now since I used cutlery I don't know if I remember how to use them, I'll probably poke myself in the face with the fork and cut my thumb off with the knife when I try and use them.

*

09.08. Monday. Hangzhou, China.

We took a taxi to see the mausoleum of a famous general called General Yue Fei. You don't care about his name though do you? This isn't the type of book where you aim to learn historical Chinese generals' names. "Well, I bought a funny book about some tranny and her blind wife but what I really wanted was to learn the names of dead Chinese generals." I could have made anything up. I'm half tempted to change his name it to General Stiffrod to see if anyone even notices. General Anxiety Disorder.

Anyway General Zod is an absolute legend in China. He was killed when the ruler at the time accidentally had him killed. Oopsies. The mausoleum itself was about as good as diarrhoea, so we quickly made our way round it and left.

After the exhilaration of the tomb we thought we couldn't take any more excitement but we mustered all our strength and tried to get a taxi to see a pagoda temple thing. Taxi drivers like most Chinese people don't actually like foreigners and don't stop for us or they get close enough see my face and floor the gas to get away as quickly as possible before they catch tranny gay disease. Eventually one did stop for us. This one however was clearly a bit special because he had difficulties in understanding the concept of a car and started driving off when I had just one leg in it. No you see Mr. Taxi Man I have to have more than one leg in your car before you start driving. In fact I'd say I need a minimum of 90% of my body inside before you can start to depart, until that moment please do not classify me as being in your taxi. You can't drive off with just my leg for this important reason — it is attached to my body and even more importantly for you, my hand, in which contains the money I shall be giving you on successful completion of the journey. Now be a good driver and stop your car, you stupid fuckwit. He didn't understand anything and mumbled something back so I said I said. "Yes, I'll have 2 coffees and a hard boiled pineapple heavy on the mayo please." He didn't understand that either.

Our entire bodies eventually got to the pagoda and walked up to see the view of the lake and the modern city behind it. At the top was a little tea shop so we decided to order some. The Chinese take tea very seriously indeed but it's not cheap stuff, for good tea you're looking at about 10 pounds for a small pot, but we thought we'd treat ourselves to try the stuff at least once. We sat outside on the terrace and admired the view then the tea came along with some watermelon, tofu, some mystery brown substance (probably poo) and lots of weird nibbles. Seeing as we didn't ask for any food and now had a table full of stuff it was surprising when Natalie asked for an extra bowl of rice. Sure enough two minutes later the pretty woman turned up with a bowl … of chicken feet. We kindly told her we didn't want them to which we got the "What the fuck's wrong with you?" look. The Chinese eat chicken feet like we eat peanuts which is just plain weird.

In the evening we found a street painter who drew nice portrait sketches for eight dollars so we got a picture made. It was super good but sitting still for more than one minute is exceptionally difficult for me and I kept getting told off, it reminded me of when we did yoga and in the middle of the class the teacher, a horrible evil Spanish woman with bad English would scream:

"Darcie, stop changing your eyes" and I was desperate to scream back, "It's moving your eyes you demented bendy bitch." She was a transphobe and hated me. It wasn't like I was in a fucking leotard. People go there to meditate and become Zen-like, not stare into the bewildering genitals of the freak in front. Still she did not approve of my existence and made it very known. Yoga was so much fun for all the wrong reasons. When the bendy bitch teacher wasn't looking, Natalie and I would try and make each other fall over whilst trying not to burst out laughing. Ah, them were the days. Then we had to chant "OMMMMMM" for some unknown reason. "Can we not sing a song instead? Here, I'll start, if you're bendy and you know it clap your shoulders, no?"

As we were drawn, an ever changing group of up to

40 people stopped to watch the artist and us. Everyone told Natalie she was very beautiful and gave me evil disapproving looks whilst many pointed and laughed at me because the Chinese are nice like that. The artist chose to draw me as a pretty female not like a bloke in a dress so we were rather happy.

*

10.08. Tuesday. Hangzhou, China.

We tried to find a new hostel because our hostel was full of annoying people that spat everywhere, talked loudly all night and listened to their TVs on full volume at 3am. To top it off, at 4am literally every night someone in the room next door decided that it would be the best time to use a hair dryer for an hour, fuck knows what was going on in there? What takes an hour on a hair dryer? Rapunzel's locks would be dryer than a desiccated coconut in that amount of time. Fuck, even my hair would dry and I have more hair than a particularly hairy sheep.

We found a new hostel round the corner which turned out to be even worse. The Chinese are pretty gross to western people. They probably think were gross but we don't spit of walls wipe our asses on walls put feet marks on as many of the room's surfaces as possible (commonly somehow including the ceiling). We spent the day inside writing and trying to plan for our upcoming trip to North Korea which was a few days later. I don't know how the idea to go to North Korea came up but it did and it's surprisingly easy to get there. You just ask for the visa, you get it then you get on a plane and go. Retrospectively we were naive and ignorant about the country and we shouldn't have gone. I don't want to give my tourist money to that evil bastard and his bunch of evil bastard buddies. But naively and stupidly we thought going there would be awesome.

Quotes from the last few days:

Natalie: I just spoke to your Mum, she said she has a cake in the oven.
Me: I hope that's not a euphemism because I don't think I could handle that.

Natalie: I'm tired of curry. Everything burns from my vagina to my throat.
Me: Um, I think you're eating it wrong.

 Me: Oh my god how much garlic was in that? I feel like I've just swallowed a Frenchman.

Natalie: Hey watch it you pie pants.
Me: Pie pants?
Natalie: Yeah pork pie pants.
Me: I don't know if that's good or not.

*

11.08. Wednesday. On a train somewhere. Beijing, China.

After a hideous five hour long train journey we got to Beijing and immediately made our way to a hotel where we would be meeting the owner of the North Korean tour group we were joining and the other members of the group for the briefing. In our group was James, a funny German, Peter a German doctor, Karen a three foot tall American- Korean who looked just exactly like E.T. (no offence to her, or E.T, it was just commentable) and two Italians. During the briefing we were told what we could and could not do whilst in North Korea. This included the following:

- Do not criticise the leader.
- Do not criticise the system.
- Do not criticise anything relating to North Korea.
- Do not under any circumstances discuss politics.
- You may not under any circumstance leave the hotel or walk around anywhere unless the guide is with you.
- Do not take pictures of the military, police or anyone in a uniform.
- Do not bring in any materials, books or tapes that might be deemed inappropriate to the system.
- Do not talk about religion.
- Don't call Kim Jong Un a fat evil cunt who should be shot in the dick.

I really wanted to ask whether I'd have a problem being trans but figured he would have told me if I was going to land and have my underwear pulled down and my genitals inspected, then I'd get summarily shot in the face for being a wrong-un. I don't like to bring gender up a lot. I can't stand those boring people that constantly bang on about being gay, trans, black, white or Asian.

Yes we get it. Well done. Now talk about something else you boring bastards. (Yes I'm aware I mention it a lot in this book, but being like this in countries around the world has interesting consequences. Normally I don't mention it).

On the Metro on the way back to the hotel, the phone rang and the tour owner very delicately told me that on the trip we'd be visiting the mausoleum of Kim Jong IL and Kim Il Sung and wearing women's clothes might cause big problems so I should either not go or 'man up.' I was going to say well fuck them then, I'm a woman and I'm not dressing as a man, why should I? But not everywhere is as liberal as the West and I'm not stubborn enough to demand they instantly are. I guess I'm trying to justify the fact I chose to man up. Basically I don't care enough for it to bother me. If they said dress like a chicken I would have done. So we went to a market to buy some trousers. We found a perfect looking shit clothing stall with lots of shit looking man trousers hanging up so I went in to commence the bargaining.

Me: Hi, I'd like some of these hideous man trousers please.
Man: Ha I knew it! I bloody knew it!
Me: you said that out loud you insensitive, rude prick.
Man: Oh sorry ppp ... hahaha. Sorry. Look good quality trousers (he pulls out lighter and holds a flame to them).
Me: What is it with Asia where you think you can prove something's quality by proving its resistance to fire?
Man: Look best quality, no fire, very good.
Me: Look, if I need fire resistant trousers I'll let you

know but I have no current plans to set my legs on fire. If however I change my mind and need to set myself on fire you will be the first person I come to for fireproof trousers. What I want is the lowest quality, shittest, cheapest trousers you've got. I will wear them once and if they are still intact having not dissolved into the crap they're made from then they will be given away, if not then they will be placed in the bin where forever they shall remain.

Man: Yes, look good quality. (He once again proceeds to show they don't burn with the lighter which is pressed that close on the material they wouldn't burn if they were made from fire lighters).

Me: Why would good quality even mean they were less flammable? How do you guys even come up with this shit? No! I want NOT good quality! I want bad quality. I have little money, I want cheap, cheap! How much this one?

Man: Twenty.

Me: No, too much I want rubbish trousers.

Man: My friend, look. (He proceeds the second quality test which involves screwing things into the tightest ball possible and releasing it to show they are still there and therefore good quality).

Me: Yes, that's nice, well done, but I'm not paying 20

euro for them for a couple of reasons. Firstly I am a lady you know, and secondly they are shit and will go instantly to the bin. I'll give you five and that's generous.

Man: My friend, I am a wholesaler. My cost price is more than this.

Me: No you're not and no it isn't. Fine, I'll go somewhere else.

Man: Okay, okay eight euro.
Me: No. (Walk out)
Man: Okay, okay, five euro. Miss please.
Me: Aww, you called me miss. Okay five euro. Can we hug?

Another thing I have never really understood is the pants/trousers thing. Everyone says pants these days but pants are underwear not trousers. I remember the first time I heard someone call them pants, an old friend asked if I was going to be wearing pants that night and I was like why the fuck do you want to know that Paul?

An hour later and sweating like Nazis at the Jewish Taekwondo convention for the mentally unstable we found a Wal-Mart where Natalie bought 13 dragon fruit and I bought about 40 tangerines and a billion pears. Fruit is too bloody heavy isn't it? If genetic modification is so good then why can't they make it weigh less? Stupid scientists.

In the evening we did more panicking and questioning our sanity. We got our nails done and then went for a Thai meal which was so spicy it caused hallucinations and spontaneous giggling for no reason.

*

12.08. Thursday. Beijing/Pyongyang.

We had about two hours sleep through a mixture of stress and excitement and we were insanely tired. We were stood at the check in looking at the sign saying Pyongyang. We swallowed hard and checked our bags in.

We boarded the plane which was one of North Korea's three planes. It was so old we were reasonably sure it was made out of Bakelite and wood. Even the Wright brothers would have called it an antique and refused to get on. All the writing had worn off the doors and seat numbers and it smelt like a sofa that had been sat on continuously for 50 years by people that ate nothing but cabbage. I hate the smell of human, it's gross, I prefer eau de cow to human smell. I actually like the smell of cow shit, I can't decide if it smells nice or I like it because it reminds me of the countryside, either way it's nice, One day I'm going to have a pet cow and not let it outside.

We sat down in our seats and tried not to focus on quite how decrepit the plane looked. It didn't take us long to notice that the non-original TV stuck to the ceiling with something resembling Blu Tack was playing some serious joke-like propaganda. We found it fascinating. We also noticed that everyone on the place was wearing the pin badges with Kim Jong Ill and Kim Il Sung portraits on them. The flight was smooth apart from when the engine noise completely stopped mid-flight causing me and Natalie to add to the plane's revolting odour. There was a weird atmosphere on board the plane as if we were now in another world and all the rules had changed, it's hard to explain but it was there.

The plane landed in Pyongyang on a runway that really, really needed resurfacing. The only thing scarier than flying into North Korea on a North Korean Bakelite antique fucking plane is landing on a runway with potholes big enough to fit cars in.

As we walked off the plane another tourist started taking pictures of the other planes that were parked up because they were all from the 50's and had missing engines and were all covered up or, in fact, just fake planes to make them look like it was a proper airport. Natalie being Natalie thought it would be a good idea to join in talking pictures to the dismay of the military people surrounding the plane who couldn't believe we were doing it. They were not remotely impressed at all, especially because everyone was warned that we have to ask before we take photos of anything let alone a fucking airport. I think they were keen not to make a scene the second everyone arrived so they let it slide. That first person to take a photo either had balls of steel or was stupid — either way we thank him because we got some cool pics of fake planes. Of the five or so other planes there I think maybe only one was airworthy and when I say airworthy I mean you probably only had a 50% chance of plummeting into the ground.

The airport terminal was like a cow shed from the 1930's. It had one massive ancient luggage conveyor in the middle and the whole room was stuffed full of seriously mean looking military people who didn't look remotely friendly. Our visas were a separate piece of paper and weren't in our passports but I really wanted my passport stamped because I thought it would be cool. I'd read online you can ask them to stamp it for you so I asked. The look of anger, disbelief and utter hatred was scary. I promptly shut my mouth and moved on.

After we'd collected our bags a woman came up to us and asked if we were Darcie and Natalie. I was so nervous I hesitated before answering. She introduced herself as Che and she would be our guide for the week. She was dressed smartly had a lovely loving smile and was probably early 40's. We went outside to a waiting green bus and drove through the eerily quiet streets to a local restaurant where we ate. On the TV there was some hard-core propaganda showing military firing guns and tanks firing all to joke-like military music, it seemed a bit like what Nazi Germany must have been like with the relentless propaganda. The food wasn't actually that bad. We had lots of vegetable type things and kimchi which is the Korean national dish; it is fermented spicy cabbage and has the reaction you would expect if you ate spicy fermented cabbage.

After the meal we boarded the bus and went to the hotel — this is the only hotel in Pyongyang where foreigners are allowed to stay. It's on its own island in the Taedong River in the middle of the city. It was quite decent and had a nice view over the city. It is widely believed that the hotel is bugged with sound and video so we behaved ourselves and didn't say anything Kim Jong Un might find offensive, like hey Kim you evil bastard, check out my surprise genitals, bet you didn't expect that did you, you evil shit haired cunt.

The bathroom was interesting; the tap gave out cold water but if you turned it to hot it sucked in air which was pretty much the exact opposite of the desired function. It was weird and fascinating so I got a glass of water and put the tap in it to see what would happen and was amazed to see it sucked it all up! This was without doubt the most amazing thing I'd ever witnessed. I got bored with this curiosity after 45 minutes which was handy because we were all to convene in the lobby around that time anyway.

The only way to visit North Korea is in a tour which has a set itinerary of stuff to do. You can't change the plan or decide to do something different if you desire. The plan is set and you stick to it. The first stop was the train station where we were to pick up two more people who had obviously seen the plane and decided the train was less likely to cause death. The train station was so odd, it was spotlessly clean and everyone was so orderly with about 80% of the people being in uniform. It was like something from a movie. Lots of people stared at us and everyone looked distinctly unhappy. The whole place just felt eerie like being in a war movie with everyone dressed in either 40's style clothes or in military uniform.

We picked up the late arrivers and took the bus to the Korean Natural History Museum which I was quite looking forward too. I expected display after display showing how the Kim dynasty invented everything from fire to the wheel to walking upright.

"Before the Kim dynasty the human race spent their days scurrying around in the mud, filth and ate their own excrement whilst head-butting rocks and trying to mate with trees, at night they would scream themselves to sleep whilst rubbing poo on their faces, then the dear leader Kim Il Sung was born and overnight he transformed the world. He invented civilization, the wheel, fire, the internet and the greatest invention of all the lean green fat reducing machine. Now bow down to his greatness or get shot in the face."

In reality however, the museum was crap. The displays were 40-year-old decaying cardboard and were about as informative as a lemon. The poor woman giving us a guided tour looked like her soul had been destroyed. Never has the look of apathy and defeat been so clear on a person's face. She had been broken and it was upsetting to see. I'd only had a couple of hours sleep and was doing that thing where I was trying not to yawn and in the process making faces like I was trying to unblock constipation whilst doing a crossword puzzle. Che, obviously noticing my weird faces, came over and asked if I was okay. I said I was tired and needed a coffee or 10. She replied that there was a coffee place next door and did I want to go with her? I thought she was taking the piss and was about to compliment her on her excellent and rather brave sense of humour but she wasn't joking because there actually was a coffee place next door.

So as the rest of the group, including an insanely bored and now pissed off Natalie were shown the origins of Korean tribes, we snuck next door to the weirdest tiny empty café in the history of the world ever! There were no people, pictures or anything other than tables and chairs. There were no menus or any sign of what the weird place was. There was just a pretty woman stood behind a counter. Che asked for coffees and had we sat down and had a chat. It was a special moment in which we talked about dancing, high heels, the lovely styles there were in the country and how they dress better than in the UK where on a Friday night it looks like the town's overrun with prostitutes because even though it's freezing cold, women wear almost nothing. I thought a bit of self-depreciation would be good and it was. Then we turned to the great imperial aggressors, America. I stated that they had declared more wars than any other country and although the people were friendly, nice and generally peaceful, the government are prone to causing shit around the world in failed wars. Che loved me. She never once brought up my gender which was nice too.

An hour later and both absolutely tripping on coffee I paid, ironically with US Dollars and we met the bored looking group outside the museum. We were shocked to see about ten thousand people that had somehow mysteriously congregated in the square outside. Literally thousands of people sat on the ground in their national costumes. We had randomly timed the trip to coincide with the national celebration of 65 years as a nation. We apparently weren't supposed to be seeing these thousands of people practicing clapping and cheering so we were quickly ushered into the bus and driven to the hotel.

We had half an hour to have a quick shower and meet the group in reception before we were taken to the Arirang Mass Games which we were also lucky enough to coincide our trip. The Arirang Mass Games are one of the most spectacular spectacles on Earth. Tens of thousands of performers in the world's biggest stadium, dancing, acting, singing, gymnastics, a wall of thousands of people holding up different coloured placards to produce images and slogans ... it's pretty much beyond description so perhaps Google it. The games happen sporadically, there hasn't been one since our trip. There can be 10 year gaps. We were just lucky.

Whilst we were all waiting for E.T. in the reception, I noticed that in one of the massive fish tanks that adorned a huge wall was a turtle — a real life sea turtle. I don't know how the hell they got it there but the last thing I expected to see in North Korea was a sea turtle in a fish tank. I have now added sea turtle to my Christmas wish list.

Eventually E.T. finished phoning home or whatever the fuck she was doing and we boarded the bus and were driven to the stadium. It was huge and very modern. We were shown to our seats and then the show began. I don't think words can quite express the Arirang Mass Games because it is by a mile the most incredible thing I have ever seen in my life. Everyone was amazed. There were a hundred thousand performers in total which is just insane.

For all that is wrong with the country as perceived from a Western viewpoint and from a point of view of someone that's never lived in a socialist country, the people are extremely patriotic, they do love their country and the leaders ... maybe it's the 24 hour relentless propaganda which is so intense even Goebbels would think it's too much or maybe it's that they have to be like that or they'll be shot. I don't know. No one knows. The country is secretive, there is very little information on anything but as much as we probed and questioned things with people the more we understood that the people didn't feel that hard done by, if anything they blame the Americans for everything and for them to participate in the games was a great honour. We think.

We got back on the bus and Che sang us all a traditional folk song. It was a beautiful moment which sent a shiver down my spine. We got to the hotel ate some god-awful food and then passed out. It had been one hell of a long day.

*

13.08. Friday. Pyongyang, North Korea.

At 5:30 am the phone rang and someone told us it was time to wake up so with stingy tired eyes we got up and dressed up for the mausoleum. My wonderful fireproof five euro trousers that we'd bargained so hard for were about 10 sizes too small and didn't even nearly close so I had to dig out my handy sewing kit and devise an ingenious system of thread, knots, loops and precariously positioned safety pins to hold them up so that it didn't look like I'd stolen the pants off a 10 year old boy (This is why we use the word trousers!!!!!) I felt uncomfortable in the wrong clothes but being in North Korea and visiting the mausoleum of the dictators who were embalmed was so much freakier, the clothes were the least of my worries.

The oddness began almost as soon as we arrived at the mausoleum. After queuing for ages we went through a metal detector, I was panicking that my safety pin thread device would set the alarm off and the guard would discover it and then a whole chain of events would unfold leading to me being spanked to death by Kim Jong Un which would not be ideal.

Soldier: Care to explain why your trousers are held up with thread and a safety pin?
Me: No I can't sorry ... but look, they're non-flammable! Best quality.
Soldier: That's not good enough. Come with me. Kim

Jong Un's going to spank you senseless.

Me: (being dragged away) Wait, wait watch I can hold a flame to them and they don't burn. Watch, I can screw them up in a ball and they're still there! Wait! Arghh!

Thankfully I didn't get spanked by Kim Jong Un and we passed through fine. We were told to get in rows of four people, then we walked up some stairs still in rows and onto an endless travelator which is where we remained unable to walk for the next 20 minutes. We were slowly moved past pictures of all the various Kims. The travelator went on for about 200 metres, it was ridiculous. There were lots of military people and smartly dressed locals coming back on the other way all looking very sombre with some in tears. As the end of the corridor approached we walked round a corner and were faced with another endless corridor with yet another travelator with lots more pictures of the glorious leaders doing glorious things like riding glorious horses, pointing at glorious machinery and generally trying not to look like two gloriously evil fucking cunts that watched their people starve as they guzzled champagne and had water slides built in their palaces because they're cunts.

Eventually we reached a big door with two scary looking army men either side. Che told us that we had to walk in our rows of four and then bow at the statue of the Kims. So we all walked into the big empty room with the massive statue of the cunts at the other end. We bowed then left the room through a side door. (Sorry for using the c word so much. I don't normally use it but no other word quite expresses my hatred of the cunts.) We then walked up some stairs and then into a room with more military people in it. At the end of the room was a small short corridor which had big nozzles covering the walls that were blowing out cold air like a giant hair dryers, it was so weird. We walked through it individually then lined up in our rows of four again. We were now in a large dimly lit red room which in the middle had the body of Kim Cunt 1.

We lined up on one side of it and bowed, then solemnly walked round to the other side and bowed again then again on the third side. The body looked quite well preserved, which can probably be explained by the fact the place was fucking freezing.

We left the body room and walked down the palatial corridor to a room with all the medals and honorary diplomas that he had been awarded throughout his life. They all seemed a bit pointless, I don't know whether he awarded himself the medals or whether he was surrounded by ass-lickers but some of them were just stupid. Honorary degree for Excellency and services to magnesium? Medal of honour for outstanding bravery and unrelenting support for chicken production? If you're going to award yourself honorary awards why not make them more apt, honorary degree for outstanding obesity and evil dictatorship. Medal of honour for outstandingly bad leadership and unrelenting support for the devil. Degree for biggest wanker on Earth. Master's degree in awful fashion sense and joke-like hair styles.

I got the message of how amazing the Kims were pretty quickly and decided to speak to Che instead who I'd decided I loved. She opened up a bit more about life. She told me that the government found her a husband, an officer in the army and that her daughter doesn't know she works with foreigners and whilst she is on a tour she is not allowed to go home or contact her family, she instead stays at the hotel with us. If there are many tourists she has consecutive groups and doesn't see her daughter for weeks on end, and she is a lucky one because when she was younger North Korea and Cuba had an agreement where the top 100 students could go and study for a year in the other country and Che was lucky enough to learn Spanish in Cuba for a year so she is one of less the 0.01 % who have seen the world outside of North Korea. Even when she was away she was banned from watching TV or listening to Western music or radio. The totalitarianism went with her. She was genuinely interested in me and my gender. She had absolutely no presumptions or prejudices, just lots of sensible questions which she nodded in approval at the answers to. I think we were equally intrigued by each other's lives.

After admiring Kim Jong Sun's amazing intelligence and education and obviously his immense bravery and services to his people (coughbullshit) we walked down some stairs and were faced with another hair dryer thing which led to the mausoleum of Kim Jong-il who died just a few years ago. We bowed at each side and left into a side room which was a room dedicated to the twat's honorary degrees, diplomas and medals.

We continued our mausoleum tour to the ground floor where we saw their car collection and the train carriage which is where Kim Jong-il sadly died — Hooray! His famous sunglasses were there as were two sets of his famous jumpsuits and more surprisingly a

Macbook Air. Nice of him to spout relentless propaganda about America being the evil imperial aggressors and them use a fucking Macbook, the cunt. Normal people aren't even allowed the Internet which makes it even more annoying.

E.T. then hobbled over and asked Che how quickly the train could come to a stop, which let's be honest was a stupid question but, because she was American, Che hated her and snapped back, "How should I know I'm not a train driver" I burst out laughing to which Che gave me a wry smile. It was brilliant. I felt like high fiving her. No one liked E.T. because she was an utter shit-stirring bitch, but that's another story. Thought I'd point that out so you don't just think I'm being mean about her because she looked like E.T. because if there's one thing someone like me doesn't do it is judge someone on their appearance. E.T's looks were incidental to her being one of the worst people I have ever met. Within four hours of meeting her she had managed to piss off everyone in the group for various different reasons. In our case she was so rude to both Natalie and me, we couldn't work out if she was joking or not. She wasn't. She should have just fucked off back to the back to Planet Bitch from whence she came.

We once again boarded the green bus of doom and rushed through the quiet deserted streets back to the hotel for lunch. We were ushered up to the roof where we went to, of all things, a revolving restaurant. Oh yes, in the country where the people have nothing there is a hotel with a revolving restaurant. We had a buffet which was so awful we instantly renamed the place the revolting restaurant. Well not audibly, we didn't want to be shot in the face. The only slightly edible thing was cold soggy French fries which were stuck together with something resembling, and probably containing, man juice. Thankfully as with every meal we were given beer so I drank it just to get some calories. I don't drink alcohol because my body doesn't process it and just get instantly smashed then get an instant hangover so I was absolutely wasted. I couldn't stop telling an Italian woman how unusual but beautiful her face was and as if that wasn't bad enough I took about 3000 pictures of her face as her husband looked on unsure what to do. Fuck it was so embarrassing.

In the afternoon, still smashed off my fake tits, we boarded the bus and were driven to a massive bronze statue of Kim Jong Cunt and his cunt son, we lined up again and then walked up and bowed to it. Yay. Then we laid flowers on the steps in front of it. Yay. There were military people everywhere all doing the same thing. Yay. They really do worship the leaders. Whether they want to or not is an entirely different question but I think overwhelmingly yes. If anything they blame the Americans for all bad things.

On a different and much more interesting note, if you can be overwhelmed and underwhelmed can you just be whelmed? How are you today? Whelmed and you? What does whelmed even mean? What do you think of your Christmas present? I'm whelmed.

Back on the bus again we drove to a bookshop where we bought some propaganda books. Who doesn't want to read Kim Jong-il's books? He's got hundreds of diplomas and degrees so he must be a genius! Everyone will be getting North Korean propaganda for

Christmas.

Outside the shop I was drunkenly flirting with Che (another reason I don't drink) and I asked her why she's not allowed to see her family when she's on a tour and she replied that there are many tourist spies and it's very difficult. She then abruptly left. In the square next to the bookshop there were some children on roller boots that came and said hello. It was so normal it was weird. I'm not sure what happened in the rest of the day because I drank more and was so drunk that probably for the best I blocked it out.

Quotes from the last few days:

Natalie: Jesus what have you been eating? Dead people?
Me: Do you want me to open the window?
Natalie: Yes, yes open the window, open the bloody wall, holy fuck it's disgusting.
Me: It's not my fault it's the falafel.

Me: I just spelt diarrhoea right. This is a new milestone in my life.

Natalie: Wouldn't it be better if the Smurfs were pink?
Me: Ooh I love a philosophical debate.

Natalie: I'm getting sick! Here have some of my saliva.
Me: What is wrong with you?
Natalie: What? We share everything.
Me: You are demented. You want me to get sick too?

Natalie: We are sickness twin buddies. Kiss me.
Me: You're not normal.

*

14.08. Saturday. Pyongyang, North Korea.

I came round naked on the bathroom floor with Natalie screaming at me. I had cleverly vomited in the bathroom sink, blocked it, tried to unblock it by what I can only assume was splashing it absolutely everywhere and thus had covered almost every surface of the bathroom in vomit. It was not good. This, incidentally, is another reason why I'm teetotal. Natalie was not amused and screamed at me. I sat in the shower and cried. It was the worst night ever and I'm so ashamed. My body just doesn't process alcohol, I could have one shot and it would be like normal people drinking 18 pints. I had learnt my lesson years previously and was absolutely fine being teetotal but once every few years when everyone is drinking I forget I can't drink. This was North Korean beer and the temptation was too great.

In the morning we boarded the green bus and drove an hour driving through the beautiful countryside to reach a massive dam in a town called Nampo. We were given a presentation about its construction which was thoroughly boring. I once again made the excuse I needed the toilet and found Che. I asked her what she meant by saying there are many spies for tourists she bluntly told me, "What is it you don't understand Darcie? We don't spy; we are not like the Americans."

I think she was bugged. She was acting so strangely.

I felt like an idiot and quickly went into undo mode and wriggled out of it. She then gave me a certain smile that very nearly caused me to cry. It'll haunt me forever. So sad. She knew. She was a prisoner in a country where everybody is a prisoner, everyone is a spy and you cannot even talk freely in your own family. So utterly tragic. I had to try so hard not to cry all the way back to Pyongyang I nearly shit myself.

My emotions were suddenly interrupted when Che jumped up on the bus, told us all to get off and to follow her. So we all literally ran down a random Pyongyang road chasing after our guide. It was a tad surreal. Somehow we had bumped into a huge military parade with tanks, armoured trucks, missiles and all the military equipment you see in these parades on TV. So we watched the military parade, you know like you do when you're in North Korea. There were thousands of people waving the parade by and there was a band playing military music. We waved at all the trucks of people and when they saw us their faces lit up with huge smiles and they waved back frantically. It was brilliant. They were so pleased to see us. The North Korean people love foreigners apart from Americans and it was nice to see the military so happy to see us. A lot of the soldiers looked malnourished, small and unhealthy and this really got to Natalie who was almost in tears. So it was my turn to try and take her mind of it. Crying at a military parade is not appropriate. We are not normally afraid to cry. In fact I'd go as far as to say I spend more time crying than not crying. I cry that much I worry about salt deficiency, - that's when you know you cry a lot. I cheered her up and we waved at the parade.

The next stop was the Pyongyang Metro system which is the deepest in the world at 100 metres underground. There are rumours that the military have their own tunnels and that the city is well connected underground for the "leaders" and their chums. There are also rumours that the metro only runs to show the tourists how modern the city is and that it's actually all an act. I can confirm that this is rubbish, it's as real as any other Metro with real people doing real things. The stations were beautiful with a kind of Art Deco meets 1940 Soviet Union.

We took the subway one stop to the Arc de Triomphe which was like all the Arcs de Triomphe in the world. Why does every country have exactly the same monument? Uh, let's make a monument to show how amazing we are. What should we make? Something original to show our unique brilliance? No, no let's just make a fucking arch the same as everyone else for the last 2000 years. If I was in charge I'd make one the shape of boobs.

*

15.08. Sunday. Pyongyang, North Korea.

Today was the day we were going to the DMZ (demilitarization zone) which is where the North meets the South on the most heavily armed border in the world. The DMZ runs the length of the country and is full of landmines and armies on both sides blasting propaganda at each other over huge speakers. We boarded the bus at 7.30 am and drove for two hours past lots of military checkpoints and hundreds of massive frescos of the leaders which seem to be on every street corner. About half way into the journey, Che came to the back of the bus and told me that the previous day I'd taken a picture in a village that needed deleting, I asked what picture and she said of some children playing near a rundown building. Of course no problem I replied but how do you know what I took pictures of? She told me that someone had seen someone sat at the back of a bus taking pictures and they had reported it, the system had worked out what bus was there at that time who was sat where then contacted the hotel who told Che. It's amazing really. I was quite impressed.

At the DMZ border itself the two Koreas have two big embassy type building facing each other and in-between them are four sheds - two blue and two white. Two of these are South Korean and two are the North's. The sheds are actually on the border itself and when inside these huts you can be in both the North and South but you can't leave through the other side unless that's how you came in. It's just weird and hard to explain.

We pulled up to the buffer zone and went to one of the few souvenir shops in the country. I bought a Pyongyang t-shirt which I'm sure will be useful in case I want to offend some people by looking like a an absolute idiot walking round London in it. I also bought a huge beautiful painting which Natalie thought was horrible. We waited around for what seemed like an eternity whilst surrounded by lots of soldiers who were armed to the teeth. It was pretty scary. Eventually we got on the bus and went down the small lane to the border. We stopped at a building where the armistice was signed, bringing an end to the war. An English-speaking general told us about the war and the Americans "defeat." The cover of the agreement had been torn off by someone not best pleased about it. We got back on the bus and went further down the road to the border and the big building with the four sheds. We could see some tourists on the south and Natalie's phone even updated Facebook by logging onto the South's network. It was weird seeing them, knowing that only 50 metres separated us but we were worlds apart.

We left feeling even weirder than ever. We then went for Korean tapas which was actually relatively edible. Lots and lots of brass coloured little bowls filled the table. A couple of them didn't taste like asshole which was nice.

In the afternoon we went to a rural museum which was utterly shit. We estimated that 90% of what we were told to be lies and couldn't be bothered listening to it. It was described as a socialist utopia but the skinny, malnourished unhappy looking people didn't correspond so we both became angry and waited outside. The next stop on the never-ending tour was to a secondary school. We were asked to sit in the school hall as bored looking children with big fake smiles sang and danced for us. Then they came up to us and dragged us to dance with them. This was about as horrendous an experience as is humanly possible for us. We hate dancing. We hate child exploitation and we hated this fucking child zoo. But then did we want to offend a bunch of children? I decided I did because it's better than dancing. Natalie danced and winced with the utter horror of the situation.

I had rented a phone from the airport for no reason other than it was cheap and I thought it would be cool to call people from there (no, I'm not very clever). So I went outside to calm my emotions and thought it would be funny to call my brother.

Me: Guess where I'm calling from?

John: If you've actually done that thing with an old Nokia, a condom and Natalie's vagina that you're always on about I swear to god I will end you.

Me: Hahaha, I forgot about that. One day we'll do that.

John: You're sick.

Me: Hey it's not even my idea. It's Natalie's. She's the sick one, always going on about how weird it would be to speak to people from the inside of her vagina.

John: She needs help. Where are you then fuckwad?

Me: North Korea.

John: No you're not.

Me: Well, I am.

John: How are you calling me?

Me: I rented a phone.

John: You're calling me in the UK from a North Korean number? You utter fucking moron. Now my phone's going to be bugged for sure. Do know how much porn I watch?

Me: Ah yes, haha, I didn't think of that. Sorry.

John: You're a fucking idiot. I'm going to have to get a new number now.

Me: Ooops.

John: What the hell are you doing in that shit hole anyway?

Me: Shit hole?? You mean glory hole, no, wait, not glory hole, you mean paradise… you moron you're going to get me shot.

John: Whatever, bye.

Me: One last thing John, Remember that thing you hid under your stairs about North Korea?

John: What the fuck are you on about you shit head?

Me: That thing hidden under your stairs. The thing you were hiding. Well I agree with it.

John: You're trying to get me searched aren't you, you cross-dressing cunt? You fucking bellend.

Me: Yeah enjoy that. And you'll hide it up your anus again won't you? So they'd better check there too.

John: You girlyboy mother fucker I am going to destroy you.

Me: Takes one to know one.

John: That doesn't even make sense.

Me: I know you are but what am I?

John: Fuck you

Me: I love you too.

John: Fucking prick.

Full of happiness and pride in the fact that my brother would almost certainly be getting surveillance, his phone bugged and potentially hopefully anally searched, we got back on the bus and drove down another completely deserted potholed motorway to a maternity and breast cancer hospital. We were all given white doctors overcoats and then followed a young doctor as she showed us round all the place whilst going on and on about breasts. She repeatedly told us that North Korea leads the world in terms of treatment and research. We must have seen about six women's breasts and felt really uneasy about it. The semi-naked women cringed as much as we did. It was horrific. If the government wanted to show us how amazing they were, they could have just told us instead of leading us round the place like it was a zoo. Fuck it was awful.

How to make breast exams and the hideous possibility of cancer worse ... get a bunch of Western buffoons to stare at you getting examined. It was absolutely fucking terrible.

All of us were flustered and feeling weird. We left and had a glorious meal of Korean food which can only be described as culinary Nirvana. It was cabbage that had been boiled in what we can only assume was poo, then plopped onto some soggy noodles. Feeling like we'd just eaten poo we boarded surely the best vehicle ever created — our beloved green bus and were driven to the art university. The University was so good that as I looked at it I saw a vision of Jesus.

Almost unable to take any more splendour we went to the film studio where two or three propaganda movies are made each year. Behold, I exclaimed, why are people wasting their money going to Universal Studios when magical places like this exist? All in all it was so amazing all 10 of us had instant orgasms and fell to the floor writhing around in our own euphoric goo. Not really. Imagine Universal Studios then take away anything good and interesting and that's what it was like. It was turd.

The next stop was the Pyongyang Exhibition Centre which was a huge hall with exhibits detailing North Korean industry. It was quite interesting especially seeing as their only industry is Chinese-run and they have international sanctions against them. The guide told us that for steel-making, the clever scientists had developed a way to create steel without the coke which is needed elsewhere. It was apparently much cheaper and more efficient than using coke which is used everywhere else on Earth. It was Peter the German that quietly pointed out that they can't buy coke due to international sanctions. It's funny at the things they believe compared to what we are told in the West. A couple of days earlier, Che had told me that there are sanctions because America didn't want the North Koreans to have a satellite. She didn't know anything about the threatening with destruction of just about every country with nuclear annihilation, their idiotic nuke tests and launching missiles into the sea. They only hear one version of the world. Strangely if you think about it, so do we to a certain extent.

I have never really understood North Korean missile launches. How can anyone hate the sea so much that they spend their time firing missiles into it?

"Take that sea, mwahahaha. Oh what was that, sea? You said I'm a short fat wanker with bad hair? Right that's it, fire another missile into it, that'll teach it"

On the way back to the hotel we stopped off at the bowling alley which was deserted apart from two guys playing. I'd read about it before but couldn't have imagined how creepy it actually was. The machine that keeps scores was totally broken and even if you didn't hit a single pin it showed a strike. It probably hadn't been reset since Kim Jong Un last played and magically beat everyone in the country. I somehow managed to win which annoyed everyone because I roll the ball between my legs like a five-year-old child. E.T. kept telling everyone that my winning wasn't fair and my winning position didn't count because I didn't bowl the ball properly. I didn't say anything back and let the other eight people, who also despised her, tell her off.

I just smiled at her which made her red with anger. She was such a bitch. If I ever write a follow up book I'll write about what she did that was so bad. Terrible human.

*

16.08. Monday Pyongyang, North Korea.

We started the day in the best way possible, with a stale sandwich containing limp cucumber and something that was supposed to be vinegar but was more than likely battery acid. It was all that was left at the deserted breakfast buffet. We then we boarded the bus and travelled two hours to Sariwon which is a little town somewhere. When we arrived, we walked up a hill to see a beautiful old traditional pavilion which overlooked the town. This was filled with English students which we doubt it was coincidence that they were all there looking beautiful in the most scenic spot in the town at the exact same time we showed up but it didn't matter and wasn't a sinister bit of planning. We spoke to the shy students and had a lovely moment. The vibe in the town was the same as anywhere else in the world. People going to and fro going about their daily business. People on bikes, walking, running. It was about the most normal we'd seen in the country.

Back aboard the green bus of doom we drove a little further down the road to an old dilapidated hotel where we were to eat lunch. The hotel was old and well before the time of the Korean War and the Kim cunts took over. It had high ceilings and faded grandeur everywhere. It was beautiful. The menu consisted of nonsensical gross-sounding dishes so we ordered some plain noodles. Some other people further down the table were however a tad more adventurous/sick and ordered dog soup. So being vegan ... we thought we'd try it. Who wouldn't try dog soup in North Korea? Yeah shut up! It was actually nice but I was instantly sick with the grossness of it all. Sorry Fido I did a bad thing and am sorry.

P.S. You're rather tasty.

The next stop on our never-ending itinerary was the Children's Palace back in Pyongyang which as described is a palace full of children. These were the "lucky" kids that got good grades and were forced to go the special school where they would be forced to have the best education and become slave genius freaks. We were shown round lots of classrooms where deeply unhappy looking children performed to the tourists. They were amazingly skilled but then I suppose they had to be. After seeing the children sing, paint, dance and a five-year-old girl play the piano better than I have ever seen anyone ever play we went to a big theatre and took our seats ready for the grand performance where Kim Jong Un can show the world that the people are amazingly skilled and happy and that North Korea isn't a hermit dictatorship socialist country run by an evil bastard who is almost certainly psychotic and evil like his father and his grandfather. The show was amazing! Literally amazing but anyone not stupid saw it for what it was and it took the shine off the display.

After a meal of cooked cucumber and other terrible things we got back to the hotel, it was our last night and we weren't so upset about it.

The stress and emotion of the whole thing along with the relentless program had taken its toll and we were fucked.

*

17.08. Tuesday. Pyongyang, North Korea.

We packed our bags said goodbye to the people bugging our room.

Natalie: Goodbye Kim please thanks for not killing us. Please be nice okay?
Me: Yeah just be a good boy.
Natalie: And stop eating so much.
Me: Fuck's sake, Nat, were just about to leave. I don't want to be shot.
Natalie: Oh yeah. Shit.
Me: Here, I'll change the subject. Check this out spies, this is what's in my pants?

I then exposed myself to put the spies out of their misery. I imagine 50 people sat in the spy centre all cheered and exchanged money they had betted on me. I curtsied and we left the room.

We went downstairs to check out. Che with whom I'd developed a bit of a special relationship, gave me a gift of kimchi and I gave her 20 tangerines. We gave her a ridiculously large tip which was way more than we could afford but I don't think we could have lived with ourselves if we didn't give it. She had been amazing and so good at her job and we just wanted to hug her constantly.

We had decided to take the train to China because it was supposed to be an amazing experience and we didn't fancy dying on the Bakelite and wood plane so we boarded the big green bus one last time and went to the train station. As we stood there I savoured the moment being surrounded my military uniformed men and women, the orderly fashion everyone did things and in particular the pretty uniformed women pushing a trolley with food around. It was just like the 1940s. So eerie yet so beautiful and unique. We said our goodbyes to Che giving her huge hugs and crying in her face and then got on the train. As we moved away we waved as we left for the real world.

The countryside was beautiful and the people working on the land looked much the same as everywhere else in Asia. We played a game called count the murals of the leaders. We got bored at 30. After four hours the train stopped. We didn't know why but out of the window a military man ran along the train waving a handgun in his hand causing us to promptly shit ourselves. Ten minutes later, a guard came into our carriage and asked to look through our bags. He rifled through but didn't find anything he didn't like. Then he wanted to look at our photos so we handed him our cameras and phones. He didn't delete any but laughed as he looked through my iPhone photos. I don't know whether there were naked pictures of us but it wouldn't surprise me by the way he was laughing. Then seizing the moment to make him like us I offered him a hard boiled sweet but unfortunately due to the heat they had all melted together and so he put a clump of about four in his mouth and we all laughed as he struggled to talk. He was a nice man.

The next people he went to see must have thought he's totally unprofessional chomping on a mouth full of sweets. We were relieved that it was over but it was short lived because on came a much more senior and meaner officer. He wasn't playing round and demanded to see our phones, he went through them but didn't find anything. Then he went through our cameras and wasn't at all impressed. He tutted and huffed as he deleted almost a quarter of our photos, thankfully the night before we had backed them up onto encrypted USB sticks knowing that this check would likely happen. After about an hour, the guards left and the train moved off. Five minutes later we crossed the bridge of the Daedong River and were in China. The difference was unbelievable, there were colours, advertising, capitalism, happy looking free people, and modern buildings. The feeling on the train changed in an instant. We all felt it. It was like someone changed the background music. It's hard to explain but in an instant everything was transformed and everyone felt it deeply. We were safe, we were free, we were alive.

Just inside China we changed train to a Chinese sleeper train which would take us to Beijing. We found some other tourists who had come from North Korea and spent hours talking about the madness and insane experiences of the week. It was a bit like group counselling, we were all traumatised by the endless fucked -up experiences and sights, the never-ending itinerary and emotional rollercoaster we had been taken on and needed to talk about it.

North Korea had a profound effect on us and changed us both deeply. It's so intensely harsh, different and strange in every way possible and yet people are still people whether they are under a fucked up regime or not. Daily life is pretty much the same for everyone everywhere. We didn't see massive hardship or poverty. We saw real life and real people and interacted far more than we thought we would have done and don't think the people know they are in a fucked up dictatorship. A few people looked like their souls had been destroyed but over all people just got on with life and smiled. They love the leaders, the military and have a shared utter hatred of America. They are not all unhappy at all from what we saw. Koreans are such beautiful intelligent people and I'd love to go back one day and see that it's changed and the people were free. Above all else I hope Kim Jong Un either realises he can change the lives of so many for the better and be remembered as a real hero instead of a butcher who carried on his family's awful legacy or he has an intensely painful slow death for being a cunt who had palaces built as his people starved and has anyone who even imagines change sent to concentration camps. In fact fuck it, I hope the cunt gets the slow painful death he deserves.

Quotes of the last few days:

Me: There's two lots of bad news.
Natalie: What? There's two lots of baboons?

Me: You made the toilet smell of asparagus pee. I prefer the smell of shit to asparagus pee.

Me: You know your eyes are huge as well, if we had a baby it would be an owl.

Natalie: Pull your skirt down Kim Jong Un can see your knickers.

Me: Those with nothing have everything.

Natalie: Aww, you came to hug me.
Me: Nope, I'm just using you for your body heat.

Natalie: Aghh, the revolving door is chasing my bottom.

Natalie: You chewed the top of the pen, no wonder you have AIDS.
Me: I don't have AIDS.
Natalie: You do now.
Me: Shit.

*

Chapter Five

18.08. Wednesday. Beijing, China.

All we wanted to do was get our Mongolian visa and leave China. Returning to a country with extreme transphobia, xenophobia, dirt, rudeness and lack of communication had gotten to us and we just wanted to leave. Even after the insanity of North Korea, China was not somewhere we were happy to be. We needed just five days to get a Mongolian visa so I had the great idea to save money and get the cheapest place to stay in the whole of Beijing. The cheapest normal hostel was $15 a night. The place I picked was $3. It was not a clever decision. It was a room in a private apartment in a small town 40 minutes outside of Beijing. Everything about the town and the apartment was revolting. We honestly don't reckon the bathroom had ever been cleaned.

The toilet was literally black and the whole room absolutely stank of shit, piss and filth. The shower consisted of an open pipe that came out of a stained wall and was not only cold but also stank of sewage. The bedroom had bed sheets which were 80% pubes and 20% dirt. There was no air conditioning, it smelt so bad and worst of all there was no fucking Internet signal. Natalie was extremely upset with me for picking the place and I felt terrible. After North Korea and sleeping on a train we deserved some level of comfort to gather ourselves and I had picked a disgustingly vile cesspit.

Angry and sad, we left the room to find go to the Mongolian embassy to apply for the visa. The sequence of events that happened next is so ridiculous I'm just going to reel it off. Within hours I'd been groped by an old man; been laughed at in my face by Mongolian embassy staff; been in a pretty serious car crash whilst in an illegal taxi, then got told by a passer-by to leave the area quickly to avoid the police, so we walked down the motorway and spent three hours lost. After we eventually found civilization, all the taxis refused to take us presumably because they were cunts. Then, when nearly back at the apartment, a guy crossed the road just to call me a faggot and I lost my temper for the first time in my entire life. Normally I just laugh it off or cry. On this day I'd had enough and I went mad — like actually mad. I must have looked like an absolute psychopath making shouting and squealing noises like a mix between a zombie and a horse.

Such were the weird noises that I think I invented new sounds. He absolutely shit his pants and ran away. I think if he would have stayed he'd have ended up being kneed in the balls. I was seriously sick of all the abuse I got in China. Why can't they just bitch behind my back like everywhere else? It was such a crazy day.

In the evening, we tried to buy some cheap sheets to put on the bed but being China even this simple task was nigh-on-fucking-impossible. We would have had better luck trying to communicate with a different species of animal. The woman stared at us as if we were talking horses. We showed her my phone with the translated message of what we wanted and knew it made sense because we translated it back from Chinese to English again but it may as well have said, "Please turn yourself inside out, drink a dishwasher and stick your big toe inside an Amazonian frog's rectum whilst singing the Macarena." It took an hour to finally get some shitty sheets. We hit the bed and passed out.

*

18 to 21.08. Beijing, China.

We spent the next few days in a coffee shop writing. We didn't want to see anything or be insulted so from 9am to 9pm, we sat in a coffee shop. It was pretty nice especially the total lack of abuse. The coffee was shit. Whilst sat there bitching about all things Chinese I thought it would be a good time to write a review for the absolute utter shithole we were staying in.

Trip Advisor Reviews.

XXXXXX Apartment, Beijing. AKA The Sewer.

What did you like most about XXXXXX Apartment, Beijing?
I liked the sheets which were 80% pubes. Pubes it turns out are rather good at keeping you warm. After this trip when I get home I'm going to carefully collect all our pubes on a daily basis and make my own blanket out of them. Perhaps I could even start selling them. Once people realise their incredible heat capturing capabilities they have they will be queuing up to get their blankets. Eventually demand will be so great I'll have to collect other people's pubes thus helping the economy.

I also enjoyed the epic filth of the place. It's a well-known fact that living in a sterile environment is bad for you because your immune system becomes weak so staying in this apartment which was effectively a sewer must have bolstered my immune system to the point where I am now completely immortal.

What did you like least about XXXXXX Apartment, Beijing?
The thing I liked least was the ceiling which wasn't filthy enough. Thankfully I helped amend this let down by smearing it in poo so now it fits with the rest of the place.

Was the location good for XXXXXX Apartment, Beijing?
Yes. As stated in the advert it was located in central Beijing, and by central Beijing they cleverly meant 40 minutes outside of Beijing and off the Metro lines meaning we had to get buses with no idea where we were going. Oh, let's not forget the rubbish dump at the end of the road which was nice to be next to. I love the smell of festering rubbish in the morning.

Did you enjoy the food?
We wouldn't have eaten in there if you paid us. We would have instantly caught the shits and died. The food in the local vicinity was Chinese and therefore revolting.

Would you return to XXXXXX Apartment, Beijing?
Not even for a million pounds … Well yeah, we'd go if we were paid but we'd want to be wearing a full radiation suits and welding goggles.

Rate XXXXXX Apartment, Beijing out of 10?
Minus 4000.

So, that was China. What an amazing country if you don't mind the fact that most of them hate foreigners, they are rude, dirty and transphobic, homophobic and racist and don't even try to be vegetarian or vegan because everything contains duck tits, hamster balls and other hideous parts of animal. To summarise in the politest possible way. We shall not be returning or ordering Chinese food ever again.

*

22.08. Tuesday. Beijing, China.

We had just three hours' sleep in the festering shit-stinking room when the alarm when off for us to get up and go to the airport. It became clear very quickly that were both in cataclysmically bad moods. They were so bad we didn't even talk to each other because saying anything would have resulted in an argument. It didn't take long before the inevitable happened though.

Natalie: Why would you book this fucking shithole, you cheapskate asshole. I can't even shower because I'll be dirtier than I am now. It's disgusting and you are an idiot.
Me: You book the fucking rooms then. Why do I have to do everything?
Natalie: Because you're a fucking asshole.
Me: Excellent I'm glad we got that cleared up then.

We dragged the bags through the spit and filth covered corridor into the spit and filth-covered elevator and onto the spit and filth-covered streets. We tried to get a taxi to the airport but no taxi would take us because they are all bastards. Literally an hour went by and our pants were slowly starting to fill with poo.

"So how did you miss your flight?"
"Well Chinese taxi drivers hate foreigners that's fucking why."

*

Chapter Six

We landed in Mongolia and instantly loved it. Even the immigration staff were nice.

Immigration woman: You're passport says male but you're female.
Me: I love you. Can we hug?

The hotel in Ulaanbaatar was nice. We had a big room which was extra special because there was a distinct lack of spit and filth. The bathroom included an actual shower with an actual shower head not just a cold pipe sticking out of a shit splattered wall. The only thing that was a tad odd was that they clearly had a problem understanding the carpet. It was on the floor which was pretty normal but also on the walls, a chair and covering a table. It was really weird. Perhaps we're all wrong and carpet should be used on more surfaces. I think I'm going to get the carpet fitter round to carpet up my ceiling, walls and toilet. Who needs carpet on a table? It pretty much defies every use a table has.

"Damn I spilt my coffee get the carpet cleaners round."

The only thing it would be good for is James bloody Dyson who would get to invent some new expensive shit vacuum: "New Dyson carpet cleaner for all your ceiling, wall and table carpet needs." No doubt it would cost a billion pounds and like all of his other needlessly expensive shit machines that we don't actually need.

In the evening the driver we had organised came

round. We had planned a four-week adventure with nomads in the most remote part of Outer Mongolia where we were assured tourists have never been before. What could possibly go wrong when two vegetarian lesbians one who can barely see and the other one is transgender woman go into the middle of nowhere for four weeks? They'd not even seen Westerners before let alone the circus freak show.

The driver came round with a friend who did all the talking and we quickly figured out why, he couldn't speak a word of English. We were pretty angry because communicating is pretty important when you're in the middle of fucking nowhere and the only way in or out is 15 hours of off-road driving. His friend he insisted he could speak English but was shy. It turned out the only words he could say were "no ploblem" and the only time he ever actually said this was when we did actually have a fucking problem like for example his getting drunk and crashing into a hole, his getting drunk and demanding I drive, his getting drunk and getting stuck in a swamp. Still when he wasn't endangering our lives he turned out to be a nice guy.

As we sat in the hotel cafe and discussed routes. Sakal the driver was sat opposite me and was literally staring in my face with a confused look on his face. Normally, people try to hide their confusion but he was sat half a metre away literally staring at me whilst looking the most confused I have ever seen anyone look. In the end Natalie lent over and said, "Yes she is."

I laughed but he didn't understand. I was just about to indicate through hand gestures that indeed I have the body of a man but am in fact a woman but I thought it might be better to know him a little longer before doing the penis and boob gestures as he stared into my face. Transgenderism is very much in the closet in Mongolia and is not seen or heard about. Nazism unbelievably is a huge problem. Lots of Mongolians are actual Nazis — no I'm not making this up, anyway as such they have a huge problem with homophobia and transphobia. In 2001, three trans people were kidnapped which scared the bejesus out of us. Call me old fashioned but I have always been averse to kidnapping. They hate our type so much they have actual street protests. Yep, that'll teach the gays, street protests. Fucking hell.

"Well I was born a lesbian but after seeing all these fat, thick, skinhead cunts protesting I've suddenly realised I was wrong to be transgender and gay, now get me out of these girl clothes and bring me some man things!"

No you, thick stupid cunts, nobody would choose this. It is utterly shit and you should leave us alone. We already got a shit enough hand in life without you protesting your hatred of our existence. Why homophobia exists is still a mystery to us and all intelligent people. You can't get rid of us! A percentage of the population is like this, it's like protesting about the existence of ducks. They exist! Just get over it you thick bastards.

"No ducks, mallards out, Donald Duck is a wanker,"

It's just stupid and so sad because LGBTQ people are bound to exist in Mongolia in the same numbers as everywhere else in the world but they have to live their lives in the closet because of the rampant homophobia. What exactly do you worry about, you thick homophobic cunts? Are you worried all us gays sit around all day planning how we are going have sex with you, convert your toilet to be gender neutral before convincing your kids to be trans? Have you met gay people? They are called gay for a reason and it's nothing to do with Marvin. It's because gay people are stereotypically happy. Just leave us alone you thick stupid bastards.

The English-speaking friend then asked if we had any very warm clothes to which we looked at ourselves in our stupid skimpy summer dresses and answered, no. We had read online that the weather would be from 18 to 35 degrees but whoever wrote that turned out to be a lying shit because it would actually be minus 20 to plus 20 which is one fuck of a range for a day. Who doesn't like to freeze their fake tits off at night and sweat them off during the day?

So after they left to talk about how gay we were and how they would dispose of our revolting gay bodies in the wilderness, we walked down the road to the local shop to buy a cheap warm top each. The shop was extra shit. It was in a Mall with about three other shops, all of which sold the same shit which was comically bad quality.

It's a bad sign when they sell sewing kits at the checkout to fix the holes in new clothes you have just bought. I bought a huge thick maroon fluffy thing and Natalie bought the itchiest maroon wool thing ever. We promptly decided to start a band together called Maroon Two. We wore nothing else but our new maroon things for the following 24 days. I honestly don't know how people lived before the invention of cotton and nylon. Could you actually imagine having to wear wool? It is a stupid substance. I'm surprised even sheep aren't so sick of the incessant itching. That's what soldiers wore in the war isn't it? Wool uniforms.

"Well you're probably going to get shot or blown up and whilst you wait for that glorious day you're going to have to wear this itchy ass wool uniform"

We went back to our carpet lined room packed our shit and prepared for the insanity the next few weeks would bring. Weirdly the room couldn't be locked from the inside. It was slightly unnerving because there were lots of scary looking people walking around and they all looked at us like they wanted us, particularly me, dead.

Quotes from the last few days:

Natalie: My Mum just took a punk out of the dog's face.
Me: I'm sorry what?
Natalie: You know, a punk?
Me: Erm, no I really don't.
Natalie: You know the punks that go into the skin?
Me: You mean a tick?
Natalie: Yeah a punk.
Me: There called ticks.
Natalie: In Sweden, they're called punks.
Me: I'm not sure I believe that.

Natalie: Have you ever vomited curry? It tastes like

curry when you vomit.
Me: Yes I'm bulimic, I've vomited everything.

Waitress: Do you want a cup of tea?
Me: Yes if you can make it without putting meat in it.

Me: Why are those children screaming in each other's faces
Natalie: Well seeing as they're both two years old and they are naked, she's probably thinking what the fuck do you have growing on your groin? And he's probably thinking where the fuck is your penis?

*

23.08. Wednesday. Ulaanbaatar, Mongolia.

It was 7.30 am and I was trying to wake Natalie up my usual way by jumping on top of her and doing my impression of a sea lion. Apparently I'm too cute to be angry at, so I do it several times a week because I get bored and need her to wake up to entertain me because I'm selfish. At that moment though a woman walked in through the unlockable door with a tray containing breakfast. We didn't even know we had it included in the price let alone being served it in bed. We would have been more pleased if it didn't look like we were having weirdo animal sex. Her face was that of absolute shock. We felt bad for her but not as bad as we felt for ourselves but what could we say?

"Sorry that was my sea lion impression, we weren't doing the sex, honestly, I do it to wake her up because I'm a thoroughly selfish little bitch and I get bored with her sleeping. Oh yes, and I have the body of a man including an annoyingly large penis which I hate but the wife loves. Anyway please don't kidnap and kill me, I'm very sorry I shall be straight male from now on I promise."

We ate breakfast and sat in the room savouring the cleanliness and relative normality of it, besides the fucked-up carpet of course. We said goodbye to the toilet and the shower knowing we wouldn't see one again for a while, and then we wrestled 20 kilos of Natalie's knickers down the eight flights of stairs because the lift was broken. We got outside and saw our beast of burden for the month, it was a 2001 Toyota Land Cruiser and was cool as fuck. I get slightly aroused by giant 4x4 cars. I don't know why. Not long after I first met Natalie, I mentioned that some cars turn me on and she replied that they turn her on too and the other day she saw an Audi Q8 and she wanted to "ride the gear stick and lick its exhaust hole."

"Behold I shall marry you," I replied. The same day I got drunk and wrote it on her family's WhatsApp group - as pretty much the first thing I'd written on there. Her family didn't speak to me for months and only liked me again after three years ... and that's why I don't drink. I'd had half a glass of wine. I hate to think how much trouble I'm going to be in for writing this. Oh god she's going to kill me.

Our first stop in the car was a supermarket to buy some food for the trip. What they call a supermarket is in fact a huge open air market with 50 stalls all selling literally the exact same things: sweets, chocolate, pickled cucumbers and instant noodles. With no exaggeration they sold nothing else. We had to buy food for 27 days which was at least easy. We'll have 68 instant noodles please, a shit ton of chocolate and half a ton of gherkins please. I wouldn't even mind if there was more than one flavour of fucking instant noodles we could buy but they all contained meat which left us one flavour, kimchi flavour — yes really. It was good but was so incredibly spicy it made your ass twitch as you ate it.

A short drive later we left Ulaanbaatar which to put it nicely, was a festering Soviet cack-fest and we entered the famous countryside which was beautiful, or at least so I heard because I was asleep. When I woke up there was a random guy in the front seat snoring, I don't know who he was because I fell asleep again and when I woke up he was gone.

The scenery was stunning, endless rolling green hills, yaks, horses and cows and the famous small circular white yurts Mongolia is famous for. Not a fence, building or permanent structure in sight and all of this blessed in the most amazing iridescent light we'd ever seen. I can't describe it but the light there is different somehow. It's brighter and clearer and it makes everything look different and more vibrant.

The roads were interesting in that they didn't exist. You just drive over the hills and mountains off road. You drive as the crow flies regardless of the ground or mountains in the way. It was mental. Occasionally there were some tyre tracks in the ground so at least you could tell other people had been there before and we weren't being led to our gay kidnap death. We couldn't figure out how anyone knows where they're going because there's nothing but open space and as someone that can spin in a circle and be lost I couldn't fathom how he knew where he was going.

Around eight hours later and with civilisation very far behind us we drove over the top of a hill and in the green desolate valley below they were randomly holding some local traditional games so we pulled up and to everyone's shock and bemusement we got out and watched. We didn't really understand the first game but it appeared like you had to run into a pack of angry wild horses armed with a stick with a rope hoop on the end and catch yourself a particular horse. I'm scared shitless of horses and to a lesser extent sticks with hoops on the end so I hid behind Natalie trying not to shit my pants. The next sport of wrestling then began. Now I've never fancied men before, well apart from one guy, a fireman called Joe ... ahhh Joe ... but anyway these wrestlers were dressed in what can only be described as uber-sexy bikinis. There's no other way to describe them. Before each fight they performed a dance which to put it bluntly was gay porn. Sticking their asses out and gyrating all over the place whilst bending over and spanking themselves on their asses. It looked like what I imagine a homosexual person's erotic dreams would be like. It was about as homoerotic as I have ever seen. Then they started wrestling each other and I swear I'm not making this up, two referees followed them round spanking them on their asses really hard every few seconds the whole time.

It was as weird, kinky and odd as it sounds. If I hadn't seen it and recorded it I wouldn't have believed it. The winner of the wrestling was the one that made the other fall on his face. Then the winner did a hugely over-the-top erotic sexy victory dance which involved ass shaking, gyrating, self-spanking and waving of his arms like a camp gay seagull that had been covered in glue. Please feel free to type Mongolian wrestling dance into YouTube to see it for yourselves. It was practically porn. I'm never being invited to Mongolia again, am I?

"First he was gay, then he was a she then he, she, it was with another woman who also liked women then she insulted our capital, supermarkets and national sports."

…Oh but it gets so much worse later on!

The final game involved riding a horse at full speed and then reaching down and picking a stick up off the ground without falling off and dying. We were in the path of the horses and having them charge towards me gave me heart palpitations so I screamed and went to sit in the car where I was safe. Shortly after we set off on the journey again.

The original plan for the day was to drive the 15 hours to the nomad family we'd be staying with but due to spending too long watching shit-scary horses and mega-gay wrestling it became dark and driving off road over mountains was to say the least just a tad dangerous. So suddenly without pulling off the road because there wasn't one he stopped the car pulled a tent out of the back, took one look at us, shook his head and put it up himself.

It was almost dark, we were fucking freezing and that's when Natalie tentatively notified me that she needed to poop. For some reason she has always had extreme toilet phobia and won't go unless she has a palatial toilet made of solid gold, bejewelled in unicorn eyelashes, diamonds and emeralds and has toilet paper made out of swan fluff. So having to go in the middle of fucking nowhere was not conducive to her poopage. I was made to stand guard in case the invisible people that didn't exist were to see the poopage, regardless of it being totally dark and there being no one around. In the end she chickened out, cried and shouted at me for bringing her to such a place. I couldn't be bothered fighting so I said we'd find a toilet in the morning even though I knew there wouldn't be one for the next 24 days.

Right before we crawled into our shit freezing stupid tent, Sakal came over babbling incoherently as he did. At first we thought he'd lost the plot with him making odd noises but then out came out a howl, as in the howl wolves make.

Sakal: No ploblem, no ploblem. Haha.
Me: That might be no problem for you, you little fuck goblin, you're sleeping in the fucking monster truck of a car over there not in a cloth fucking tent. Do you know what wolves do to a transgender lesbian couple? After they finish laughing, they fucking eat them.
Sakal: No ploblem, no ploblem.
Me: Yes fucking ploblem. I don't want to be fucking eaten.
Sakal: No ploblem.
Me: Look Sakal, I'm only going to say this once, it's pronounced problem not ploblem and we do have a fucking problem because we are rather averse to being dinner.
Sakal: No ploblem.
Me: Fuck.

We climbed in the tent and lay on the cold freezing rock hard floor because there was no mattress. The comfort wasn't even on the radar though. No, the rocks in our backs were nothing compared to the thought of being torn apart by a pack of ravenous angry wolves. So we sat there hour after hour feeding off each other's fears making each other increasingly scared. The whole night was spent wide eyed in terror wondering what the fuck we were doing in the middle of Outer Mongolia in a tent when there were wolves around. I obviously got the blame and was a stupid person for thinking it would be fun.

Natalie: You're an idiot Darcie and I hate you.

Me: Well thanks Natalie, we're just about to get fucking eaten to fucking death and you want to tell me you hate me. Well that's just bloody great.

Natalie: I can't even poo. I need to poo and I can't because there's no fucking toilet.

Me: You are surrounded by toilet, the whole area is a toilet. Toilet, toilet as far as the eye can see. In fact I'd go as far as to say you'd be hard pressed to find somewhere within a hundred fucking miles that could be considered not toilet

Natalie: I'm not going in the middle of bloody nowhere.

Me: It's fucking pitch black, who do you think is going to see you?

Natalie: A fucking wolf Darcie. I'm not shitting in a wolf field are you mad?

Me: I'm sure when the wolves smell your shit they'll run away.

Natalie: Fuck you. You know I have toilet phobia why would you say that? Why do you always try and be funny? I hate you. I hope when the wolves come they eat you first.

Me: You'd prefer to watch me being eaten before being eaten yourself? Your last moment on Earth watching your soul mate being torn apart and munched to death? You're not very nice are you?

Natalie: Fuck you. You know what I meant.

Me: Yeah, you'd like to spend your last living moments watching my hideously brutal death. Look you insane cow, we'll find a toilet tomorrow stop crying you're not going to shit the bed and even if you did it wouldn't make it any less hospitable than it is now. If anything it'll keep the wolves away.

Natalie: Right, that's it. In the morning, I'm going back to Ulaanbaatar.

Me: Fine. I'll send you a postcard okay?

Natalie: Fuck you.

Me: No, fuck you.

Natalie: Hug me, I'm cold.

Me: No, we're fighting, hugging is against the rules of fighting. We have to make up first.

Natalie: Fine we're friends again. Now hug me I'm cold.

Me: I love you.

Natalie: I love you too and I don't want to watch you being eaten.

Me: Well that's good to know.

*

24.08.   Thursday.   Ulaanbaatar,   Mongolia.

We didn't wake up because we'd not slept. Every rustle, noise and draft and we shit ourselves thinking that a giant wolf would burst in and eat us. It was the worst night we'd ever had and we have had some shit nights, including once having a night in which one of us (Natalie) did actually shit the bed. But it's best I never tell you that story because I'm already likely to be murdered for telling you about her wanting sex with an Audi Q8.

It was 6am. We were sat cross-legged outside the tent with our matted hair blowing in the wind. We had broken looks on our faces and a thousand yard stare. Sakal emerged from the car, looked at us and laughed hysterically. He just would not stop laughing. Eventually he managed to stop laughing long enough to gesture the question if we'd slept well.

"Um, how about fuck you Sakal. Next time we'll sleep in the car you can get eaten by a wolf you bastard."

Fuck knows what he found so funny, maybe it was the stupid weird white tourists that couldn't even make it one night. Whatever it was, he laughed so hard and for so long that it cheered us up and put us in good moods.

Half an hour later and still laughing like a deranged hyena he grabbed a pan from the boot and got some water from a nearby stream which we boiled to make coffee. Then came the search for the cups which Sakal cleverly didn't own. Why would we have cups? Who needs cups for coffee? Only pretentious, materialistic pussies that's who. Real people don't need shithead cups. No real people instead drink directly from the rusty pan. After rummaging for a while he triumphantly produced two paper cups. They would have actually been good had they been from this decade. They were utterly porous so after having boiling coffee pour over our hands we had the ingenious idea to line them with sandwich bags that we had dragged with us from Sri Lanka for absolutely no conceivable reason.

We set off over hills, valleys and mountains stopping at yurts along the way to ask for directions. Or GPS as Sakal joked. You know the terrain is difficult to navigate when you're driving to your own area (we were staying in Sakal's family area) which you have driven to a million times and still get lost. He got lost several times and would have to drive an hour back over the same hills the whole time shouting. "Nosh!" which means shit in Mongolian. We both decided nosh was the best word in the world and joined in shouting, "Nosh!" when things went wrong. Sakal thought this was hilarious and it soon became the only other word we could communicate with apart from "ploblem."

After another five hours we crossed the crest of a hill, Sakal pointed to three yurts in the valley below and indicated we'd be staying there. Soon enough we pulled up and met the beautiful happy family of nomads. We were shown the yurt we'd be staying in for a while. It was beautiful. The wooden sticks holding the roof up had all been beautifully painted with intricate patterns. The wooden trellis circular walls had beautiful blue cloth covering them. In the middle of the yurt there was a square metal fire with a stack of wood next to it. On the three sides there were beds which were also used as sofas, tables, workstations and all other things people use flat surfaces for.

There was a small Buddhist shrine with lots of

trinkets on it. All over the yurts you could see the grass growing through the floor which was strange for us. The material at the sides of the yurt didn't touch the ground properly and you could see outside and more importantly the freezing air could get it. There were three other yurts next to us in which the extended family lived in. All the family shared the thousand strong herd of horses, cows, goat and sheep and all the work responsibilities. It was how humans have lived for tens of thousands of years before we became a disease to the planet. It was a bit like seeing living history. The only modern things they owned were some metal tools. People five thousand years ago could have walked in and felt at home. There was nothing modern. No electricity, TV or Internet and the people were the happiest most stress-free people we have ever met.

The landscape was stunningly beautiful, rolling green land as far as the eye could see. A few hills here and there and the bluest sky we'd ever seen. It was just a huge beautiful expanse of space with nothing in it. It was pretty much how you'd expect heaven to look.

We unloaded our bags unto the yurt as the family looked on with shocked open mouths. We had more stuff with us for a short trip than they own between the lot of them. It was so embarrassing. I couldn't be bothered blaming Natalie and her obsession with useless stuff and knickers so I just accepted that we looked stupid. It all barely fit in the yurt. One entire half of the place was stacked with our bags. They couldn't believe we had so much shit and spent the next few weeks trying to look in our bags to see what we had. I would have loved to have been able to tell them knickers, high heels, candles and about a thousand too many dresses. Would you like some knickers as a memento?

Once we had settled, in we were invited next door to a smaller yurt. We sat on the bed and were presented with the most hideous thing since chicken feet snacks. A substance so monstrous it should be banned under the Geneva Convention: alcoholic horse milk. Let me try and describe it to you, imagine the worst thing in the world, times it by ten and you're still nowhere near close to how fucking hideously bad alcoholic horse milk is. The Nomads want you to drink it constantly and it's extremely rude and insulting to refuse. Well I fucking hate milk! I'm a fucking vegan. I don't want the fucking breast milk of any fucking animal let alone a fucking horse. No, just fucking no! It's fucking disgusting! Not to mention I don't drink fucking alcohol because it fucks me up. And the taste … it tastes like your worst nightmares. It's a bit like rancid three-week old milk that's been left in the sun then been mixed with half a bottle of vodka and a handful of cat shit.

Bodo, the leader of the household, handed me the bowl with the evil bubbling shit in it and I took it. Then Sakal slapped me on my hand and I was like, what the nosh are you doing, you nosh head? Then he indicated you can only accept things with your right hand as the left one is rude and an insult. So I took it with my right hand had a sip and had to try not to spit it out all over all everyone's faces. It tasted like Satan's asshole. It tastes exactly how you'd expect the fermented breast milk of a horse would taste like but a thousand times worse.

Trying not to gag and at the same time smile as if it was nice was acting so fucking good I should have been given an Oscar. I handed the bowl back to Bodo with my left hand and got slapped again. I wouldn't fucking mind but I'd already read not to give or take anything with the left hand before we even got to Mongolia. As is traditional, Bodo had a sip, topped the bowl up and handed it to Natalie. I had to pretend I wasn't relishing her response to drinking it because she is a whole load worse at hiding her feelings than me. She took the bowl and drank. Her face of utter disgust and repulsion and at the same time the urgent need to smile and pretend it was nice was so funny I nearly shit my pants trying not to laugh.

As we sat in the yurt a steady stream of family members and locals came to say hello and drink more horse juice with us. All of them were dressed in beautiful national dress and brought with them a bottle of vodka for Bodo. There were about 25 of us packed in the tiny circular yurt which could have comfortably sat five. Most people sat on the floor. Everybody was talking it in turns to ask us something before realising we didn't understand a single word they said. Then despite it being one o'clock in the afternoon, the vodka was opened. I adamantly tried to explain that I didn't drink alcohol but instead of respecting it they all started bullying me. Vodka and traditions are very unique in Mongolia.

There is only one cup for a start and everyone drinks out of the same one. The man of the house decides who gets given the cup and the way it gets handed round follows some kind of order we think. You have to drink the whole amount in three sips before handing it back. Then it is refilled and passed to the next person. Everyone is bullied to drink, from old women to 10 year olds. It's just so weird. I made it three rounds without drinking and they were most displeased. It's pretty insulting to refuse but I don't bloody drink. I hate booze. The fourth time, I was passed the cup the bullying stepped up a notch, everybody including a woman who was clearly 400 years old was angrily telling me to drink ... so I drank it. It took approximately 10 seconds for me to become absolutely smashed off my tits.

Along with the booze we were given dried horse cheese which I don't want to disrespectful to so I'll phrase it politely ... it is repulsive. You'd think two fussy vegans would think of going somewhere more logical than Outer Mongolia where they eat nothing but animal but no, we're not very clever. It tasted exactly how you'd expect the dried mouldy breast milk of a horse to taste like, but worse, so much worse. There was zero point trying to explain we don't eat cheese because they already thought we were weirdos for not eating meat and they were letting us for free to show us their culture so our diets and beliefs took a backseat for a little while for the greater good.

The vodka kept flowing and everyone was wasted. I'm a quiet introspective drunk who just sits contemplates life and cries a lot. Natalie on the other hand falls into the category of babbling talkative, annoying drunk. No one understood her including me. She didn't stop babbling away for three hours.

Up to this point, they thought we were just friends but kept pointing to our wedding rings and asking where our husbands were. I wanted to say we were just friends so we didn't blow their minds or worse, get us killed, but before I could say anything Natalie was explaining through gesture alone that we were together as lesbians but I was also born a man. I could feel my heart pounding in my chest.

These were simple people. Not simple stupid, but with a simple way of life. Gay, lesbian and trans people simply did not exist openly here. It was unheard of and saying all this stuff to them was almost like explaining that we were aliens from the planet Zoog. Fuck them thinking it's weird, we think it's weird and it's us that are like this. Bodo nodded with a confused drunken look on his face and his wife, Jeffna, grinned like a chimpanzee. Other family members looked decidedly less pleased but then they were absolutely wasted and probably thought they were understanding Natalie wrong. Even I could barely follow her but the gestures of penis and boobs are pretty hard to mistake though. If I hadn't been hammered I'd have died with embarrassment.

All in all though, it had gone well. I think because we were the first foreigners they had ever seen they thought everything about us was weird so they let it go. The men were always weird around me but I get that everywhere. In general men don't know how to act around me.

"Do I ask him, her, she, it to play darts or try and shag it? Fuck, this is confusing. I shall just act like they are a leper for all eternity"

It was now 3pm and we were all absolutely wasted. It

feels so wrong to be drunk in the day because you can't do anything but carry on drinking or pass out. We eventually made it to our yurt where we sat wondering what happened to us. I would have passed out had it not been for Natalie's urgent need to poop so we went for a wander expecting to find a little shed type thing or at least something to hide yourself. But no, there was nothing, just flat land as far as the eye could see. We went and found Sakal who was slumped over outside. We gestured "toilet" to which he laughed and indicated that it's everywhere. Natalie was not at all pleased. The rest of the day was a blur.

*

24.08. Thursday. Somewhere in Outer Mongolia.

I got woken up at 7am by a fully clothed Natalie telling me she needed the toilet right bloody now and that I'd better hurry up or she was going to shit herself. I was absolutely broken. I'd not drunk anything other than my North Korean beer in seven years and had the worst hangover ever. It was horrendous. I bolted for the door and was sick. Then I sat in mounds of animal shit because the ground was covered in it and I wasn't capable of standing. I sat there crying with my head in my hands trying not to die for four minutes before a very angry Natalie came to get me. I imagine being stabbed in the brain with a rusty garden trowel would be less painful than my headache. Natalie was not sympathetic in the slightest and shouted, "You help me shit right bloody now or I swear I will ruin you."

In the 12 years we'd been together she'd never mentioned poo once. She always went out of her way to deny she did it despite me assuring her it's a bodily function that is as normal as breathing.

Natalie: I'm washing my hair.
Me: It's 2pm your Mum's just come to visit and we're having a barbecue. Ah, you need to poop. **Natalie:** No I don't, you do, fuck off.

Or another classic:

Natalie: I'm going to phone my Dad upstairs.
Me: Right, okay then, um, it's five in the morning where they live. Ah hold on, wait you need to squish one out don't you?
Natalie: Fuck you.

There was absolutely nowhere to go. The land was flat and there were people roaming round tending to animals so her new idea was to barricade ourselves in the yurt where she would poop in a plastic bag then dispose of it later. I pointed out that there are no locks on the doors and the small child that was always following us kept climbing on the roof and spying on us through the hole which was impossible to close and apart from that it was disgusting, wrong and the thought made me feel physically ill.

Me: You want to poo in a carrier bag? No! God no! What's wrong with you? It'll stink. Where are you going to put it? They'll find it, open it and then wonder why the fuck we have a bag of poo in the yurt. They already think we're fucking weird and now you want to shit in a bag and store it until later like it's a normal thing? The only place you could hide it is your pocket and I'm not sure I could still love someone who stores poo in their

pockets. How do you even shit in a bag? What if you miss? Oh sorry about that Mrs. Nomad. I just took a steaming dump on your floor.
Natalie: Yes.
Me: No.

I pointed to the small hill in the distance and said, that's the only option. Without saying anything she stormed off towards it. Thirty minutes later, we were at the foot of the hill which, up close, was actually fucking huge. Natalie still wasn't happy because the nomads' only modern possession was a set of huge binoculars and we were pretty confident they would be wondering what the hell we were doing and would almost certainly be spying on us. So, squishing one out at the foot of the mountain would be the worst idea ever. So she started climbing the bastard at a speed no normal human can climb. I was close to death. I heaved then vomited all over my shoes whilst wishing myself dead to end the pain. I sat there and cried more. Natalie shouted that she needed me to see if there was anyone around because she can't see. So I got up and ran after her.

We got to the top which was not only fucking freezing but also the windiest place on Earth and then just over the crest I told her the coast was clear and stood guard like a good wife whilst she did her thing. She was most happy. She literally came bounding over like an excited Labrador. A few days later we were told that the mountain we appropriately named Mount Poop was in fact sacred to the family and it's where they buried their dead. I can't begin to imagine how insulting it would be if they climbed it and found the grossness and toilet paper, a product they don't use.

In the afternoon we were asked to help milk the horses. I'd already tried to explain that I hate them and would happily have them all shot and eaten by the French but they didn't understand or care.

Me: No you don't understand, I will cry, I fucking hate them.

Natalie: Stop being a pussy, Darcie.

Me: Fuck you, you bitch why are you on their side? I swear to god I'm divorcing you. Why is this funny for you? I hate you.

Natalie: Sorry.

Me: I want a divorce, you pig. If I get eaten by the fucking horse I hope you never forgive yourself.

Natalie: Horses don't eat people Darcie I have told you this before.

Me: You weren't there Natalie! They do! They are fucking evil and I hate them and I hate you.

So, with a lot of bullying and encouragement from everyone, particularly Natalie the back-stabbing cow, we went to the place where all the horses had congregated. I soon found out why they were all there, it was because they had captured the foals and tied them to a low rope line. All the mares were stood around to be with their kids but they couldn't suckle them because the rope was so low it made it impossible. To milk the giant hairy dicks you had to untie the foal and wrestle it over to its mother, then you let it suckle for a minute to get the mares juices flowing, then, whilst being careful not to let the mare see, two people wrestle the still hungry foal away and milk the horse dry whilst it thinks it's still the foal suckling. After all the milk has run out you release them both and the foal desperately tries to work out why their mother is so completely shit at producing milk.

Here's something you probably didn't know, horses can control their supply of milk. As in they can turn it off. A couple of times the horse realised the trickery we performing and switched the milk off. It's weird. Cows can't do it and neither can women, but horses can. A very useful fact to know I'm sure you'll agree. If you ever find yourself in a situation where you need to milk a horse now at least you know.

It was my turn and I was literally pushed next to the semi-wild bastard and told to hold the bucket and start squeezing its tits. It was monstrous. I protested and protested, then tried to stand up but they just firmly pushed me down again. I tried to stay calm because I could feel the panic attack bubbling and that would have resulted in being kicked in the head for sure. I looked at Natalie who realised I was in a really bad state and she said it was her turn to get me out of it. I ran 20 metres away and tried not to hyperventilate and cry. As Natalie was milking it, it bolted and ran away. Natalie fell backwards but it could have been worse. They laughed. We shit ourselves. They are not domesticated horses. They are semi-wild and about as dangerous an animal as you could work with. Fuck horses.

The rest of the day was spent with my head in my hands in agony being laughed at by countless nomads. Natalie played with the kids and watched a goat being killed, butchered and cooked before running back to tell me all about it.

Natalie: They stabbed it then reached in and pulled something out.
Me: No, god no, please god stop talking, just stop talking.

Natalie: No I have to tell someone I'm traumatised.
Me: So am I. Stop talking, it's traumatising me.
Natalie: No, so then it was bleating but no air was coming out because its head wasn't attached to its body.
Me: Fuck off, Natalie.
Natalie: Then they cut it in half and there was steam.
Me: That's it, go away or I'll tell everyone you shat on the hill.

I just wanted it to be the night so I could sleep but because the yurts are living spaces for all the family, they are the kitchen, bathroom — not toilet! — and workplace so curling up into a ball in bed was not an option particularly as they were also hung-over and were working their asses off. I would have sold a kidney for a soft bed in a clean place but I had to wait for eight hideously long painful hours before I could end the day.

We both slept really well until about 3am at which point it was too cold to sleep. It must have been about minus 10. Sex was out of the question because in the bed opposite ours were three children and in the other bed there was a fat man. We have no idea who he was and never saw him again but in the morning there was a huge purple bra on the floor and nobody knew whose it was. It was so weird. Everyone that came in for a week afterwards picked it up looked at me and Natalie and we had to try and explain through hand gestures that it wasn't ours and that there was a fat man sleeping in the bed. No one understood us and they just thought we were even more weird. We barely slept and spent the night shaking and moaning.

*

25.08. Friday. Somewhere in Outer Mongolia.

We woke up well aware of our own stench. The bed itself didn't smell but Sakal had his own hard-core sleeping bags that were about 20 inches thick and made out of camel hair. They were supposed to be amazing but were in fact about as warm as ice and they fucking stank. Ugh, god I can taste the smell typing this. It smelt a bit like condensed BO with a hint of animal. It wasn't nice. Maybe when they said camel hair they meant camel toe hair, from a woman with some diseases and no access to sanitation. Okay, I went totally too far there, sorry. There was no alternative to the sleeping bags so we made do but we smelled like condensed anus. We hadn't got round to asking where the washing facilities were because these people lived the most hard-core basic life ever.

They live in what are effectively small tents in a place where it regularly gets to minus 50 degrees Celsius. We had planned to wipe ourselves down with a damp cloth but we were never alone and it was always too cold to get wet. Plus the general interest in my body was even more than usual. It's normal for people to stare at my tits in bemusement and intrigue but the nomads literally just stared at them constantly trying to work out what trickery I was using. So having a cloth bath thing wasn't really an option.

In the afternoon, Sakal came bounding through the door singing a song as he always fucking did. For the entire month we were with him he sang the same verse which was something like, "Something, something mongol ... mongol, mongol, mongol." We found it amusing to join in each time to which he'd laugh himself into a coughing fit. When he regained in his composure we asked him about how we were to wash ourselves. He pointed to a bucket and showed us how to wash. About once a week you took the bucket outside where you placed it on the ground, stood in it, in the freezing weather and poured cold water on yourself. Well we're no pussy bitches (we are total pussy bitches) but standing in the middle of the minus 15 degree tundra in a gale on a huge flat plain where everyone wants to see my lack of tits and what the fuck is actually between my legs, whilst pouring cold water on ourselves was not something we were prepared to do. So we didn't wash for the next 24 days.

A short while later, Bodo showed up in his beautiful green traditional clothes with a giant fucking gun on his shoulder. He indicated that I and only I should go shooting with him. I am pretty paranoid about my perceived gender and felt like he just walked up to me and said, "You're a man aren't you cunt face? It's time for you to man-up, you pussy bastard. Come shooting with me and grow a pair." I know he meant no harm even if that's really what he was thinking and I really didn't want to make them think we were weirder than we actually are so I wished Natalie good luck and told her it was nice knowing her and to tell the world I was shot dead by a nomad for being a tranny.

Off we set over the hills for about an hour on our way to shoot a wild animal in the face like real men. The walk was tough, it was freezing cold, raining and Bodo was extremely fit and strong and, well, I'm not. All of a sudden he stopped and told me to be quiet. Well I wasn't going to burst into a chorus of "The hills are alive." He lay on the ground and told me to lie down too. He pointed his gun into the distance and we stayed there for 35 minutes, which incidentally was the longest I'd ever been quiet and still for in my life. I spent the time praying to a god I that don't believe in that there would be no animals being shot. Thankfully the animals were too busy to be shot in the face so we got up, said "nosh" to each other a few times whilst I pretended to be disappointed at the lack of animal death then we and set off back to the yurts. I was rather happy at not being shot.

In the afternoon we decided to make something for the family. We had almost no ingredients but muddled enough shit together to make flapjacks. We had the following ingredients: oats. There was no sugar, raisins, honey or anything else so we tried to improvise. I went to the car and came back with five Werther's Originals which we boiled down to make sugar sauce. We then added the oats, small bits of overripe semi-rotting apple that had likely been in the car since the 1980's and mushed the resulting mess into biscuit shapes. Then came the problem that there was no oven, just Sakal's tiny rusting cooking pot which sat over a little butane camping stove which was totally shit and inefficient. So we decided to cook them on the yurts fire which Natalie had somehow made so fucking hot the metal lid was actually glowing. Our system worked well; they cooked and were in the shape of biscuits. If you ignored the fact they were drier than eating desecrated chalk that had been rolled in salt and fallen into a clay oven for a year, they were nice.

We proudly went next door with a huge plate of the bastards and handed them over. Now it was their turn to feign delight. "Mmm-mmm" they all said, whilst putting them down on the table or hiding them when we weren't looking. Ironically we were then offered the bowl of dried horse cheese which we took nibbled on and hid in our bras when no one was looking. It was pretty funny later in the day when we discovered we both hid the hideous stuff in our bras and pulled it out at the same time. We had a right old chuckle to ourselves.

As we sat there something amazing happened. Bodo's cousin pulled up in a Toyota Prius. As in she drove the thing over the fucking huge hills, rivers and mud that the massive land cruiser struggled to get over and pulled up outside like it was normal.

"Oh look there's a Toyota Prius," I said as my brain tried to work out what the hell was going on.

The cousin was an English teacher in the town's school, 45 kilometres away. She had driven for four hours over the hills to see us. It was amazing to speak with her and the family. We had so many questions but the only one I could think about was where do these people have sex? Where the fuck do they fuck for fuck's sake? They all live in the same room where there is zero privacy, ever. I was on the verge of trying to ask but then my one and only brain cell told me it was an idiotic thing to ask.

In return for our "cookies" or just because they're nomads, out came a bottle of vodka. I was absolutely fucking adamant I'd never drink again ever ..... and so the bullying started. At first it was just Bodo but then Sakal joined in and then everyone else. Vega the English teacher whispered, "Darcie it's very rude not to accept the drink." Yes but I don't fucking drink. It's not rude if I don't do it. What if I was a Muslim would you say the same thing? Even fucking Natalie the treacherous wench joined in.

Natalie: Just drink a bit and they'll leave you alone.
Me: Fuck you Natalie. I'm still hung-over from the other day. My one and only pair of shoes smell of the vomit I covered them with.

Then a grandmother tapped me on the shoulder and sternly told me to drink the shot. I have no idea what her actual wording was but she was not happy.

Grandmother: Drink the vodka.
Me: No, no, I can't.
Grandmother: Drink it, bitch.
Me: No, no. I don't drink alcohol.
Grandmother: Drink it, you stupid foreign bitch.
Me: I still have a hangover from the other day and my shoes smell of vomit.
Grandmother: I said drink it you STUPID TRANNY BITCH OR I'LL FUCK YOU UP.

I lasted another five minutes before I gave in. Thirty minutes later we were all absolutely smashed off our tits. Bodo decided he'd treat us all to some traditional songs which would have been lovely, if their style of singing wasn't to Western ears, absolutely fucking hilarious. Type Mongolian singing into the Internet to hear it. It's pretty hard not to burst out laughing when someone is doing that in your face. We love culture but this was a sound like you'd expect a stoned alien to make, or if you asked a small child to produce the most insane hysterical noise they can come up with. Both

Natalie and I were biting our lips trying not to laugh. We both knew that if we even had the slightest of eye contact with each other we'd both lose it completely which would not be good. So we both spent his 20-minute sing-song facing different directions trying to think of things to stop ourselves laughing. I was desperately thinking of the day my beloved cat got run over and later Natalie told me she was thinking of her Dad's hairy back which is just fucking weird. Either way, not laughing was one of our biggest achievements in our lives.

He eventually stopped singing, turned to me and through Vega told me it was my turn to sing. "No, no. I don't sing" I protested but he just wouldn't take no for an answer. I tried to change the subject and I even went outside to the toilet to make them forget the idea but nothing worked. I was told it would be of great insult if I didn't sing or recite a poem. I tried with everything I had to get out of it. I begged Natalie to do it for me but she said she would rather die.

"Yeah me too, don't make me do this, please I'll do anything you want, please, I can't sing and I don't know any fucking poems."

It was no good Natalie was having none of it and for the second time in the night she was a turncoat treacherous cow. The family started to get angry with me so I told Natalie that I hated her and wanted a divorce and whilst turning a funny shade of purple I recited the only thing I could remember, the time honoured favourite ... Baa Baa Black Sheep. It was horrendous. I nearly died from embarrassment. I said it slowly and thoughtfully as if it wasn't a shit nursery rhyme. It did the trick and they were actually impressed all nodding in approval and then clapping. They asked what the poem was about and were thrilled to hear it was about sheep. Never in my life did I envisage being sat in a yurt in Outer Mongolia with a bunch of nomads, pissed out of my face reciting a nursery rhyme to great applause

I was rewarded for my bravery when Boda appeared with a wolf skin that he'd shot.

"Here have a wolf, it was eating my sheep so I shot it in its face."

Fuck yes! It wasn't a refined fur, it was literally a giant fucking wolf that had its insides removed then had two sticks jammed inside it. It was so fucking cool. It's extremely honourable to be given a wolf skin and they are only given to those that are respected. I felt most pleased with myself. I know we're vegan but the nomads live alongside nature the way humans should, they of all people have the right to shoot the wolves that are killing their animals and give the skin away to stupid foreign tourists. I especially loved the wolf's head, dangling feet and tail. Months later I took a leg to my brother's house to freak the fuck out of his dog. It worked and the dog went nuts and ran into a glass door — the dog has been in the same house for 10 years so presumably the wolf freaked him so much he forgot about the giant glass door. It was one of the highlights of my life. I thought it was hilarious but apparently laughing at scared animals that run into things isn't funny so I got shouted at. Still funny as fuck though. I still laugh about that once a week when it pops into my head. Just the way his ears pricked up he let out a weird yelp then launched himself into the glass. So funny.

In the night we desperately needed to pee so walked hand in hand about 30 metres away from the yurt as is customary. Natalie did her thing whilst I guarded her and then I let loose whilst stood up, because it makes sense to make use of one's equipment especially in the middle of the night when there's no one around … and that's when we saw someone looking at us. It was pitch black but we had the most powerful torch on the fucking planet with us that we'd bought in China. I have no doubt they all had a nice natter among themselves. Had it not been for the fact there were children sleeping in the bed next to us, I'd have used a bottle to pee in. I couldn't care less. It was fucking freezing, there were wolves, horses, yaks and goats about and goats are weird and I don't trust them, their eyes are in backwards and it's not right, and well you already know how I feel about horses. Basically wandering around in the dark was the most terrifying thing imaginable and there has to be one single advantage of having this ridiculous appendage stuck to my body.

Quotes from the last few days:

Me: Okay, faucet is being added to the list of banned words. It's a tap.

Me: Ryvita, who knew cardboard was edible?
Natalie: I've got such bad stomach ache I hope you don't mind if I shit the bed 'cos it's a very real possibility. You're probably going to wake up with shit

all over your face.

Me: I've eaten so much today I think my body is trying to tell me something.

Natalie: Yeah you're fat.

Me: Fuck you.

Natalie: Do you like yogurt?

Me: Yeah.

Natalie: Do you really like yogurt?

Me: Yeah.

Natalie: I like sloths.

Me: I don't know how that's related to yogurt.

Natalie: Do you like yogurt?

Me: You're freaking me out.

Natalie: Do you like yogurt?

Me: Stop it stop it. I'm freaking out. Seriously, stop talking.

Natalie: Do you like yogurt?

Me: No, no, no I don't. Shut up.

*

26.08. Saturday. Somewhere in Outer Mongolia.

At 5.30am there was a single knock at the door and then Jeffna was there in her beautiful traditional clothes telling us to get up and milk the cows. We both wanted to say, "Um, no thanks. It's early, cold and have you seen us? We're rubbish pathetic little snowflakes."

But we didn't want to look like the pussies we are, so we put on the same stinking clothes we'd worn every other day and stumbled down to the cows. Now, you might not believe this but I am not actually scared of cows. I like them. I like their eyes and faces. They are like massive simple hairy children. They're lovable and as mental as this may sound I have always felt a bond with them, so I jumped at the chance. I was not particularly good at milking them. Their nipples are weird and slippery but still I was better at it than Natalie who didn't even manage one single drop of milk.

The work was hard and it was fucking freezing. We had borrowed boots but, like idiots, we had short pop socks on so our toes were so fucking cold they felt like if you bent them they'd snap off. I doubt embalming your feet in ice would have made them any colder. We both quickly covered our single warm top in cow drool and shit. I was quite keen not to look rubbish at absolutely everything so persevered and really tried to do a good job. Natalie on the other hand stood in the corner and sulked. I used her sulking time to get extra good girl points like a naughty sibling kissing their parent's ass. Natalie not only looks like an angel but is one. She's always helping any way she can and everyone loves her and wonders why she's with a freak when she could have a nice normal girl or boy so it felt nice to be the good one for once.

"So Mrs. Jeffna" I said sucking up to her. "Should I get that cow now? Okay, come here, Moo, you big stupid slobbering bastard. Here you go Mrs. Jeffna, cow delivered. Would you like me to do anything else? Perhaps kiss your backside?"

Around midday we suddenly realised that we hadn't told our families that we'd be out of contact for such a long time and our parents would be worried sick.

We decided that we needed the Internet too urgently

to tell them because waiting another 20 days would be unacceptable, selfish and wrong. Sakal was not remotely amused but we were paying him so we all got in the car and went towards the nearest village with Internet five hours away.

The village was like something out of an old Western movie. There was a single dirt road where there sat one single building, an old fashioned wooden structure that looked as if it had been put up by Natalie and I. This was the one single shop. Let me tell you about the shop. So we walked in and the old man practically fell off his chair. He couldn't believe his eyes. After a minute or two, he noticed I wasn't all as I initially appeared and had the look a confused dog has when they tilt their heads. Then we tried to communicate with him so we said, "Hello," but he just couldn't figure out what was going on and stared blankly ahead. He then decided our apparition was hilarious and laughed as we searched the single shelf for something not made out of animal, alcohol or sugar. We didn't find a single thing. Just sweets canned meat and alcohol. We didn't want to insult him by not buying anything so bought a small can with Russian writing on it that we had no idea what it was but the can looked interesting then we decided to buy some vodka and sweets for the family.

Instead of driving straight back home, Sakal took us on a relative-visiting spree because they all lived close by. You remember how when you're a kid and you are forced to see your distant relatives because your Mum's forced you into it but they're all dicks and to be quite honest you'd rather eat shit but you do it anyway because your Mum will spank you to death if you don't?

Well that's what we did. We'd spend half an hour driving up and down hills in the middle of nowhere, mile after mile of nothingness as far as the eye could see trying to find the yurt among the nothingness, then we'd find it and have an hour of nomad hospitality which is truly wonderful — if you like horse cheese, alcoholic horse milk you can't refuse to accept and vodka.

At least, by this point, we'd become very good at hiding the cheese. One of us would point to something, like pretty beams or a nice piece of furniture and as everyone looked we'd hide the cheese in our handbags or bras. We still hadn't thought of how to actually get rid of the stuff and our bags were starting to fill with the shit. Really I'm not exaggerating when I say that it's the worst stuff in the whole world ever.

Family to family we visited. By the sixth family we were drunk, again, as was Sakal. We were being fed things that made our skin crawl and being spoken to in a language we didn't understand. I don't know why some people think that if they speak slower and louder you will somehow understand them? No! I don't speak the language. If you said one word a minute I wouldn't all of a sudden be able to understand it. I'd have better luck understanding you if you communicated using only the sound of fart. "Fart, fart, fart, fart." Ah, you like cabbage. Okay that was way too far and now I feel sick. You can't really tell what food fart came from anyway can you? Right it's quiet time for me.

On the way to yet another relative we spotted a wild fox. We were expecting Sakal to say, "Wow, look a fox! Let's observe the beautiful creature as it gracefully meanders through the stunning landscape." Well, the

Mongolian equivalent which would sound something like "Shgkkk;da; dkfskjhadj;';./lk'sk'.;/@:>:afd" — that's literally how they speak. But instead he floored the gas and tried to run the poor thing over. We screamed "Nooo! Sakal stop!" but he either couldn't hear us or was choosing not to. He was likely too busy thinking about how nice a new fox hat would be. We chased the little furry thing for two minutes driving about as dangerous as is possible. Thankfully the little furry fellow found his hole in the nick of time and was safe.

The next house we went to there were three women sat around the fire cleaning intestines and then putting them in the huge cooking pot which was already boiling away with numerous organs and two goat heads. Our stomachs churned. Mongolian cuisine is famous for its boiled sheep heads. Watching them bubble away in a soup of its own organs was reasonably disgusting for us but I think if you eat meat you should eat the whole animal. Animal is animal whether it's the leg, ass or eyeball. As I think I might have mentioned a few dozen times we're vegetarian pussies so it was utterly revolting and our mouths were watering with nausea. I'm definitely turning into one of those people that constantly goes on about their vegetarianism aren't I? God I hate those guys. You know the ones, they mention it in every single sentence.

Me: Hi I'm Vegetarian Rachel, I'm vegetarian. I don't eat meat because I'm vegetarian, did I mention I'm vegetarian? Because I'm vegetarian.
A: Really? Thanks Rachel but I don't give a fuck.
Me: Is that because I'm vegetarian?
A: No it's because you're a boring bitch.

I've got a friend like that, well I call her a friend but in actual fact they're a total bitch. No offence Vegetarian Rachel the Vegetarian.

"I only eat ecological kale that's grown in the wild from a sustainable source. I don't believe in farming. I don't listen to mainstream music. I only listen to vinyl records I have recorded myself using the sounds of whales mating."

Oh do fuck off. Here let me shit in a cup for you, there you go, it's organic. Enjoy.

I'll tell you what though, I'm vegetarian (I did mention I'm vegetarian right?)

Anyway I'm vegetarian, but some animals are so hideous they look like they should be eaten. Have you actually seen a turkey? They are literally the ugliest animal on the planet. You know some animals are so ugly they're endearing? Pugs for example? Well turkeys are so hideous they look like they should be eaten. What the fuck's that thing on their heads? Flobble, wobble, wobble. Gross, everyone should eat them so there's fewer of them. (I don't really mean this).

By the time we got back it was dark and we were once again drunk. We sat on the bed enjoying a brief moment of solitude for the first time in forever. We emptied all the cheese out of our bags, bras and pockets and admired the mountain of the stuff. It was ridiculous.

*

27.08 Sunday. Somewhere in Outer Mongolia.

In the morning, Jeffna once again gave a solitary knock and was standing over our bed telling us to get up. It would have been easier if I didn't still suffer from that thing boys sometimes suffer with in mornings. God, I would love to have it ripped off. I hate it. Still there's worse problems to have. Some people are born with extra fingers, toes and heads. I'd love a sex change so badly but the surgery is in its infancy, the failure rate is unacceptable and we want kids, oh and most of all Natalie, as the owner of a normal functioning vagina has become rather fond of ye olde courgette so we just make do. Like you do. There are worse birth defects to have I suppose. Still when I see it, it upsets me each and every time. It shouldn't be there and makes me question myself and forces me to spend my entire life trying to hide the bastard. So despite Jeffna's encouragement I couldn't just get out of bed. I wouldn't have been able to if I was a man either. I don't think the reaction would have been good.

"Aghh, Aghh, Darcie. There's is a python in your underwear!"

She left confused and we quickly got ready. We thought we were going to be squeezing the juice out of cow's nipples again but we were taken to where the sheep chill during the night. We were given a bit of rope each with a hoop on the end and told to catch ones with particularly shitty asses. It was not my ideal job.

"Hmm what would you like to do today Darcie?"

"Well I'd love to catch a sheep and clean its butthole."

Natalie couldn't see the difference between the sheep because to her there were a thousand identical white furry blobs. She took it in good spirits and laughed at her lack of vision. She would have loved this only a few months before.

I managed to catch one. Then Jeffna ran over to it picked it up and body slammed it onto its back. Then she produced a large pair of scissors and proceeded to cut away the hair around its lady bits and asshole so it didn't get shitty butthole vagina disease. She handed me the scissors and asked me to continue.

"You want me, Darcie, with the shaky trembling hands to give a sheep a Brazilian with this massive pair of scissors? Um no, this is not a good idea."

The sheep breathed a sigh of relief when I handed the scissors back safe in the knowledge it wouldn't have its vagina cut off by a weird looking freak. I bet it ran over to its mates and told them all about it and they were like, "Yeah honey, sure that happened".

"It did it did, this weird he, she thing caught me, then I was body slammed on my back then the it tried to cut my vagina off"

"Sure thing, lay off the drugs, okay?"

We spent two hours catching sheep, pinning them down whilst Jeffna did the Brazilians. Natalie it turns out would be very good at Judo because no one can throw a sheep on its back quite like her. She couldn't catch the bastards but was the one that did the best job overall. For a five foot tall Hobbit she is strong as hell. The unfortunate result of all this was that I had lost all my cow milking brownie points because for the next three days all anyone talked about was how amazing at sheep wrangling Natalie was.

We spent the afternoon sat on top of poop mountain because we both needed to go. It was the first day it wasn't minus bloody 30 so we sat there just by ourselves. It was delightful and absolutely stunning. Rolling green hills as far as the eye could see, tiny white yurts dotted around and huge birds of prey flying acrobatically overhead as if for no other reason than to show off their flying skills. It was a lovely moment provided the wind didn't blow the revolting scent of our freshly laid poop into our faces.

By the time we got back to our yurt it was full to the brim with relatives and locals. There was nowhere to sit but it turned out they have funny rules for that. The respected men are to sit at the back of the yurt on the floor and the women get to sit on the beds at the sides. I was told to go to the back with all the men which instantly pissed me off. Natalie sat on the bed. Then the horse alcohol came out. We had already had too much of it, we were repulsed by it and had reached the point where we couldn't hide the grimacing. We'd take a sip, pull a disgusted face like we'd just bitten into a lemon whilst staring at the hideous bodies of our gyrating naked grandparents, then had to follow this with a forced smile that must have been so clearly fake it would have been better just to shout, "Fuck, this is disgusting and I'd prefer to eat dog turd sandwiches."

Thankfully after being it handed to us ceremonially five times the horse filth went away and out came the vodka. The only time I have ever been happy to see it.

An hour later everyone was plastered yet again. Vega had showed up again so unfortunately she was there to tell everyone that I am very good at reciting poetry.

"No Vega, fuck you!"

This time I sensed the futility in trying to get out of it so instead tried to get Natalie back for being treacherous bitch and joining in pressuring me to do it the first time. I said I will do it but only if Natalie sings a song too. I expected them to all jump on board with the bullying like they did to me but instead they turned on me.

"No Natalie only sings if she wants to."
"Well how's that fair then? You bullied me to sing, I nearly cried but now you won't bully her?"

They were having none of it. Apparently only they could decide who to bully. I collected my thoughts and dignity and very purposely recited Baa Baa Black Sheep again. Trying to make it sound like it had meaning and wasn't about, well, I don't know what it's about, it's just stupid.

Baa black sheep have you any wool? - Oh you're a sheep and you don't talk. Would you like me to give you a Brazilian wax so you don't get shitty butt hole vagina disease?
Yes sir yes sir three bags full. Aghh What the fuck? You do talk! A talking sheep. I'm going to make so

much money off you. Come with me you woolly bastard. Oh and if you call me Sir again I'm going to turn you to kebab you hear me?

One for the master, one for the dame and one for the little boy who lives down the lane. Look sheep I don't know what you're on about but if you could try and make sense that might maximise my profits.

I was more drunk than I had ever been in my life. I had drunk a litre of vodka or more and was wrecked. I don't remember any of what happened next but apparently I decided to do another rendition of Baa Baa Black Sheep on my own accord then spent an hour talking about Elton John despite the fact no one had heard of him.

The next bit definitely happened because the proof was in Natalie's hair... I vomited all over the bed then somehow I switched sides and Natalie slept in it. At around four in the morning, Natalie found me whimpering at the end of the bed whilst completely naked. At that point she realised I had vomited all over the bed and her hair and went absolutely mental.

I was unresponsive and so she tried to get sense into me with violence by slapping me. This didn't work and instead made me go outside in the minus 20 degree weather whilst still naked. Natalie realised that being nice was probably more conducive to my not actually dying. She found me 40 metres away by the stream where I apparently told her that I couldn't find the toilet.

She had to drag me back, clean the vomit and make

sure that I didn't die. I then apparently spent the remainder of the night crying and apologising for being a monster. Bearing in mind that there were three children we were sharing the yurt with and it makes the whole thing so much worse. Apparently they didn't wake up. They are used to sleeping metres away from family and just switch off.

*

28.08. Monday. Somewhere in Outer Mongolia.

I woke up still completely drunk with the worst headache known to man. Let me tell you, you might think you have experienced a hangover in the past but you haven't. What you experienced were effectively orgasms compared to my hangover. The room was spinning and I felt sicker than Captain Sick who'd just drank 18 bottles of diesel and spent an hour on a roundabout. God, it was so bad that I genuinely contemplated suicide to make the pain stop. Imagine being stabbed in the head? Well, that would be like tickling compared to my pain.

Natalie was still absolutely livid and wasn't speaking to me and still had vomit in her hair. I think there's something about having vomit in your hair and the inability to wash it that makes people see red. I was tasked with heating up water and washing it for her but I couldn't because I couldn't actually move. I could stand up for about 30 seconds before the spinning made me lie down and vomit. I crawled outside through the mounds of animal shit and wrenched my guts up. I had never been in a worse state. As I lay there in the shit, Natalie would emerge every now and to shout at me and tell me how terrible I was. None of this concerned the nomads who went about their lives whilst laughing at me. It's a pretty normal sight for them. I couldn't even respond, I was 90% sure I was going to die. Natalie heated the water herself and I helped wash her hair in between vomiting at the smell of the hair vomit. Added to her anger was the fact we had no shampoo or soap because we're stupid and didn't bring any. The small pot of water washed some of it out but it stank and was disgusting. Her hair was revolting and it was all my fault. To give you an idea of how angry she was, I was in trouble for two months and I daren't ever mention it again for the rest of my life because she might actually kill me. If we ever have a copy of this book in the house I'm seriously going to have to blank this bit out. In my defence however it wasn't my fault. The nomads made me do it. I don't even bloody drink. I got bullied by nomads who are all alcoholics. The other way around I would be the same though, well less angry, but still. Having someone's vomit in my hair would cause me extreme distress.

Feeling like death, I got put in the car and got driven to meet a thousand more local relatives. We had specified that we wanted to meet lots of nomads and experience the culture but at that point I would have given everything I owned to be alone in a bed at home. We pulled up at the yurt but I physically couldn't handle it so I slept in the freezing car. Then we went to see a shrine where I also experienced its joy by sleeping in the car. In fact I slept, whinged, wriggled in pain and vomited for the following five hours. To help me and my hideous state, Sakal thought it would be nice to literally visit every single nomad family in the entire fucking country. I wouldn't mind so much but Natalie had drank the same amount as me but she can handle it whereas I cannot. It was one of the worst days of my life.

Quotes from the last few days:

Me: I don't have my toothbrush.
Natalie: Just use the toilet paper but not the first piece.
Me: No shit.
Natalie: Exactly.

Me: There's a problem with the sky.
Natalie: What?
Me: It's raining.

Natalie: When we were little I was really hyperactive me and my brother used to climb on top of the table and eat newspapers.
Me: This explains a lot.
Natalie: Yeah and my Mum would run to the doctors saying that we've eaten a newspapers and are we going to die.

Me: I, Fredrick Fredrickson son of Frederick hereby take you Frederick, son of my great uncle Frederick and my great aunt Frederick in front of my mother Fredrick her mother Fredrick and my son Frederick. To be my lawful wedded Frederick. (Have no idea why I said this).

*

29.08. Tuesday. Somewhere in Outer Mongolia.

I woke up still hung-over with the worst headache

ever (again). I convinced myself that I was dying because I'm a hypochondriac and no human has ever had a hangover for more than a day so therefore it had to be an alcohol induced brain aneurysm. Natalie told me to stop being a bloody idiot and get dressed. I told her that in order to get dressed she would need to take the children that literally sat on the other bed staring at us at all times away because they were making me too nervous to get up. So she took them outside to play volleyball. I went back to sleep safe in the knowledge there was no one to harass me or children staring at me. Thirty minutes later a very angry Natalie, who was still exceptionally angry about the vomit in the hair incident, came in pulled the covers back and told me that she'd fallen in shit whilst playing volleyball and the whole time I'd been a bloody sleep and I'm a stupid selfish bitch. She had cow shit all over her clothes, face and hair. I had to use every single bit of energy I had to not laugh. Have you ever tried so hard not to laugh you cry? Well that's what I had.

"Oh no, that's terrible," I said through pursed lips with tears of pure hysterical joy pouring down my face.

After helping wash filth off Natalie for the second time in 24 hours, we were given our task for the morning: to refill their water barrel which they use for absolutely everything. The water source was a natural spring which just appeared out of the land. It was really amazing to see.

There was nothing but land and then a stream was there. It would have the best water source we'd ever seen had it not also been popular with horses, goats, cows, sheep, yak, and every other animal in the known universe, all of whom thought they'd take the biggest dumps imaginable in it. I'm not exaggerating when I say the water was full to the brim of poo. We had been drinking it for days and hadn't died but it wasn't particularly nice to think of. Jeffna showed us how to get the water, skimming the top away with a scoop to reduce the amount of shit as much as possible. She left us to it and we set about slowly filling the buckets up.

After we'd been there an hour freezing our boobs off, the little seven year old rat-kid whose name we never learned because it was literally unpronounceable came bounding over telling us over and over again the only thing he'd learned in English, "No, no, no, no, no!" He could genuinely do everything better than us and had taken to telling us off for absolutely everything. Making the fire, "No, no, no, no!" Milking the cows, "No, no, no, no!" Making love to Natalie, "No, no, no, no!"

Well no fuck you rat-boy I'm doing the water so you can fuck off. He looked in our buckets which to be fair were full of particles of shit, dirt and grossness, said, "No, no, no, no!" and emptied the bastards out. No Ratty no! That's taken us ages. He then stopped us from filling them up whilst he went slightly upstream to the shallow start of the spring where for some reason he made a damn out of … wait for this … horse shit. We were like, "Fuck off Ratty, you are not helping," but he wouldn't listen.

"What are you doing? Stop making waterworks out of poo".

We have no idea what he was trying to achieve but,

after 20 minutes, we got bored and carried on filling the buckets up regardless. Every time he came and said, "No, no, no, no!" we replied, "No, no, no, no!" thus creating a giant no-no-no-off. It was pretty surreal. An hour later we were soaking wet and freezing cold and Ratty was still there telling us off but we had our buckets filled so we carried the heavy-as-shit water back and filled up the big barrel by the yurt door. Then the little bastard snitched on us and said all the water was dirty. We spent fucking hours collecting that and all you did was make a dam out of all things, actual shit. Everyone sided with Ratty and made fun of our water collecting ability and were yet more convinced we were rubbish at absolutely everything. Still, they drank it anyway.

At some point over the few days we'd been there we had offered to make the family a meal so in the afternoon we set about cooking for 15. We only had limited ingredients but did our best. We named our meal, "Anal explosion of the worst kind" It tasted pretty good but caused such hideous problems with gas I'm surprised no one died. Here is the recipe:

Ingredients:
Entire cabbages x 2
Tins of mixed beans x 2
Onions x 10
Decomposing potatoes x 5
Packs of instant noodles x 3

Method:
Put everything in a pan and cook until mush.

Disclaimer: I am not responsible if anyone actually

makes this and has fart related deaths.

The gas problems were so unbelievably bad that we were only half joking about sleeping outside in the arctic weather just to avoid having to breathe each other's farts all night. To make matters worse, the kids in the opposite bed had multiplied and now there were four of them sleeping in the same bed which is just what you want when you're all revolting fart monsters. The third bed had a random woman in it. We never saw her before or after but assumed she was the woman behind the mystery purple bra that was still in the corner. Natalie took it over to her and through some hideously embarrassing hand gestures indicated if it was hers. It wasn't hers. It was so cringeworthy, I hid under the covers until the very real risk of gassing myself to death made me gasp for air. Sorry to be so crude by the way but it genuinely was that bad. I know girls aren't supposed to fart, poo or do anything else unladylike but this was so, so bad I just couldn't leave it out.

*

30.08. Wednesday. Somewhere in Outer Mongolia

We woke up, drank three coffees each because even though we had no food, soap, shampoo or electricity, coffee is one of those things we can't go without so we had a huge stash of instant Nescafe we'd brought along. Ratty turned up to drink a coffee with us and practice his "No, no, no, no's." He was seven years old but drank about four cups of coffee with us a day. In fact every time we had coffee he'd appear out of nowhere demanding a cup. We were going to ask his parents if he was allowed coffee but we never figured out who his parents were and he drank alcoholic horse milk all the time and the odd sip of vodka so the coffee was the least of his troubles. As you'd imagine a seven-year-old on coffee to be, he was the most annoying human on earth, running around and babbling shit non-stop. It drove Natalie mad but I thought was hilarious. His annoyingness climaxed when he decided to start counting as quickly as possible and wouldn't shut the fuck up. He literally followed us round counting for about 25 minutes.

It stopped being funny after a while and so I very politely told him to fuck off. He didn't understand so I thought I'd give him a taste of his own medicine and started counting too. This made Natalie pull a face of utter exasperation that was so hilarious it nearly put me off my counting. I learnt an important thing that day, never have a battle of annoyance with a child because they have inbuilt skills that can never be matched. In the end we gave him a coffee sachet on the condition he went away.

In the afternoon we went outside and unbelievably the sky was blue and had this mysterious yellow orb in it. Off in the distance was Ratty on his horse and I don't know what came over me but I thought, yes I want to do that. Yes I know I'm terrified of them but the fear causes me quite a few problems in life as you have seen, so I really wanted to try and conquer my fear of them with the use of the oldest, slowest, friendliest horse ever that a seven year old child could ride. It must have been at least a hundred years old and was so close to death I actually thought sitting on the big brown bastard might actually kill it. My heart was pounding out of my chest as I went over, stroked its big stupid nose and asked it nicely not to kill me. Bodo then came running over with a big smile on his face, he then literally picked me up and put me on the thing. Thankfully Mongolian horses are short, I am light, and Bodo was strong as fuck. I felt a mixture of absolute fear, exhilaration and hot flushes at being picked up.

"Look I'm on a horse!" I shouted to Natalie. "A horse, a real fucking horse!" Natalie came over with the camera and shouted at me not to show any fear because they can sense it and they can throw you off.

"Well thanks for telling me that, I feel a lot better now. How do you not feel scared when you are scared? If you have any other wise words of wisdom maybe keep them to yourself" I screeched back.

Over the next three minutes I learned to ride the thing. They have pretty easy controls. Left, right, go and stop, STOP, STOP NOW YOU GIANT HAIRY BELLEND. FUCK. FUUUUCK STOP, STOP, PLEASE STOP YOU BIG HAIRY TWAT, and No I didn't mean the hairy twat bit but stop and let's talk about this like adults. Fine then, fuck you, I hope you end up in some cheap hamburgers you cunt. AGHHH, I'M JOKING. HELP ME, JESUS.

Apart from the odd terrified shrill when it did something unexpected like eat grass or drink water I was pretty good and soon enough I was trotting round the place like a pro.

Someone: So did you conquer your fear of horses, Darcie?

Me: Yes I did.
Someone: And how long did it last?
Me: Well let me tell you...

I was happy with my ancient small horse and having finally conquered my long-standing fears. I was pretty high on life, taking selfies of myself. Is that a double negative? Taking selfies of myself? Hmm? I don't care, on with the story... so anyway I was taking selfies and getting Natalie to video me triumphantly trotting around then shortly after we got summoned over to help milk the horses and I nearly got kicked in the head. With no exaggeration I genuinely nearly died. It missed my head by centimetres and would have probably killed me outright. The horse bolted away taking a fence post with it. Vega said, "This horse is a very bad angry horse" Well don't tell me to milk it then! How about that for a good idea? Then they expected me to carry on milking other horses as if this near death experience was nothing and it was normal to nearly have had a hoof through my face. I was having none of it and stormed off safe in the knowledge that all horses were indeed bastards and the French were right for eating them. Natalie had a better excuse for not helping and kept saying she couldn't help milk them because of her eye disease. It made absolutely no sense but worked. My fear of horses had been cured and then come back stronger than ever all within an hour.

Later in the day we were all sat outside on the grass, well I say grass it was 70 percent poo, 20 percent crickets, locusts, spiders, ants and 10 percent withered grass. Sat with us was Jeffna's daughter who had been staying with a relative for the week to help them with their animals. She was about 13 and her passion in life was Mongolian wrestling. She had decided that she wanted to wrestle us both which I really, really didn't want to do. I'm not strong in any way but still it just felt wrong but she wouldn't take no for an answer. Thankfully Natalie went first and surprisingly she actually put up a fight, eventually though the girl got bored picked her up and dropped on her head. Then it was my turn. I tried so hard to lose but what could I do without looking like I'm giving up. All I needed to lose was my head to hit the ground but she couldn't pick me up. I desperately wanted to leap into the air and then land headfirst on the ground but couldn't. It was horrendous. Then she opted to rapidly lift me up between my legs and throw me down.

"Well love there's some rather sensitive but unwelcome things that live in that zone and they hurt like fuck when effectively whacked."

I promptly fell to the ground in agony. Everyone thought it was absolutely hilarious apart from me and the girl who obviously didn't know about me. It took me about four hours to recover and made me the laughing stock of everyone for miles around. They told the story to every visitor that came round for the entire time we were with them. I have no doubt they are still laughing and will continue to do so for decades to come.

After yet another lunch of instant bloody stupid noodles we were told that we needed to make hay whilst the sun shines. That's literally what they said. So we jumped in the car and were driven to some meadows. We were each given a scythe and shown what to do. We both tried desperately not to be shit at yet another thing but we were appalling, and I mean laughably bad. Natalie managed to cut approximately zero hay. I made a small mound which they laughed at. We did make ourselves useful by boiling water and giving everyone lots of coffee. Four hours later and the nomads had a shitload of hay. We then had to pick it up and make haystacks out of it which even we could do. We worked our asses off to try and prove ourselves and they nodded in approval at our work which made us feel good. We didn't even complain that the hay was full to the brim of shit and therefore so were we. No, we stood there covered in filth and shit with sweat dripping down our faces feeling most proud of ourselves.

We got back to almost a hero's welcome. So it was decided that the family would teach us how to make vodka. I won't bore you with the details only that they make it from horse and cow milk, a whole heap of weird looking apparatus that sits above the fire and after two hours you have fruity nice tasting vodka that's about 30% alcoholic and strangely delicious. I pretended to drink because I would have rather died than drink more alcohol.

At night we had about five minutes to ourselves so set about trying to wash our festering stinky bodies so we wet a sock and used it to wipe ourselves down. It wasn't effective for a couple of reasons. Firstly, because I'm pretty sure Natalie picked a dirty sock instead of a clean one so we were effectively wiping ourselves down with stinking foot sweat on our already stinking revolting bodies. And secondly the water we used hadn't been boiled and therefore consisted of about 20% poo. Not only that, but the camel hair sleeping bags had become so smelly you could actually smell them outside the yurt. They fucking stank. We hated them passionately but didn't have a choice. It was either them or freeze so we just smelled really bad. Even the goats looked at us like we're revolting skanks.

*

31.08. Thursday. Somewhere in Outer Mongolia.

We were woken up by a lot of commotion outside the yurt. We got up and went out to see what was going on. Someone had managed to shoot a marmot and so they would be having a lovely special meal to eat the bastard. Marmots are huge giant rat things that live in burrows all over Mongolia. That's nice I hear you say. But no! It's not! Because quite importantly ... they carry the bubonic fucking plague! Thousands die every year after eating them.

Would you like the marmot recipe? Well you don't get a choice because this is my book and I can do what I like, so here it is…

1. Shoot a wild, plague carrying marmot in the face.
2. Blowtorch its fur off.
3. Pull its head off, gut it and squeeze the remaining poo out of its anus.
4. Take red hot stones out of the fire and place them inside the carcass.
5. Tie the neck hole closed with wire and watch as it balloons up and hot steam escapes out of its holes filling the air with the stench of cooking rat, shit and plague.
6. Look up at the weird white transgender lesbian

beast monster and ask why they look green and like they are going to vomit on you?

7. Slice it up and eat it (the marmot, not the lesbian).

8. Die of the bubonic plague.

We both stood there looking green. It was fucking gross. But, then, we are vegetarian, I did mention were vegetarian right? Because we are vegetarian you know. It was probably delicious if you weren't vegetarian like us vegetarians. The whole family appeared and sat on the "grass" and tucked into the plague-carrying rat. We didn't have any because we are vegetarian.

We had a pretty chilled out day sat by the fire drinking coffee and playing with Ratty who we'd decided was the best child in the world. Towards the afternoon the sky turned black and there was a massive rain storm. The daughter came running in telling us to help put stuff on the bed so it doesn't get wet. Well, she came in screaming like she'd just seen a massacre and we stood there wondering if she'd lost the plot. We cottoned on after far too long of a time and helped.

The yurts being just big tents have no foundations drainage or any ground works so when it rains a lot the water flows in. Water also pours in through the only window which is in the roof above the fire. The sound of the rain hissing as it hit the red hot metal was relaxing.

As it was getting dark Sakal came to see us. He pointed to our bags and indicated that we would leave in the morning. We had no idea. He babbled for 30 minutes but we had no idea what he was on about. We went next door to sit in the small yurt with Bodo and

Jeffna and another 12 family members being force fed horse cheese and horse milk. Everyone sang folk songs into the early hours. It was beautiful especially not being bullied to drink or sing.

Quotes from the last few days:

Natalie: Oh my god, once I had the most amazing tapas. It was breaded breadcrumbs that were fried, they're called migas and they are divine.
Me: Did you just say breaded breadcrumbs?
Natalie: Yeah they are breaded breadcrumbs.
Me: Surely breaded breadcrumbs would just be bread? You can't have breaded bread crumbs which are breaded with bread as it would just be bread.
Natalie: You're stupid.

Me: What's this music?
Natalie: You wouldn't like it, it's good.

Me: I need to stop eating spicy food. I think I've broken my ass hole.

Natalie: I want to play the meringues.
Me: The what?
Natalie: The meringues.
Me: I think you mean the maracas.
Natalie: Oh yeah.

*

01.09. Saturday. Somewhere in Outer Mongolia.

In the morning, we packed Natalie's mounds of

useless shit up and stuffed it the car. Once again the family stood around aghast in shock at how we had more with us than they actually own. We sat in their yurt one last time and drank fermented horse milk and told them how lucky they were to have a beautiful family and life. We were all sad that we were going and I had to think of some really deranged stuff to stop myself crying. They loaded us up with horse cheese, milk, and yogurt because as far as they knew we loved it all. They have so much pride in it and even though we'd spent a week hiding it in our bags, bras, pockets and vaginas, it was infinitely better to have them think we liked it and throw it away later than have them know we find it more revolting than eating actual shit.

We waved as we set off over the hills and into the distance. The whole day was spent in the car which would have been boring had it not been for the joint sing-song we had to Mongolian radio. Obviously we had no idea what we were saying but tried to sing along regardless. This made Sakal laugh so much he nearly crashed into boulders, holes and off a cliff.

Nine hours of being thrown around in the car as the car lurched around on the never-before-driven-on land and we were absolutely knackered. Natalie had a bad stomach ache and was in agony. Normally the only thing that fixes her when she gets these stomach aches are baths or hot showers. Nothing else works and she's tried everything so we asked Sakal if he knew of a hotel. I thought it was pointless asking seeing as we hadn't seen a structure not made out of cloth in a week and we were in the middle of Outer fucking Mongolia. Sakal laughed then thought with a serious look on his face for a few minutes before saying, "Hotel, no ploblem." We were equally surprised that a hotel actually existed as that Sakal knew other words apart from "no ploblem." Sure enough. Two hours later, we came across a dirt road which led to a wooden structure which looked so old it had been built by dinosaurs. Sakal was over the moon having actually found it.

Inside there was a small decaying café with a beautiful woman sat behind a vodka bottle-covered bar. There were two unconscious nomads at a table in the corner. We sat down and began the annoying spiel about how we want food without dead animals in it (because we're vegetarians) It took us about an hour to make her understand and another hour to make our food. Mashed potato. It was delicious and would have been even better if there was enough for more than one very small anorexic mouse.

After our meal we were shown to our room. We weren't hopeful but would have been happy with a shower and bed not harder than granite and a room that wasn't cold enough to make Santa shit his pants and start torching elves. Just to be alone would have been a treat. What we were presented with was a room so bad we laughed out loud. It was a small room with black mould covering the ceiling and walls. It smelt like a mixture between condensed dog and damp. The wood was disintegrating and bits of it were all over the floor. There was electricity at least, there were no sockets, but there were electric cables jutting out of the walls seeming positioned just to take out eyes or kill someone if they were live, which they probably were. The best part of the room was the sink which had a functioning tap but no pipes to take the water away. The water just went on the floor. Oh and the water was brown.

We were too tired to argue and we didn't want to sleep in the tent so we paid the two dollars for the room and sat on the bed wondering how the fuck we were here and if we got raped and killed would anyone ever know what became of us. Natalie's stomach ache had gone so at least there was that.

We'd only been sat on the bed for two minutes when Natalie noticed something moving. This would make the rest of the shitness look like nothing. One word: beetles. They were everywhere we'd squashed three of the bastards within a minute. John, Paul and George were dead where the fuck was Ringo? Oh there he is, inside the fucking bed. I tried to play it down so Natalie could relax but this was the exact opposite of what we needed. Natalie cried and I tried to comfort her as best I could whilst at the same time not crying myself. It was no good so we both cried. It was a release of a week's worth of tension and insanity and sadness at sleeping with the beetles and not having a choice about it.

We were both fragile and didn't want to see the toilet because we knew it'd set us off again but as Natalie gracefully put it she needed to "squish one out." Classy, Natalie! So we went in search of the toilet. We would have been happy with a hole or just the abyss of the plains to be honest but there was a sign for toilets so we went in. Unbelievably the toilet was not a piece of wood over a shit hole and nor was it a latrine. Unbelievably it was a western toilet. Now we have seen some shitholes in our lives, literally, but this one was so dirty we couldn't tell what colour it originally was. After 20 years of never being cleaned it was black and the most revolting western toilet we'd ever seen. We went behind them and did our thing.

*

02.09. Sunday. Somewhere in Outer Mongolia.

I don't know how many beetles were in that room but it must have been hundreds. They were everywhere. I woke up at 7am in a blind panic because there was one in my hair. I had the biggest fit ever which would have been amazing on camera. I literally jumped up and started running around scratching at my head, ripping clumps of hair out, pulling my clothes off whilst doing my levitating deranged chicken flapping dance. This commotion unsurprisingly woke Natalie up who opened her eyes and without moving or saying anything watched me flapping around like an idiot unsure of what she was witnessing or if it was even real. She only realised she was awake and not having an insane dream when I screamed that there was a fucking beetle in my hair. She jumped up and, within about two minutes, we had vacated the room. It was the quickest we have ever left a room. Natalie's bags normally explode all over the room after her being in there for 10 seconds and it takes her at least an hour to cram all the shit back in them again.

We were itchy all over and felt dirty to our bones. We still hadn't showered and now we felt all beetley and gross. We went next door to the cafe for the free breakfast. This consisted of stale bread, some butter which we assumed was pulled out of a horse's rectum and to wash this filth down, a cup of plain boiling water. Sakal thought this breakfast was the best thing in the world and sat there for 45 minutes stuffing his face with the endless supply of stale bread. We went to sit in the car because it was clean. As we were sat there, Natalie started screaming. I had no idea why and thought she was dying or something. Then she screeched, "Aghh, aghh. There's a fucking beetle in my knickers. Arghh it's in my ass."

I quickly replied, "Is it Paul McCartney? Because regardless of not liking men and him being a million years old, I wouldn't mind that." I thought it was a hilarious reply and was quite happy with myself about it. Natalie did not find it remotely amusing and had a girly flapping fit of her own trying to get something out of her knickers whilst being sat in a car. It was one of the most amazing and strangely erotic things I have ever seen. She repeatedly grabbed at her crotch, then resorted to sticking her hand down her knickers all whilst wriggling around. I helped by watching and becoming increasingly aroused. Then she ran out of the car behind a shed to search for Mr. McCartney who was no doubt about to set up shop in her vagina. She never did find the beetle. I still joke it's probably laid eggs in her vagina and one day millions of beetles will come crawling out. I'm nice like that.

Trip Advisor Reviews

The rotting beetle filled barn in the middle of fucking nowhere in Outer Mongolia, aka "The Cavern"

What did you like most about "The Cavern"?
It's always nice to have insects in your hair, vagina and anus for a number of reasons. Firstly it gives them

somewhere to hide, which is nice for them. It also provides months worth of paranoia that they are in your hair, which means you scratch and itch like crazy which is actually proven to increase hair growth. I also particularly liked the sink too. Like I always say – plumbing is for idiots.

What did you like least about "The Cavern"?
Every single surface

What did you think about the location of "The Cavern"?
Being in the middle of absolutely fucking nowhere is great, so long as you don't need edible food, cleanliness, a hospital, toilet, clean clothes, toilet paper and any other semblance of normality.

Did you enjoy the food?
Yep. Stale bread provides the haw with lots of exercise and according to Orbit chewing gum adverts, this is good for teeth. There was no horse cheese or milk, so that was nice. The butter on the other hand tasted like Satan's anus but worse.

Would you return to "The Cavern"?
Yes, because sometimes you just want scabies

Rate "The Cavern" Shithole from 1-10
Minus 150 to the power of 40

A few hours of shit driving later and we turned up in a town, a real life actual town. I don't want to be too mean about the town because I'm sure it was lovely (compared to hell) but it was a bit shit. There was a row of shops that all sold the exact same things which were all shit. Literally three aisles of alcohol, five aisles of sweets and one of instant noodles. It was an absolute total fuck-fest. We left with nothing. Actually no, that's a lie. We left with condoms. Not that we use them but because they were branded "Itche condoms" I was so amused by this I bought three packets to give to various people for Christmas. How do you make condoms more hated than they already are? Make them itchy.

A: Bloody condoms I can't feel anything….. Oh hold on yes I can…. AGHHH, AGHHH! FUCK!

B: Honey, I think we should have a romantic time tonight.
A: No fuck off. It's taken three weeks for the rash to go.

The reason we were in the town was to see the ancient capital of Mongolia which was used during Genghis Khan's time. It was okay I suppose. We could have just looked on Google Images though. It was just a bit wank and then there's the thing about Genghis Khan, he was one of history's most hideously brutal genocidal mass murderers. He and his cunt mates killed 40 million people which was 10% of the world's population at the time and yet he is the undisputed hero of Mongolia. I don't care if it was centuries ago because they were still men, women and children murdered in cold blood. Fuck Genghis Khan. They should erase him from history not celebrate him. Could you imagine Germans in the future celebrating Hitler? There's no difference. They are both psychotic heinous genocidal cunts. Wow, that went a bit political didn't it?

We walked round the site thinking this would have been quite a nice building hundreds of years ago but it's fucked now and the guy who built was a bastard so can we go now please? We didn't want to insult or disrespect their national hero so we feigned interest.

Whilst we were in town we thought it would be an excellent idea to see if there was a hotel to wash our revolting stinking bodies, which had started to attract flies. We did indeed find one, the poshest one on Earth. Unbelievably this marble covered palace cost $150 a night. Who the fuck would pay that? There was nothing in the area to see, well apart from the decaying ancient buildings built by an epic prick which were wank anyway. Regardless of all this we were half tempted to pimp ourselves out for sex to pay for a bed and a shower. I don't know how much we'd make. I doubt I'd make very much.

Pimp: So would you like, the hottie or the tranny?

Skank: Um, the hottie! In fact I'll pay just to make the tranny go away. It's putting me off. Actually wait, I have premature ejaculation so can you get the tranny to rear its repulsive little head after about 50 seconds to help me last longer?

We had no idea of where we were going or any plans because Sakal, the guy with the answers, could only say, "No ploblem" and now the word "hotel." All we knew was that we were going to see some fun places in Mongolia and visit different nomad families. We got back in the car with no idea of where we were going. Seven hours of being thrown around the car later and he stopped, looked at me and told me that it was my turn to drive. I jumped at the chance and had a massive grin on my face as I drove over the hills and mountains off-road. He was most impressed with my driving which was amazing because no one else on Earth ever has been.

It was dark by the time we arrived. We had no idea where we were but hated it instantly. There were about 60 yurts all packed together with white Western dreadlocked topless idiots playing bongos and shit German techno. Nothing shows the world you're an idiot quite like being a topless white dreadlocked guy playing the fucking bongos. I fucking hate the bongos and anyone that plays them is an idiot. And white people with dreadlocks? No, just no! You should be shot in the face as far as I'm concerned and even that's too kind. How do you even get you shit hair to do that? With Blu tack, Pritt Stick and filth by the looks of things. And put some bloody clothes on you idiot. Do you see anyone else topless? No!

Yes I'm sure you are proud of your toned abs but everyone else thinks you're a smug prick. And bongos? Fucking bongos? The instrument of wankers. I hate them. There's always one idiot on a beach that thinks everyone wants to hear them bongo-ing away. No one wants to hear your shit noise you wannabe hippy prick. I hope you get rabies of the face you twat.

So we hadn't even entered the place and we hated it. Sakal desperately tried to explain something but we had no idea what he was on about. He rushed off and came back with a woman who spoke English. She explained that this was a hot spring and there are thermal pools. We instantly went from being angry to almost crying with happiness. We both wanted to rip our clothes off and run into the water, and in the process probably removing anyone already in it.

"Ugh what the fuck is that? It has the face of a woman but … ugh god I'm going to be sick. Oh my god what's that smell? It's the freaks, arghh, run."

Unfortunately the springs had closed for the night and we needed to rent a yurt to sleep in. We paid the money, about £30, which was well over budget but we didn't really have a choice because the tent scared the bejesus out of us and, after wolf night, the very thought of it gave us heart palpitations. The yurt had three tiny single beds. We desperately wanted to be alone but Sakal invited himself to sleep in one of them. We preferred that to his sleeping in his car because we're not assholes but still, if he'd insisted on sleeping the car, we wouldn't have argued. The English-speaking woman then showed up and told us sadly that she had to sleep in a tent because the place would not give her a bed. She was hinting she wanted our other single bed forcing Natalie and I to share a single bed made for a dwarf anorexic child. We're not monsters so we agreed. We also agreed that she would tag along on our trip and we'd pay her for her translating services. She wanted £2 a day for the whole day's work. This was far too low and so started the most bizarre negotiation when we were trying to pay more and she wanted less.

Natalie: We will give you ten pounds a day.

Her: No, only two please.
Natalie: No, that's too little. We will pay you ten and we pay for food and accommodation and tip you at the end.
Her: No, no just two. Please only two.
Natalie: No, you're getting ten.
Her: No, two.

Natalie: Look if you don't stop this, we'll increase it to twelve.

Her: Fine, fine. Thank you very much. I will take ten.

We crammed ourselves into our tiny single bed which was barely big enough for one and tried to sleep. Within about two minutes we had decided to never be kind or chivalrous again because the woman snored all night at a joke-like volume. Imagine a pig with a megaphone — well that wouldn't come close. She sounded like she was doing an impression of someone doing the worst snoring in the world. I can't stand snorers and I'm an ex one myself. When I'm drunk I become chief pig of the universe. I think everyone should take Natalie's approach of dealing with snorers and beat them until they stop. I used to wake up covered in bruises and I'd have no idea why. I'd had the snoring beaten out of me. Nothing wrong with it. Well maybe there is.

Friend: Darcie, have you been beaten up?

Me: No, I snored and the wife beat me up in my sleep.

Friend: Wow, she sounds like a great woman.

Me: She is! I love her.

Both lying there in a tiny bed and being unable to sleep with the fear of beetles, spiders and the fact it was fucking freezing and then having to deal with the snoring pig, we both were thinking reasonably evil thoughts on how to shut her up. We both speak basic Spanish and amused ourselves by whispering ways to end her. You will like me less if I tell you what we said because it was evil and totally uncalled for but I'm going to say it anyway ... I said I hope the bed breaks and she falls through the floor into some cow shit (she was rather large). Natalie said we should hold her nose closed … and her mouth. Totally evil considering she was a lovely woman, but being unable to sleep well in weeks and being kept awake all night by a pig makes you like that.

*

03.09. Monday. Some utter shithole in Outer Mongolia.

In the morning we somehow made the fire ourselves. We would have been quite happy about this feat but the pig was still snoring which was making us shake with rage. We made a coffee and sat there depressed, tired and angry. Eventually she woke up and asked us if we slept well. Not shouting, "No, you snoring pig bitch," and then launching ourselves at her was a physical and mental achievement

We put on our swimming stuff. I wore a short skirt and a black tee shirt covering what was clearly a bra containing fake tits. I looked reasonably stupid but the alternative look of man-beast was not an option. We walked past bongo prick who shouted good morning to us.

"Yeah, fuck you, Wank Shaft. I hope you get trampled by a yak," is what I thought.

"Good morning," we cheerily answered back. I think the 10 days had turned us evil from the lack of sleep and untold hardship for pussies like us.

As we got close to the spa the smell of eggs hit us.

"It's just the sulphur it's good for you," I said to Natalie knowing it's not actually good for you.

The spa consisted of three small pools with steam rising up into the freezing morning air. The views were spectacular, rolling hills fading into the distance and a beautiful steaming river winding through it. It was idyllic.

"Wow, Darcie that sounds lovely, I can't believe something was nice for you."

Oh I haven't finished. The three pools had never once been cleaned. It makes me heave to think about it. They looked alright until you were in them and that's when you noticed you couldn't actually see the bottom of the shallow pools through all the filth. Within seconds Natalie pulled a huge clump of hair and filth from the bottom and that's when we got out. It was actually disgusting. Hair, skin and fly soup that stank of eggs was not in any way a nice thing. We were really pissed off. There wasn't a cleaning system whatsoever and it was pretty much like bathing in stinking filth. I told the staff what I thought about it then stormed off ... directly into the men's changing rooms.

Old habits…..

Our only demand for the trip was that we didn't want to go to any tourist traps. We didn't want shit like this though. We came for culture not a dirty bath with a bunch of fucking idiots. All we'd ever said is that we wanted to avoid tourists and he'd bought us to a shit hole with nothing but tourists, including dreadlocked Bongo McWankface. We had no doubt he got a commission for bringing us there and he was quite happy to meet up with all the other drivers he knew from bringing every other numpty tourist there. We went slightly over the top, letting off steam about how pissed off we were.

We then apologised and tried to explain again not to take us to cack fests like that again.

To piss us off more, as we were sat in the car waiting to leave, Sakal took an hour chatting to his friends. We were in horrible moods and sat there bitching about him. Then the English speaking snoring pig got in the car and told us that our homosexuality must have been a terrible for our parents and we are very lucky they still speak to us and that it would be a great dishonour to do this to parents in Mongolia. I was so enraged I sat with my mouth open unable to speak. Then by brain clicked into gear and the rant to end all rants ensued. I said that anyone who thinks this is a choice is an idiot. Do you think we enjoy the stares, the hatred the increased risk of violence, rape and suicide? Do you think we like knowing everyone is talking about us and thinks were revolting and weird? Fuck the parents if they are dishonoured. They are dishonouring us and our will to be happy.

The rant went on for about 15 minutes. She instantly regretted saying what she had said and wanted to leave but every time I'd stop berating her Natalie would start, then I'd get riled up and start again. She had a 30-minute dressing-down including Natalie shouting and crying in her face.

She was white with fear, regret and shock. I don't think she meant to insult us but we were on the edge of losing it before she opened her big, snoring, pig mouth and said something insulting. Stupid bitch. She strangely decided she did not want to come with us as a translator after that. We were quite happy about it.

We made friends with Sakal again by singing along to the Mongolian radio and shouting, "Nosh!" every time he hit a rock or drove into an animal's burrow and, after a couple of hours, he stopped being scared of us. We spent the entire day in the car again with me driving most of it because he wanted to sleep off his hangover. I didn't mind because driving because he drove too fast and was generally a tad shit at it. He was constantly moving the steering wheel for no reason. Even on a straight flat road. He'd turn it every few seconds which made us feel sick but we hadn't figured out how to tell someone they were shit at their jobs without sounding like we were telling them they were shit at their jobs.

As it was getting dark, we pulled over in middle of nowhere between a huge canyon-like gorge with a hundred metre sheer drop into the river/certain death, and 50 metres on the other side there was a dirt road. We couldn't understand what he wanted to do but then he got the tent out of the back and told us to put it up. "Um no, Sakal, I don't bloody think so," we both said simultaneously. He gave us the look that said we were pathetic and started to build it himself.

Natalie: No, Sakal, no. There is absolutely no way we're getting in that thing.
Sakal: No ploblem.
Natalie: Yes ploblem. We sleep in car. You sleep in

the bloody tent.

Sakal: Ha, ha, ha. No.

Natalie: Well fuck you then, you wanker.

We stood there like angry teenagers with folded arms but he didn't care and made the whole tent himself, put our bags in it and looked at us as if we would actually be happy. Natalie asked through gestures and howling if there were any wolves and Sakal instantly nodded but said, "No ploblem." He also, for some inexplicable reason, indicated that there were bears too and they were more dangerous. We promptly went berserk. Berserk's a great word, people don't use it enough. I have thought of loads of cool words lately that go to waste, Berserk being my favourite followed by berk. Such great words. Bring back berk, I say. There's so many good words going to waste, berk, pillock, bubble-fuck, you stupid Johnny. We should stop calling people shit stabbers and donkey licking poo magnets and bring back berk, pillock and stupid Johnny's. I digress … So anyway we went absolutely berko.

Me: Ploblem, Sakal. Big bloody ploblem.

Sakal: No ploblem.

Me: There is no bigger ploblem, you fucking twat. We're not staying in the fucking tent and getting eaten. You can fuck off. We're going in the car. You can get fucking eaten by fucking bears and wolves.

Sakal: No.

Me: Yes.

Sakal: No.

Me: Yes.

Sakal: No.

We then both started crying. Mainly because we were

upset, distraught and terrified but also because it sometimes gets you what you want. Sakal however thought our crying was funny and whilst laughing got into his car/wank pit and left us to it. Bastard.

Not only were we terrified of wolves and bears and the huge chasm of certain death but we were close to the road and everyone in the entire country drink-drives. It was a shit place to camp. A fucking huge canyon we'd probably fall down whilst trying to pee in the night, fucking wolves and bears and a road full of drunk driving twats.

We climbed in the tent and sulked in bed for the 10th night in a row. It was absolutely freezing, even fully clothed and in the stinking camel hair turd bags we shook and trembled. It must have been about minus 25 degrees, maybe more. It was so cold our faces hurt.

Quotes from the last few days:

Natalie: *Interstellar* is officially the worst movie of all time.
Me: Yeah they owe me money for watching it. They owe me two hours of life back.
Natalie: I don't really like movies in space they're all shit.
Me: *Apollo 13* was good.
Natalie: *Pretty Woman* was good too.
Me: Yeah 'cos that's a well-known space film. The universe was in Julia Roberts' mouth as I remember. It's easily big enough.
Natalie: You're an idiot.
Me: Ah yes, I thought so. When I first heard about the

Interstellar movie I thought it was a chick flick about a guy who was really into a girl called Stella. You know into Stella.

Me: I wish I was hungry because the food might actually taste good.
Natalie: Do squats for an hour to work up an appetite.
Me: Yeah okay, I can't feel my legs. Give me food.

Natalie: Stop following yourself.

Me: Go sip your unicorn milk from your Faberge egg.

*

04.09. Tuesday. Between a gorge and a road somewhere in Outer Mongolia.

At 3am we both simultaneously bolted upright with pounding hearts because there was a fucking wolf howling and we were in a fucking tent. We had never been so scared. We absolutely shit ourselves. There's something about wolf howling that plays on your innate fears, a bit like snakes and spiders. Natalie cried and I would have cried too but crying sounds a bit like a distressed dog and I didn't want to attract any attention. We were petrified to the point where we were genuinely worried we'd have heart attacks. We didn't sleep for the remainder of the night and just hugged and told each other we loved each other and that all this travelling was stupid and we should be doing normal things like having kids and jobs and why the fuck were we in Outer Mongolia in the middle of a wolf infested-forest in a fucking tent. Words can't express how scared we were. I know now that wolves generally avoid people and bears were unlikely to rip our faces off but for us this was like having a gun to our heads and we were absolutely convinced we were going to die.

Having survived the night we celebrated by eating a huge jar of gherkins we found in the car. They were delicious but we were so hideously dehydrating and there was no water. Thankfully Sakal found an animal shit filled hole so we drank about three litres of poo water each.

*

Chapter Seven

Okay so I just showed what I've written of the book so far to Natalie who says it's all a bit negative so, for her sake, here is some positivity.

We had breakfast of undercooked peas with half a kilo of salt which was delicious, who doesn't want to fart themselves to death whilst suffering from kidney failure? Not us! We like kidney failure. We then jumped in the beautiful car and drove over beautiful ground to a beautiful school where we were shown to a beautiful classroom with a beautiful English teacher who was beautiful.

Although we had nothing to say to the beautiful teacher other than that she was beautiful we stood there in a wonderful awkward silence as she showed us round the Soviet-style school which wasn't at all depressing. We both rejoiced in the fact we could smell alcohol on her breath. Alcohol makes people more social and a drunk teacher will almost certainly be able to teach better after half a bottle of vodka. In fact all teachers should be force fed vodka at the start of every school day for the good of the students. The highlight of the school was a stuffed yak in the entrance which looked like it had been made by someone with no eyes who had been given the description of a yak by someone high on LSD.

"Behold" I exclaimed. "What a fine example of a yak. Whoever made that is clearly so talented they should be made president of the world and worshiped as a god"

254

After leaving the beautiful school, beautiful teacher and beautiful life-like yak we drove for two hours to a beautiful and fantastic National Park which is famous for its amazing and beautiful volcano. Natalie had a brilliant and totally sensible hissy fit because she needed to poop but there was no pristine Western toilet in the woods on the side of an active volcano. She shed beautiful and worthwhile tears before I calmly and nicely told her to stop being a complete moron because there was no one anywhere around apart from bears and they, according to legend, do in fact shit in the woods themselves. Although some dispute this.

We then climbed the glorious and amazingly active volcano, you know, like you do, and we sat on the top and hand fed cute and amazing chipmunks some crisps, again, you know, like you do. At the top there was a French speaking Mongolian guide along with three French tourists so I gathered up all my French knowledge to ask her when the volcano last erupted. "Quelle age a BOOM?" I cleverly asked. Nine hundred years ago she answered. I promptly declared myself bilingual and the most amazing person since the maker of the sacred amazing stuffed yak to walk the face of the Earth.

On the way to the next place, we found a superb little shop with a fantastic range of about three items. One of these items was chocolate ice cream which was so incredible we all instantly orgasmed with joy. The joy was amplified to levels of Nirvana as we realised it wasn't actually chocolate and was instead just chemicals to taste similar to it. The chocolate industry is bad for the planet and the farmers are often treated badly. By purchasing this weird brown substance we were not only helping the planet but also the poor farmers.

Okay enough of this positivity! Back to my normal self. The chocolate ice cream had about as much chocolate in it as fucking cheese. Fuck knows what it was but it wasn't chocolate. It was disgusting so Sakal, the greedy fat fuck ate all three of them.

After a few hours' driving we ended up in the most beautiful place on Earth. No I'm not being sarcastic again. It really was spectacular. There was a huge crystal clear lake stretching out over the horizon, beautiful green land with yaks, yurts and trees. It was just spectacular. We found a small yurt camp with five yurts on the side of a hill and rented one for the night. I decided to make the fire whilst Sakal watched and laughed. I tried really hard but managed nothing else other than filling the room with smoke. Half an hour later and Sakal came over, literally pushed me away and lit it himself in about 10 seconds.

We went for a little walk through the hills and along the banks of the lake. It was just stunning. So pure and clear. I reckon you could have drank directly from the lake without dying. We took some cool pictures then went for a joint poop on a hill which would have been a hellish, unimaginable experience just a few weeks earlier but was almost a pleasure now there was definitely no one there and we didn't have an arctic wind blowing up our bits. Not to mention how much better a beautiful desolate hill is to using a literally festering shit hole that stank like Satan's asshole. It was amazing. Natalie had gone from someone who hid the fact she pooped for the 12 years I'd known her to someone who said this:

"This mountain's amazing because I need to go and squish one out." I'm not sure which version of Natalie I preferred, the cute angel one or the gross one. It was funny though.

We got back and sat in the yurt and Natalie cooked the national dish of Sweden. She somehow had failed to make or tell me of its existence for the previous 12 years.

Me: So let me see if I've got this straight? We've been together 12 years during which at no point have you mentioned you can make this amazing food which happens to be the national dish of your country and this is the first time I've ever heard of it?
Natalie: Yes.
Me: Well that's not very nice is it?
Natalie: No. Sorry.
Me: Unforgiven. Fuck you.
Natalie: Oh I thought of something else funny. In Finnish a bunny is called a poopoo.
Me: What? How have you not told me this before?
Natalie: I just remembered.
Me: You're fluent in the language. You must tell me these things. I have to know them.

The meal is called *putti panu* and is made with small chunks of potato and whatever else you have knocking around. It was really nice. As we were eating, Sakal came through the door with a random French guy who wanted to tag along our car journey for a couple of days, no doubt paying Sakal for the privilege. We were having none of it because we'd paid enough for the car and driver and didn't want to be second place to a random guy. Plus we'd had a bad experience in a similar situation years before with some Frenchies who were the worst people on Earth. We'd gone out of our way to help them and they left us in a snake-infested field in the middle of nowhere whilst they found the farmers who could have rescued us all but instead they left with them without even coming to tell us. It still annoys us now. This French guy was sad and it was a tad mean but, fuck him. He had dreadlocks for a start and being French, the same as the previous assholes meant that it's only right that he should be judged and punished for the mistakes of his fellow countrymen. He was not impressed but we didn't give a fuck and carried on eating the yummy meal.

We had finished the meal and were talking about the difference between cows and horses and if you could describe the difference a cow and a horse purely only describing the physical features (not as easy as you think) when who should turn up at the door? The Frenchy again. This time he bought a friend with him and they both started pitching us as to why we should forfeit our prepaid expensive trip to take a random person who had dreadlocks. Then mid-sentence he stopped, asked if we were together and grinned like an idiot then started looking at me with a confused look on his stupid face whilst his friend carried on babbling about how they would help pay for the fuel. I wasn't in the mood and was pretty pissed off with everything so I quickly said,

"Firstly you can stop staring at me, yes I have a penis and secondly we already said no. Sorry".

We felt bad for about five minutes until we started talking about the two French bitches that fucked us over years earlier and were happy with our decision. Oh god this makes us sound like monsters doesn't it? Well we are the nicest people ever and do anything for anyone nearly all the time but these guys were, fuck it, I don't need to justify it.

The only interesting thing to happen in the night was when going to pee behind the yurt at around 11 pm there was a huge fucking yak there, chomping on grass, so I went to get some of Natalie's dinner to throw to it. I'm not sure what I was expecting? Maybe it saying, "Why thank you Miss, that's awfully kind of you. Mmm this is delicious. Your wife is a superb cook." But what happened was that I threw it and the yak absolutely shit itself and ran away. Don't throw things at animals in the dark is the lesson I learnt that day.

*

05.09. Wednesday. Somewhere in Outer Mongolia.

The first thing you do in the morning when you're a nomad is make the fire because it's fucking freezing. I woke up before anyone else and thought I'd look rather impressive if they woke up to a roaring fire so I gathered some sticks and tried to light the bastard. I started with tissues, then placed some sticks on top and lit it but the tissues instantly burnt and the sticks didn't even get warm. Then I decided paper would be better so I got our travel insurance papers because it was the only paper we had and I'm not very clever. I folded them nicely and tried to light them. This achieved a lot of smoke which stung my eyes like a bitch, whatever bitch's sting eyes like. At this point, Sakal woke up looked at me and laughed like an idiot for 19 minutes.

All nomads laughed at my fire ability and winked to each other over what I probably wrongly assumed is confirmation that indeed, as a woman, I can't make fire. Which is insulting in so many ways and doesn't even make sense because it's the women that mostly make the fires in Mongolia. As he was laughing I was getting increasingly furious and wanted to punch him. Then the yurt boss guy came to deliver us some hot revolting horse milk. He sat down next to Sakal and joined in laughing at me. The laughs soon stopped and turned to approving nods because I grabbed our alcohol-based hand sanitizer which we needed to not get bacterial infections and die, and emptied the fucking lot all over the wood and paper, then I lit a match and watched as the entire thing went up like a fucking firework.

"Oh who's laughing now dick head? Me that's who, master of fire, supreme leader of burning, hahaha."

After a minute the alcohol burnt off and the fire went out to the great amusement of absolutely everyone who thought it was the funniest thing ever. It *was* pretty funny. Sakal then literally pushed me out of the way causing me to fall on the floor and got the fire going in about a minute. The stupid bastard.

Natalie and I spent the whole morning fighting. I think the stress and tension had built up and something had to break. The argument was the same one we always fought about. Natalie is deeply angry that I was in the closet for a lot of the time I was with her. I had known I was female since the age of three but hadn't told her and this abused her trust. We had talked about babies and had got married all whilst I had this dark secret. It wasn't right and I should have told her before we married. I was truly sorry and had said so a million times. It's not easy living with a freak show. She looks like a normal woman and I do not which cause her lots of problems too. Yes we love each other but still, she didn't sign up to being in a lesbian relationship with someone who looks weird so she is angry that I wasn't honest with her.

Do you want to hear how I came out? Okay sit down and brace yourselves because this is about to get hideous. Okay so I had known all my life I was female. I have memories of being in nursery school aged three and knowing I was a girl. There was never any doubt. Everybody must have known deep down because the signs were everywhere - in my mannerisms, the way I acted, the toys I played with and the fact I only wanted to be with the girls. I was female. The only thing not female about me were my body, the clothes I was dressed in and the toys I was bought. I remember standing at the school gates aged five and telling my Mum I wanted to be a girl. I was told to stop being silly and had it explained to me that I shouldn't say things like that because it would cause bullying. From about this age I'd started to steal my sister's clothes and would prance about in front of the mirror. I was never interested in boy toys and would steal her dolls which also got me in trouble.

My school life was absolute hell. I was bullied badly by just about everyone, including, get this, by some teachers. The boys hated me for being a "sissy" and most of the girls hated me for being different, weird and wanting to be one of them. This was in the early 90's and I went to a rough school in a rough part of town which the Liberal world hadn't reached. Coming out as gay or transgender would be like signing your own death warrant. It was that simple. It was just terrible and I hated every single minute of it. I didn't have any friends and spent my time in any classroom I had access to, in order to get away from the bullies. They found me anyway. I was abused all day every day for 10 years both mentally and physically.

My school life was about as close to hell as you could imagine. In my early teens, as puberty hit, I went into denial and tried to act male. This lasted about three years, at which point I was extremely depressed. I hated myself passionately and had developed pretty serious anorexia and bulimia which I still struggle with now. I couldn't see a way out and the thought of ending it all was on a continuous loop of horrendous thoughts that went through my head. Everything I saw, I thought of how I could use it to kill myself. At some point I started self-harming by cutting my wrists and arms which covered me in deep wounds and scars. Then, one day I'd just had enough. I took the cord from an extension cable and went to the garden. I tied one end around a tree branch, and the other end around my neck and I jumped. I fell to the floor with a thump as the branch bent and snapped. Such was the severity of my mental state I thought this was funny.

I was in such a bad way. I was horrendously underweight, covered in cuts and scars and now had a bruised neck. I went into my brother's room, I don't know why. I stood there as the seven-year-old slept and said my goodbyes, ready to do the finish job properly with a different branch. I looked at him and all the toys in his room and completely lost it. I fell to the floor crying. I didn't want to ruin his life too so the next day I went to the doctor and told them everything. I was fourteen.

Within two days, I was institutionalised in a mental hospital. I was in there for fifteen weeks. I'd decided in those minutes in my brother's room that I would never commit suicide and so tried to fix myself. It took five years in and out of loony bins before I'd beaten my demons. I was still in the closet but I was stable.

It was only in my late teens that I accepted that I was a woman on the inside. No one else knew. Well, I suspect they all must have known but I was in the closet and not around the type of people or family where I could just come out as a woman. It was unheard of in my world and was totally unacceptable. In private I'd started buying and wearing women's clothes. By the time I met Natalie I had a small collection of women's clothes and a wig hidden at the back of the wardrobe that I would wear when she was out. I didn't get turned on by wearing them. I was never a transvestite or a cross dresser. I just felt a sense of relief and normality. I never once wore female clothes without crying and wishing I was different.

Then, after we'd been together a few years the desire to be the real me started to eat away at me. Year after year it became stronger and stronger. I thought I could be in the closet forever just to be with my soul mate but the pain just got worse and worse. I started dropping hints.

"I'm the least manly man ever," I'd say.

"That's so nice even if I wear it."

"I can't change a tyre, have you seen me I'm a total girl." (Yes I know it's sexist)

She always knew that I was about as far from a stereotypical man as was possible but had never put two and two together. I honestly thought she knew I was a woman; it was so obvious. Then one day I just said, "You do know I'm a girl on the inside right? And I'd love to be one on the outside too."

She went absolutely crazy saying she didn't want to be with a woman, she's not lesbian, it's embarrassing and she could never be with someone like that. She didn't mind other people like that but didn't want to be with one herself.

I was not expecting that response. I tried to undo it and said I wasn't really a girl and that I was just going through a bit of depression and was just being mental. Our relationship nosedived. We fought daily. Everyone in the apartment block heard the crazy gender arguments because the shouting was so extreme. Our relationship went very bad very quickly. I was devastated at both the prospect of losing my soul mate or keeping her and living a life in the closet. Either way was a shit life. (I'd have picked to stay in the closet by the way because she *is* my soul mate).

The fighting didn't get any better and I went to stay with my brother for a week to give her space. On the third day she called me and told me that she wanted to give it a go. It started slowly. I stopped pretending to be a man as much which, in itself, was like releasing a huge weight. I wore very slightly more neutral clothes. The change wasn't anything noticeable. I was scared to make any noticeable changes because I didn't want to lose her. Then after a couple of months I was sat at my desk at work on a normal working day when I got a message. It was an image of my black dress which she'd found hidden in the wardrobe. The following text changed everything. "I want to see you in this," it said. I cried.

So there I was, all dolled up locked in the bathroom, my heart pounding with nerves and refusing to come out. I was so, so nervous. I had my dress, makeup and a wig on. I looked like the woman I was. After years in the closet I unlocked the door and stood in front of my wife. It wasn't the relief I'd always expected it would be because I thought she'd hate what she saw. That feeling ended quickly when she told me I was hot, I was really good at makeup and looked good in a dress. She then practically launched herself at me and we had sex.

It turns out she'd had a few lesbian experiences of her own and had a rather big thing for women. I told my brother about it the next day and he said he knew, that everyone knew, anyone who hadn't figured it out was an idiot. I didn't mention that to Natalie.

I still am not at one with myself. I never will be. I have the wrong genitals and seeing them upsets me daily. I have a male voice and there are signs of my birth gender everywhere. I don't understand this condition any more than you reading this will. I think it's ridiculous and weird and wish I could just learn to be a man. It would make everything so much easier and what would it matter? I already have my soul mate. I don't understand why I can't just learn to be normal. I'm so high maintenance because of it and would do anything to turn it off. I hate it. I always have and always will. Still I'm lucky in that I have been told I look female and am not ugly which is just luck, but I am thankful for it. I have issues with the way I look and think I'm hideous but other people say I'm pretty. Some trans women have the bodies and faces of big masculine men and for them it's even more difficult.

Bloody hell that went on for a bit. Right so where were we? Yes so we'd argued most of the morning enlightening the Frenchies and everyone within a mile radius about our woes and how embarrassing it is to go out with a freak show and how terrible it was that I'd lied to her. Then, once we got it all out of our systems, we decided to make up because we loved each other a lot.

We set off in the car with absolutely no idea where we were going. We both had dead phone batteries which although had no signal and hadn't had Internet for that long we were both suffering with acute Internet withdrawal symptoms. We still liked to check just in case. We expressed to Sakal that we needed electricity, a word he unbelievably knew. "No ploblem, no ploblem, electricity."

We found a café with electricity behind the counter so we handed our phones over and looked at what they had available. The options were easy because they only had two things. Yak butter tea and horse meat stew. After an hour, Sakal thought he'd point to an aerial in the corner and say the fourth English word he knew...

Sakal: Internet.
Natalie: There's Internet? Thank You God, Jesus and Santa. Woman, hand me my phone I need to internet myself to the afterlife.
Me: Here you go. Oh god, I think I'm going to cry with happiness.

We both grinned insanely reconnecting to our online lives. I don't know whether it's normal to be so happy to have the Internet you nearly cry with happiness? It was amazing.

After 30 minutes of pure Internet joy, I downloaded the bloody Kylie Minogue song on Spotify which had been in my head for three weeks and put the phone back to charge behind the counter.

One hour later, when I went to collect my phone and I had managed to download every single song she'd ever made and let me tell you she has made a shit-load of songs. Then, after several days trying to delete them individually, I was so fed up at hearing bloody Kylie songs I opted for a mass delete but due to being an idiot I deleted everything apart from one song ... *Africa* by Toto.

Natalie: Darcie why have you been listening to *Africa* by Toto on repeat for two hours?

Me: Well, Natalie that would be because I accidentally deleted all my music off my phone apart from that one bloody song, Spotify has now decided that I'm now in the wrong country to download new songs and I'm stuck in the middle of nowhere without any music apart from bloody Toto.

Natalie: Why did you delete them?

Me: KYLIE BLOODY MINOGUE. IT'S HER FAULT.

Why does Spotify even have that download button at the top? Just so you can accidentally delete all your music in as easy way as possible? It's just bloody stupid and can fuck off! As can bloody *Africa* by Toto. It's a great song for the first 20 times then it starts to make you feel physically sick. By the 50th time you hear it you're thinking fuck the rain down in Africa.

We arrived at a small yurt in the middle of nowhere where one of Sakal's relatives lived. The yurt was in a small valley surrounded by forest. Outside the yurt were the bodies of about 12 lambs which a wolf had killed the previous night. I don't know why they kill so many.

Apparently they only eat one and kill the rest anyway. Seems a bit pointless to me. We were sad to see the wasted life but it's just nature and in a roundabout way it would help nature by feeding the birds of prey, foxes and other critters.

Inside the yurt we met the family. There was a mother who was about 50, her husband and a son who had Down's syndrome. I mention this because the son did the exact same duties that anyone else would do. He brought in the sheep, milked the animals, and did everything expected in a son without Downs. It was lovely to see and he was happy as Larry, whoever Larry is. The yurt itself was plain, cold and about as prehistoric a residence as you could imagine. There wasn't anything even made of metal. The family all smiled constantly confirming our beliefs that a natural life is a happier life.

Within minutes of being in the little yurt we were fed fresh horse milk fresh out of the horse's tits. It was fucking revolting. Then the dreaded alcoholic version of the vile substance was ceremonially offered which can't be refused. I had a sip, gagged, smiled and told them it was lovely. Then Natalie had a sip gagged and told them it was lovely too. This was usually the end of the hideousness shit we had to consume but then the woman produced a bowl of horse milk yogurt which was somehow fizzy and easily the worst thing I have ever put in my mouth ever. We heaved and gagged.

Natalie: I'd prefer to suck on a tramp's ball sack than have that shit in my mouth again.
Me: Fucking hell, Natalie can you perhaps not be so fucking insulting? What if they understood?
Natalie: They don't speak English, Darcie, stop being an idiot. That shit was the worst thing in the world ever. Seriously how can they eat it? It tastes like the shit from a diseased kangaroo.
Me: Well I wouldn't know, dear, but can you please just try and save the insults until we're not sat opposite them?
Natalie: No, it's fucking disgusting.

The food just would not stop flowing, Yak and horse milk rice pudding. Dried sour yogurt biscuits which we were then shown how to make. Yep, that's useful.

"Hi there Farmer Giles, mind if I squeeze the milk

out of your horse's tits, then make some revolting yogurt out of it before letting it go dry and squishing it into biscuit shapes?"

We were stuffed and I had the overwhelming urge to purge the filth out of myself. I said was going to the toilet but Natalie knew me too well and said she'd come too because she knew I'd be sick. It wasn't nice. I wanted to shout, "Please stop feeding me I'm bulimic. Seriously just stop feeding me, this is fucking with my head." If only we'd done our research I could have invented a milk allergy. It was too late though and the pride in their lives is their milk produce. We were fucked.

It was going dark and we were already stressed about where we'd be sleeping. Sakal told us to come outside with him then pointed to the tent indicating we should set it up. We both went into full angry flapping chicken mode refusing to sleep in it. He thought it was hilarious as did the family but this time we had no intention of staying in it.

Me: You fucking get eaten by the fucking wolves and bears, you asshole. No, we're not getting in it. No way. You can get fucked. You wanker. We're not staying in the fucking tent.
Sakal: No ploblem.
Me: Fuck your "no ploblem." We're not getting in and it's that easy so you either think of a plan B or we'll be here a long time because we're not sleeping in that.

The car was his little wank pit and he hadn't given it up before because it's not really suitable for two people and, well, it's just better than the tent which he obviously knew. We were having none of it and stood there with folded arms refusing to entertain the idea. In the end he gave in and slept on the yurt's floor whilst we got the car.

Whilst in the car, the morning's argument flared up again because Natalie told me that she wished she had a man who could actually look after her and protect her. It was needlessly harsh and upsetting so I hit back with, "Let's get divorced then, because I'd prefer to be with a kind woman instead of a hurtful bitch." Then we entered screaming mode for the second time in the day. We were still not talking to each other as we went to sleep in the tiny space of the car which made it an interesting situation.

Natalie: Give me the blanket you hog. I hate you.
Me: I hate you more. You deserve to be cold, bitch.
Natalie: Me? You deserve to be cold, you bastard. It's like your heart, cold.

Me: Did you just call me a bastard? You bitch. I hope you freeze.
Natalie: You're an idiot.
Me: You're an idiot.
Natalie: You're a prick bastard.
Me: Let's break up. Seriously you're a bitch.
Natalie: Fine. Good luck finding a partner that wants a chick with a dick.
Me: Fuck you. Good luck finding someone who wants to be with a bitch you bitch. Seriously I'm breaking up with you. You are the worst person ever and I hope you get eaten by a bear.

Natalie: Me too at least I won't have to be with you.
Me: Fuck you.
Natalie: Can we be friends now I'm tired of fighting.
Me: Yeah me too.
Natalie: I love you.
Me: I love you too.
Natalie: I'm really sorry.
Me: So am I.
Natalie: Make up sex?
Me: Um, I don't think it's possible and this is Sakal's wank pit. I don't want to take clothes off in case I catch something.
Natalie: Yeah good thinking.

The car was freezing, damp and uncomfortable but we had one of the best night's sleep in ages.

*

06.09. Thursday. Somewhere in Outer Mongolia.

We woke up full of energy and happiness, skipped along past the dead lambs which were still there and into the yurt. We wished everyone a good morning. We were fed numerous horrific things but having slept everything seemed bearable. We took some photos of the family then jumped in the car and left.

About midday we arrived in a small town in the middle of a wide plain between two huge snow-capped mountain ranges. Mongolian towns are curious in that they would be exceptionally dull if it wasn't for their roofs. Everyone has a different colour roof making the towns look like kaleidoscopes of colour which is beautiful. The strange thing about this town in particular was that absolutely all the women were wearing miniskirts. It was so weird. Nowhere else did Mongolian women wear them, not even in the capital, Ulaanbaatar, where you'd expect it to be more liberal.

A few bone-rattling hours later we arrived at the other fuck off lake. This was the biggest lake in Mongolia and the fifth biggest in the world. It was like a sea. It would have been rather pretty had there not been a monsoon the entire time we were there. We rented a yurt for four dollars a night which was made even better by the fact that for the first time in weeks we were alone. No random people, children, snoring pigs, wolves or Sakal. We were alone in a room with a bed. So we promptly locked the door and had sex. Our revolting dirty bodies and odours made it kinky somehow. You should try not washing for a month and having sex. It's great.

Across a muddy field the place also unbelievably had a Western toilet. I wanted to hug it. It was white, clean and well, a toilet. I almost cried with joy. I ran back to Natalie to tell her of the news.

Me: Behold wife, I bring glorious news from my brave ventures into uncharted territory.
Natalie: Speak normally you idiot.
Me: Fine then, we can poo, there is an actual toilet, a real life normal toilet.

Now I don't know whether it was Natalie just being a dumbass or that she was just too elated to be with a proper toilet but later in the day she called me from the toilet to tell me she didn't have any toilet paper.

Natalie: Hi, can you bring me toilet paper .I don't have any and I just squished one out.

Me: Please can you go back to being poo phobic, dainty and body-shy because that's disgusting and you're a total skank.

Natalie: Yeah, but I'm sat here and, um, really need it.

Me: Did you not check beforehand? I consider that as the only requirement of needing to poop. "I need to poop do I have toilet paper? Yes, okay good." Everything else is pretty easy

Natalie: I thought it had it but I didn't.

Me: You're a dumbass.

Natalie: I know. Look just bring me some because, um, I'm dirty.

Me: Ugh, that's gross, hold on… Um err um umm oh. Right do you want the good news or the bad news?

Natalie: What?

Me: Well, we don't have any toilet paper, there's no one around and we don't even have tissues.

Natalie: Fuck what's the good news?

Me: Well there's a shower in the next room to the toilet.

Natalie: Ewww, no.

Me: Fine, stay dirty then but you'll be sleeping outside.
.

The phone went dead and I took the towel to her but by the time I reached her she was crying because the situation had gained a secondary disaster. She now had a "floater situation" and there was someone waiting to get in. I thought this was hilarious and practically rolled around the floor.

"For god's sake Natalie, calm down there's people

starving in the world and you're crying because you have a floater."

She hobbled to the shower still crying while I dealt with the disgustingness. It was this poo-tastrophy that promptly ended Natalie's brief weird flirt with open liberal poopage before becoming shy again. Then the next problem was that the showers didn't work because they only got turned on for one random hour in the afternoon because the owner was a control freak weirdo. So the situation all got a bit gross but I think you have probably heard enough revoltingness for the day. Okay no more poo stories for a little while, I promise.

We sat by the fire and ate instant bloody noodles for the 15th night in a row and enjoyed being alone. We had such high hopes for the night in our clean private yurt by ourselves. We put loads of logs on the fire, had a cup of tea and snuggled up in bed. We were just drifting off and that's when we heard the scurrying. I think deep down we both knew but it took a further 20 minutes of panicking before we saw one of the bastards. A fucking mouse. We quickly spotted a second one then a third then we lost count because they were fucking everywhere.

So once again we were in bed petrified and frozen in fear. There was no light because electricity hasn't reached Mongolia yet, it was fucking freezing because, like a pro, I killed the fire with too much wood and now there were dozens of terrifying mice running around. We tried to calm ourselves down by telling ourselves that they were just mice and they couldn't hurt us but, almost as soon as we said this, one was on our bed. Natalie screamed as it ran over her neck. We shat ourselves. We used the lights on our phones to light up the room. There were about 10 of the bastards running round. We got up and started making loads of noise to scare them away which was totally ineffective. Then we set about putting the cardboard box containing all the food which we had cleverly left on the floor out of mouse range.

This wasn't so easy because yurts are effectively fucking tents and there's nowhere to hide things. Eventually we made an upside down pyramid structure using a small table and a bin bag. I don't know why we assumed this would deter the mice and they wouldn't just bite through it, which of course they did in about two minutes. Not only were there mice everywhere including our bed but they were in our cardboard food box eating and pooping all over our food, the only food we could eat in the country because everything else contained fucking sheep tits and goat balls. We were so, so stressed. We couldn't think of a way to protect the box and were too scared to open it to see what was happening inside in case a mouse jumped out and attacked our faces. (Yes I know) but we were scared.

Quotes from the last few days:

Me: Good news! The spider has left the realm of the living.
Natalie: You're mean. You should've just put it outside.
Me: What a good idea. Maybe I could pick it up with my face and we could go for a cup of tea as well? Maybe talk about the old days and end up having a sexual

affair.

Natalie: There's something seriously wrong with you.
Me: I fucking hate spiders.
Natalie: So you killed it?
Me: Oh hold on, wait, I know CPR, I shall bring it back to life. Quick, put its loose legs on ice maybe they can be reattached by a surgeon.
Natalie: Don't be an idiot.
Me: One, two, three. Quick help me put it in the recovery position.
Natalie: It's not funny, Darcie. Don't kill things.
Me: I didn't he's just having a rest without his legs or insides.

Natalie: No offence but you look like shit.

Me: I'm going to poop in your pants then, when you put them on, you're going to get a smelly bottom.
Natalie: Are you four?
Me: Are YOU four?

Natalie: Can you pass me the slapper to turn over the potato.
Me: The what?
Natalie: The slapper thing. What's it called?
Me: A spatula.
Natalie: Oh yeah.
Me: From now until the end of time I shall call it the slapper.

*

07.09. Friday. Somewhere in Outer Mongolia.

Imagine spending the night freezing cold room with 20 mice scurrying everywhere including your face and when if you actually did managed to drift off to sleep for just a minute your partner would let out a blood curdling scream directly in your ear as a mouse ran over their face. Oh and then waking up with no shower, no electricity and worst of all no Internet. It was one of the worst nights we'd ever had. Absolutely horrific.

Once again, as the sun came up we were huddled on the grass outside, too scared to be inside. We looked over the grey lake with our mangled filthy hair blowing in the wind as the drizzle soaked our dirty unwashed clothes. We had the same thousand-yard stare we seemed to have every morning in Mongolia. We had reached our limit and were done. We fought Mongolia and Mongolia won. It was too much.

At around 8 o'clock Sakal showed up, looked at us and had one of his laughing fits. He just wouldn't stop laughing at us. This time we weren't in the mood and just sat there sulking as he fell around choking on his own laughter. We explained the mouse situation and he couldn't understand what our problem was. There were fucking mice on our faces, Sakal. One was in our fucking sleeping bag. It was a big fucking ploblem, Sakal.

It rained all day so we sat inside and tried to make fire. We both gave up after an hour and called the owner over to his delight and amusement. He did however bring with him a small bottle of butane and a blowtorch. So, as he was showing the stupid girls how real men make fire, I repeatedly pointed out to him that "real men" don't cheat. The guy was a prick and didn't care.

In the afternoon we went for a walk to see the shit lake but gave up because it was cold and wet. Nothing looks good in shit weather.

We prepared for the night by putting all the food in the car. We were quietly confident that there would be no mice. But the second it got dark they turned up again. They were everywhere. On our bed in the bed, absolutely everywhere. They must have had a plague of them because there were fucking millions of them. If I sound like I'm exaggerating I'm probably doing to opposite. It was like sleeping in mouse filled cage. It was just the worst thing ever. We didn't sleep and spent most of the night screaming and crying. Even a few months later writing this I am still scarred by the experience and frequently wake up thinking there are mice on me. I fucking hate them.

*

08.09. Saturday. Somewhere in Outer Mongolia.

We loaded up the car ready to leave the mouse-infested shit hole when the owner of the camp came over to us and handed us the bill which was not only written in Mongolian but was also too much. We asked him for an English explanation and were unbelievably told we had a charge for hot water. Natalie promptly lost the fucking plot and went berserk:

Natalie: Look here you little shit stabber, there was no fucking hot water because you only turn it on for an hour a day when everyone is somewhere else the rest of the time you run off with the only key because you like the feeling of power don't you? You little wank stain. Tell me this you little fuck goblin, does it look like I've had a shower? I haven't washed in over fifteen days. FIFTEEN bloody days. Smell me! SMELL ME! Do I smell like I've had a shower? Hot water? Hot bloody water? Why not charge us for champagne and a Jacuzzi as well? This place is appalling. The fucking cheek of it? You own a yurt camp but clearly have a fucking mouse infestation. You have seen the million mice you have running around right? Kill the fucking mice! Buy a cat! Buy 20 fucking cats. Use mouse traps, poison or bloody Napalm, just get fucking rid of them. You might like having them running over your face in the night, you revolting scrubber, but we don't. There's fucking hundreds of them and it's disgusting. They ate our noodles. You should be paying us for more noodles, you prick. You're getting the worst Trip Advisor review ever. It's going to be so bad that you're going to cry.

Man: Okay sorry. Mistake, no hot water, shower broken. Sorry.
Natalie: You will be.

She then gave him $2 which was half what it should have been and got in the car. I didn't know whether to say, "Um, it's supposed to be four," or just follow her. I decided not to risk her wrath and got in the car and let Sakal deal with the fallout. Sakal, not wanting to risk Natalie's wrath either shrugged his shoulders and got in the car too and we drove off.

We sat in the back dozing off as Sakal tried to joke about chasing foxes and marmots. He really thought we'd think it was funny but we couldn't be bothered and snuggled and whimpered feeling sorry for ourselves.

After a few hours' driving, and once again with no idea where we were going, we arrived in a small town and were told to stock up on food. This was handy because we weren't keen on eating mouse shit. Typically, the shop had the Mongolian staples of sweets, meat paste, gherkins and vodka. All very well if you're planning an early death but if you actually want food you have to settle for instant noodles which ironically contained meat paste and gherkins. There was nothing to buy so we bought four jars of gherkins and a jar of honey which leaked over the whole box covering everything. Is there a worse substance in the world than honey? I think not. It's evil stuff. They should use it in warfare.

"The bombs aren't working, bring forth the honey."
"Nooo, not honey! Okay we surrender."

The only thing worse than honey is tuna fish oil. That is fucking evil stuff. It not only stinks but you can't get rid of it. I honestly think I'd rather head-butt a spike that be covered in tuna oil.

We were tired to the point where we could have slept almost anywhere, on a toilet floor, on a bed of nails, under the sea. It wouldn't have mattered but. In the fucking car, driving over natural hills and valleys made the car shake and bounce so much that every few seconds you were launched head first into the windows and each other so we couldn't sleep.

The landscape had started to change; gone were the open plains and yurts and now there were thick forest with impossibly narrow unused forest tracks. Sakal treated these tracks as his playground without giving any care for his car. We both winced as he scraped past branches that cut into the paint.

"Um, Sakal, I'm not sure whether you know this, but that dreadful scraping noise you're hearing is not in fact a good noise, No, in fact, I'd go as far as to say it's the worst noise you can hear when it comes to the shiny appearance of this rolling lump of shit because you see, my not very intelligent friend, it is scraping the paint off the fucking car. Now if this is your car then that just makes you a bit stupid but if it's rented then that makes you a selfish little pig doesn't it?"

We decided he was a total idiot because, shortly after scratching all the paint, we reached a flooded swampy path and, instead of using any of the cars immense off-road gear like four wheel drive, a low gear, traction control or just plain old driving skills, he just took a run up and tried to get through it using speed. Needless to say we got stuck in the middle. We couldn't believe he did it nor could we believe the shock on his face. Well yes, you dim-witted turd sniffer, you just drove through a patch of swamp of unknown depth and now we're stuck. What the fuck else would happen? We were still in filthy moods and sat, unimpressed, with folded arms in the car as he faffed about trying to work out what to do. He asked us to step out about five times and we just blanked him. Then he appeared angrily at the door holding wellies for us.

"They're nice," I remarked. "I hope you enjoy eating them."

He just stood there, confused, waving them in our faces as if we didn't know what they were for. I eventually grabbed them, put them on and jumped in the ankle deep mud and water. The car was totally stuck and the path was completely impassable. I don't know why he even bothered trying. It would have been difficult in a hovercraft let alone two tons of car. Natalie then got out and started commenting on his life choices which displeased him no end. He was not only stuck but was now getting a telling off by two lesbians one of whom can't drive due to not being able to see. He stormed off to go and check the rest of the path which was clearly impossible whilst we got back in the car and helped it sink more.

A few minutes later, he came back with a random guy that must have been chilling in the woods fucking trees or whatever people in the middle of a massive forest miles away from anything do. They both looked at us sat in the car and shook their heads disappointedly. We realised that we were ourselves not that clever and were probably making the car sink further. The men hatched a plan which involved putting sticks and twigs under the submerged wheels then using the car's winch and our pushing to drag it out. We were covered head to toe in mud but it worked and we all cheered as the car was dragged free. Sakal gave the mystery guy a bottle of vodka from his stash of about seven bottles he kept in the glove box to thank him for his help. Then the inevitable happened, they opened it and drank it all. We went from being two angry, annoying women to two nightmare bitches from hell.

Natalie: We're not getting in if you're drunk.
Sakal: No ploblem, no ploblem.

Me: Yes ploblem, you wankshaft. We're not getting in with you drunk.

Sakal: No ploblem.

Me: You can barely fucking drive sober, you asshole. You're not drinking that. I don't allow you.

Natalie: Seriously, Sakal. I'll tell on you.

Sakal: No ploblem.

Natalie: I'll show you a fucking ploblem, I'm going to shit on your face when you're asleep.

Me: He'll probably like that. I'm going to tell everyone we had sex.

Natalie: That's a bad threat and it's insulting to me.

Me: Oh yeah sorry. I'm going to say I shagged your Mum.

Natalie: You're an idiot Darcie.

Me: And your Dad.

Natalie: You really are thick.

Me: And your cat.

Natalie: Stop talking, Darcie, seriously just stop talking.

They both left us with the car and went off to sit in the woods to get smashed together. We stood around bad-mouthing him and swearing about all the stuff we were going to do to him when we were back in Ulaanbaatar.

Thirty minutes later, the bottle was empty and the random guy vanished back into the woods to finish fucking his tree. Sakal, the tit, came back whilst repeatedly saying, "No ploblem." He was wasted and singing loudly whilst touching us as much as possible which we really didn't like. I have issues being touched in general and have always disliked it. We felt unsafe and scared.

We then had a really scary fight with him because I wanted to drive due to there being less chance of death but he was pissed and aggressive and insisted he drove. He actually put up a good fight until Natalie mentioned the police. The look on his face was that he would bury us in the swamp. We were pretty scared. He had total contempt for us. Thankfully his single brain cell kicked in and he reluctantly threw the keys at me. So I jumped in the driver's seat and sped off ... at a speed so bloody slow it would have annoyed a stoned snail. Soon enough we got to another boggy bit so I thought I'd teach Sakal how one uses one's car. I'd never even driven a 4x4 before but knew the logic behind them so I loudly explained how to use one.

"Right so I need to put it in a low gear with full 4x4 wheel drive on, traction control on, and slowly forwards."

We went through the deep water and mud and came out the other side like I was a pro. I turned round and high fived Natalie. Sakal, being a drunk piece of shit, saw this as an insult to his job, talent and size of his minutely small penis. Five minutes later he blew his top. He was so angry he summoned from his three brain cells a new word. Change.

Sakal: Change.
Me: No Sakal. You're drunk.
Sakal: Change. Ploblem.
Me: Yes, you're the fucking ploblem.
Sakal: CHANGE NOW!
Me: Okay, don't hurt me.

Back in his position of power, he became like a

million stupid people before him and thought he'd show off his great driving ability by driving really fast.

"No Sakal you gimp, we've already discussed this, only idiots drive fast. My fucking hamster could drive fast and I don't even have a hamster. The ability to move one's foot onto a gas pedal involves zero skill. There are people without feet, arms, legs, heads or bodies that can drive fast pushing an accelerator down is skill-less. The skill is in driving safely"

He made it an hour before the crash we knew would happen, happened. The moment came as Natalie shouted, "Slow down, Sakal for god's sake!" ... screech! ... Smash into tree. The noise was horrific and we were thrown forwards. It was a bad crash and we were both in complete shock. We left the car and sat on the grass, whilst hugging and crying. Sakal sat at the wheel unable to comprehend what had just happened as steam and car juices poured out of the engine.

It could have been much worse, had he been going only slightly quicker because the car had no seat belts because this was Mongolia and that would have been too clever. Unbelievably someone had actually taken scissors and cut the seatbelts off. We saw it in a various cars in Mongolia. I struggle to think of anything stupider.

"What the fuck are these pieces of material for? They look stupid. I'm going to cut them off with scissors"

By this point, we'd already become scared of Sakal and were now scared shitless because he'd just destroyed his car, he was drunk and aggressive and clearly decided he didn't like us whatsoever. He got out of the car and was livid.

He was faffing around his smoking ruined car and Natalie and I decided to hide in a small patch of forest 70 metres away in case he decided to kill us.

Our pain and anguish soon became slightly better when, out of habit I looked at my phone and there was not only phone signal but also one bar of internet. Somehow Sakal had managed to crash near the only village for hundreds of miles that had Internet. I mean it was slow Internet, I could have made a better connection with yogurt pots and string but it was Internet and if there's one thing we like most in life it's the Internet. One of the most enduring images I have of Mongolia is hiding in the forest as Sakal angrily faffed with his wrecked car whilst we smiled away as we reconnected to Facebook world. It was so surreal.

The sequence of events that followed are best summarised with this message I put on Facebook.

Bad news: Smashed car into a tree.
Good news: We're alive.
Bad news: The car is not.
Good news: We crashed in the only small village in the whole of Mongolia with Internet.
Bad news: We're being force fed horse milk by friendly locals that we are now staying with and we can't say no.
More bad news: We are vegan.
Even more bad news: Horse milk is utterly disgusting.
Good news: Internet, Internet, Internet.

Bad news: The family's pet dog won't leave me alone and it has developed a permanent erection and everyone's laughing.
Good news: I'm going to smack it in the balls in a minute see if it still likes me then.
Bad news: There's no room in the yurt so we are staying in a small shed which is in fact a fully functioning beehive with bees. Fucking bees!

You couldn't make this shit up...

The car had been towed away with the tent inside it. Sakal had gone somewhere with his car and to drown his sorrows with more vodka. We were alone with a random nomad woman who was dressed in rags. She had no teeth and looked like she'd had the toughest life in the world. To her we may as well have been aliens. I'm not sure she entirely believed we existed and weren't imagined. We didn't know why we were left with her but after staring at us for 30 minutes she led us to a shack and indicated we should go to sleep. The shack would have been inhospitable and shit beyond reason even if had not been a bloody active beehive, with actual bloody bees! It was a crudely-made shack that was so badly made that I could have built one myself using only my big toe and my tongue. The walls were planks of recycled battered old wood that had been nailed together by someone who I can only assume had no hands, eyes, or a body. The workmanship was so bad an embryo could have done a better job. There was an old warped piece of corrugated tin covering half the roof, leaving a nice gap so any bees that didn't want to use the huge gaps in the walls could use. Inside the shack were five bee hive boxes stacked on top of each other with a tiny space in front of them which was just about big enough for two people to squish into, carefully minding not to impale your face and body on the five million rusty nails were poking out of the wood. The space was not in any way made for human habitation. It was like sleeping in an iron maiden with bees.

We lay down on the filthy floor and wondered what insane set of circumstances had led to us leaving our stable normal lives in London to be sleeping in a beehive in Outer Mongolia. Still we had Internet and what else mattered? Neither of us are scared of bees and compared to wolves, bears, yak, horses and mice they may well have been cute kittens. Apart from the dangerous absolute freezing cold and the odd scream when a bee landed on our faces it was a bizarrely peaceful night.

*

09.09. Sunday. Somewhere in Outer Mongolia.

It was 6am. We lay there hugging as bees buzzed about us. It was minus 15 degrees inside and we were both blue and shaking like crazy. I thought Natalie was asleep and lay there stroking her hair and trying to hug some warmth into her. She opened her beautiful blue eyes and softly said, "It's too cold to cry Darcie, I want to go home."

"Me too" I replied. It broke my heart. We sat there in the beehive not knowing if anyone knew where we were, where Sakal was or whether we'd ever find our way out or whether we'd just disappear, leaving our families to despair over our disappearances.

We tried to cheer ourselves up by talking about how many stories we would be able to tell people and whether they'd even believe us.

"Yeah so we slept in a nail-filled beehive in Outer Mongolia because the driver smashed the car into a tree."

We talked about how lucky we were to be able to travel even if the reason behind it was so shit.

We then decided that we should carry on travelling until either she was blind or we ran out of money. I tried so hard not to cry over her words but it was no good and I sobbed uncontrollably and had to be consoled by Natalie telling me everything would be okay as long as we had each other and there are so many people worse off out there. This made me cry more. She is very matter of fact about her sight loss. She accepts it and moves forward without ever stopping smiling or thinking about others. She is easily the best human on the planet.

We then decided that we should carry on travelling until either she was blind or we ran out of money. I tried so hard not to cry over her words but it was no good and I sobbed uncontrollably and had to be consoled by Natalie telling me everything would be okay as long as we had each other and there's so many worse people off out there. This made me cry more. She is very matter of fact about her sight loss. She accepts it and moves forward without ever stopping smiling or thinking about others. She is easily the best human on the planet.

As we had internet I thought it was only right that I should make a TripAdvisor account for the place and leave a review.

TripAdvisor Reviews: The freezing bee filled iron fucking maiden - Outer bloody Mongolia.

What did you like most about The Freezing Bee Filled Iron Fucking Maiden - Outer bloody Mongolia?
Nothing. It was a fucking bee hive full of fucking bees and rusty fucking nails and was colder than Pingu's fucking testicles on a windy fucking day.

What did you like least about The Freezing Bee Filled Iron Fucking Maiden - Outer bloody Mongolia?
IT WAS A RUSTY NAIL FILLED ACTIVE FUCKING BEEHIVE.

Was the location good for Freezing Bee Filled Iron Fucking Maiden - Outer bloody Mongolia?
Yes. If we would have frozen to death, been stung to death or impaled ourselves to fucking death no one would have ever found us which would have meant they always had hope that we were alive somewhere.

Did you enjoy the food at The Freezing Bee Filled Iron Fucking Maiden - Outer bloody Mongolia?
Well we were surrounded by delicious honey, however the only way to get it would have involved sticking our unprotected freezing hands directly into the bee boxes which would have resulted in being massively stung then in panic we'd try to escape only to impale ourselves face first on rusty nails. So to summerise....

NO.

Would you return to Freezing Bee Filled Iron Fucking Maiden - Outer bloody Mongolia?

Yes if I felt I couldn't take anymore of life and wanted an unusual and creative way to end it all. I think it's safe to say that there were medieval torture devices that were nicer than this place.

Rate Freezing Bee Filled Iron Fucking Maiden - Outer bloody Mongolia from 1-10?

I don't think there's a number low enough. I was never very good at maths. Minus 72 gazillion. Is that even a number? I don't care it's not bloody low enough even if it is.

Two long hours later Sakal appeared a few hundred metres away and came bounding over with a huge grin on his face.

Sakal: Good morning.
Natalie: Well done, you learnt a new word but we don't like you because you're a prick, a drunk driver, aggressive and you don't really like us you're just pretending because you're scared about losing your job. Well, we're not falling for your fake happiness mind games, you wanker.
Me: Um, we need him to help us escape or we'll be here forever and I don't want to spend my life in a nail-filled beehive.
Natalie: Fine.
Me: Sakal, where car?
Sakal: Ploblem.
Me: Yeah, no shit, there's a ploblem, you drove in into a tree whilst pissed you absolute cock-womble. What

are we going to do? Are you going to give us piggyback rides?

Sakal: No ploblem.

Natalie: I think we should take pre-emptive action and kill him before he kills us.

Me: No, I'm not living in a beehive I told you. Let's just see what his plan is.

Natalie: Probably to drink vodka and kill us.

He babbled away to himself laughing and joking regardless of the fact we had no idea what he was on about. He then called someone on the phone and told us we needed to wait. He came over to look inside our beehive and thought it was the funniest thing ever.

"Yes it was hilarious, Sakal. It's a miracle we didn't stab ourselves in the face with rusty nails, freeze to death or be stung to oblivion by a bunch of angry bees."

Half an hour later, a "car" turned up. I say car, it looked like the car you drew in nursery school aged two, except that your picture was probably better. Fuck knows when it was made but we estimated in the year 1712. It was Russian and was utterly, utterly shit. Actually there weren't enough utterlys in there! It was utterly, utterly, utterly shit — wank beyond measure, a turd on wheels. Shitter than a ruptured colostomy bag. Shitter than an explosion at the sewer works. So shit that given the choice of getting in it or rubbing myself with dog food and punching a lion in the balls ... well, I'd get in the car. I'm not completely insane. I could have built a better car out of used toilet paper, poo and Pritt Stick.

Its suspension had broken up decades or centuries earlier and, unable to fix it, they had simply welded the wheels on so, every time we went over anything bigger than a speck of dust, the car would leap two fucking metres in the air causing us to whack our heads on the roof. It was like being inside a washing machine on spin cycle. It would have been more comfortable method of travel to launch ourselves forward into the air, land on our faces, get up and do the same thing again until we reached the destination.

We still had no idea where we were going. We were talking about what possible craziness could happen next. Would we be staying in an igloo, in a lake, inside a camel's rectum? I mean nothing would have surprised us at that point because Mongolia was the land of the weirdest happenings in the world ... and that's when we pulled over next to a guy holding a giant rifle and a duffel bag.

The armed man proceeded to get in without acknowledging our existence even though we happily said hello to him, which was just fucking rude. He proceeded to rest the gun in the foot well but pointing directly at Natalie's head. I said, "Um, please can you point that thing somewhere else if you don't mind?" But he totally blanked me and just laughed with Sakal whilst indicating that it wasn't loaded.

"I couldn't give a fuck whether you think it's loaded or not. I'm not sure whether you've heard of this place called America? Well, in America people get shot daily by being idiots with guns they think they are not loaded so point that fucking thing the other way you absolute fuck dumpling" He tutted and moved it. There was something not quite right about the guy. Mongolians are super friendly but this guy was a prick.

We bounced around in the back for two more hellish hours, reasonably sure we were being driven to our deaths. We then arrived at two small wooden cabins in the middle of the woods.

We were shown into one of them. There were two decrepit old beds either side, one of which was missing a mattress. The room was full of prehistoric farming equipment and about 40 years' worth of dirt. We were not amused, less so because there was no fucking fire and no one slept in Mongolia without a fire because there's a strong chance you wouldn't be waking up again. We'd just spent a night practically in the open, in the beehive and were not prepared for another freezing night. Sakal and the gunman were sleeping in the other cabin which did have a fire, probably beds and other nice things. We told Sakal we wanted to go to a hotel but he just laughed at us so once again we resigned ourselves to the fact that even though we were paying for Sakal and the car we were not in any way in control. Sakal sat us down like we were children and tried to explain something. It involved lots of gestures of shooting. We figured that if they were going to shoot us they probably wouldn't be telling us about it first so we relaxed slightly.

We realised he was trying to say we were there to hunt and this was a hunting place. Great! What better place to bring two vegans than on a fucking hunting trip?

Sakal: Bring forth the gun. Let's go shoot some animals in the face.

Me: No fuck off, you wank shaft. Just how thick are you? You know we don't eat meat yet didn't make the connection between us being unlikely to want to kill an animal? Fuck it's a miracle you remember to breathe.

Maybe we didn't mention to him that were vegetarian enough because something we rarely mention as vegetarians is that we are vegetarian because as vegetarians our vegetarianism is something we rarely mention. (Okay I promise to stop this now).

Sakal and the horrible gunman got in the car and went off to murder some animals for fun whilst we sat in the cabin deciding how to make noodles when there was no fire. We hatched a plan so clever we should have been awarded to the Nobel Prize for goodest cleverest humans in all of humandom. We looked under the bed found a campfire, turned it on and cooked our vegetarian noodles.

There was no sign of Fuckwit and his gun-toting idiot companion so we lay down on the shit single bed and tried to snuggle some warmth into each other. We drifted off into a shivery sleep that lasted for about 20 minutes because that's when the fucking mice turned up. I don't know what the odds on them being in this place were? Maybe they came in our bags? Maybe they made a nest in the bag containing 58 pairs of Natalie's dirty underwear? Who fucking knows but they were there, about 10 of the little squeaky bastards. We didn't even have any food but that didn't stop them looking. They were on our faces, bed, bags and everywhere.

Once again we spent the night in absolute terror, dangerously cold and crying in each other's arms.

Quotes from the last few days:

Natalie: (dropping toothbrush on floor) Now I'm going to have mouse teeth.

Natalie: Hello noodles, my name's Natalie and I will be eating you.

Natalie: What cheese do you like more, Liechestershishire or Golsesteshashire?
Me: There's so much wrong with that question, I don't know where to start.
Natalie: I don't know. I'm not English like you, you stupid head.

Me: I'm going in the shower.
Natalie: What.
Me: I'm going in the shower.
Natalie: What?
Me: I'm going in the shower.
Natalie: Ah I thought you said no bear brushing.
Me: What???

Me: Right, we're in a two man tent and I've just killed a mosquito that was full of blood and neither of us have been bitten … Is there someone else in here?

*

10.09. Monday. Somewhere in Outer Mongolia.

It was around 3am when we reached our limit and decided we had to get the fuck out of anywhere with mice, spiders, bees, beetles, bears or fucking wolves. We just wanted to sleep well just once. We had aged about 10 years in a week and it had stopped being fun. Adventure is great until you're crying every day and sleeping in a fucking weird gunman's house in the middle of nowhere in minus 20 degree weather looking into your soul mates face and it's blue with cold and there's mice running all over you for the second time in three days. So we woke Sakal up at 7am and told him we wanted to leave and go back to the nomad family we loved. He smiled and strangely had everything ready for us to leave within minutes. It all happened so quickly. I think him and Gun Wankshaft got into a tiff or something because he didn't even say goodbye to him. We just loaded up Natalie's knicker bags, got in the shitmobile and set off.

We stopped in town to see his smashed-up car. It really brought home how bad a crash it was. It looked like people would have died in it. It was completely destroyed and anyone that saw it would assume it would be written off and turned into some Coke cans. Yet unbelievably as we sat there watching, he met a man who showed him round it whilst pointing to various parts and shaking his head, then he was given the keys got in and drove it to where we were waiting with open mouths of absolute disbelief and shock. We couldn't believe it. Amazingly it ran and, apart from the odd clunking, screeching and steam, he planned to actually drive it. The front was smashed to bits and bits of metal, plastic and wires hung down. It looked exactly like it had been driven into a tree at high speed. The bonnet which was so ruined its only use would have been to be taken off and placed on the roof of a beehive, had clearly annoyed whoever had tried to fix the engine because they had lost their temper trying to open it and resorted to using what we can only assume was a sledgehammer, then closing it again using the same method. It looked weird with all the odd dents where they had tried to smash it open and then smash it closed again.

The windscreen was still in place but was shattered to bits making the strong Mongolian sun reflect into a billion fragments which blinded anyone in the car, next to the car or within about a three mile radius of the car. It was a wreck of a car. I asked him if it was safe to drive to which Natalie piped in, "I'm sorry, Darcie, but it's clearly not safe to drive in. I can tell that and I'm almost blind."

What he replied was complete gibberish with the word Ulaanbaatar thrown in which we correctly assumed was that he needed to get it fixed in the capital because in the middle of nowhere it wasn't being fixed or being made into cans. It would sit and rust.

"Great plan, Sakal, you take your wreck back to Ulaanbaatar and risk our lives once again whilst doing it. We don't mind being driven for a week off-road in the middle of fucking nowhere in this movable lump of turd."

We didn't have a choice so we got in and were driven off.

Our first stop was back to our beehive area. As we drove over the hill and saw our beehive of doom we both started shouting "No, no fucking way. Fuck off!" Sakal laughed like a gibbon.

Thankfully weren't sleeping there. We were there to see how honey was made. Get this… They use bees! Fucking bees! Who knew? Weird right? It was the best honey we'd ever tasted. It was nice to taste something that was actually nice and wasn't instant noodles or something squeezed out of a horse.

The highlight of the day was finding a supermarket in the "village" - the village consisting of one shop and nothing else. I'd assume the definition of "village" would be more than one building but who am I to judge? The shop was actually good because they sold some new products apart from the four same bloody things all the other shops in the country sold. This one had tinned pears — we bought 10 of those — as well as a tin of green olives and some sausage-flavoured crisps. We were over the Moon. We jumped back in the battered shit-mobile and set off again.

The funny thing about Sakal smashing the car to bits was his enjoyment in the attention it got. Every now and then we'd find a random yurt and we'd all traipse in for fucking horse milk and to ask for directions then the men would all go out to look at the car and they'd roll around laughing. All we were thinking was, how is your drink driving into a tree funny? You caused about 10 grand's worth of damage. I don't know how the fucking thing moves considering it looks like, well, like you drunkenly smashed it into a tree, you stupid twat. Maybe he was a millionaire and thought it was funny. We didn't. We also didn't think it was funny when the gift he gave to the nomads was our fucking crisps.

"I'm sorry cunt features but they're ours we need them. Give them something your own you stupid prick".

A few hours' driving later we stopped on top of a hill so Sakal could fill up the car's juices from the various bottles he needed in order to stop it melting. We decided it would be a good moment to eat because the view was incredible. Green hills as far as the eye could see, huge limestone stacks jutting out of the ground like something out of the Roadrunner cartoons. It was absolutely beautiful.

Natalie was tasked with filling the cooking pan with some water from the stream and came back with water so full of mud and animal shit it looked like poo soup and was totally unusable. But I didn't want to highlight the fact she couldn't see the chunks of dirt and poo floating around so for the greater good we boiled the poo water ready to make fucking instant noodles again. It's all we had eaten in what seemed like a decade and we were so sick of them. Neither of us are foodies, I still battle anorexia and bulimia and I despise food and eating in general. Natalie couldn't care less about food either. We are the worst dinner guests ever. Give me a raw carrot, a Granny Smith and a raw red pepper and I'll be happy. Anything else and I'll have to pretend I like it whilst trying not to spew it into the toilet at the earliest conceivable opportunity. As we tucked into the food it was Natalie's turn to have a tantrum.

Natalie: FUCK INSTANT NOODLES! Fuck them. They're stupid and I fucking hate them
Sakal: Ploblem?

Natalie: Yes there's a ploblem, Sakal, we have nothing to eat apart from these fucking noodles. We didn't like them to begin with and we've eaten nothing fucking else for fucking months. We did have crisps but you gave them away didn't, you wank features? Oh and to top it off today they taste decidedly faecal for some reason.

Sakal: No ploblem.

Natalie: Oh go away. Sakal. Go get drunk and crash into a tree. That's a joke — don't really do that or I swear to god I will pull your face off and make a mask out of it to scare children with.

Me: Fucking hell, Natalie that's a bit harsh. Good job he probably thinks you're complimenting him.

Natalie: Fuck him. Hey I forgot the pears. We have pears and olives. Okay, sorry Sakal. Darcie, bring forth the pears. This shit's going down.

We obviously didn't have a tin opener and the can obviously wasn't a ring pull but we did we fret? No. We were hardened Mongolian veterans so we took the one and only knife and hacked them out of there in five minutes of demented stabbing fury. Even Sakal looked over at the stabbing fury and swallowed hard. The pears were glorious. They made the noodles so much easier to eat. Not that we mixed them, that would be disgusting, noodles and tinned pears, bleughh.

No, we ate one can whilst we waited for the noodles to cook in the shit-filled water and another can afterwards to take the taste of eating noodles and poo away.

As we sat there, Sakal thought he'd teach us something: how to tell the different animal poos and how to say them in Mongolian. It was a skill I am sure we will never need.

"Hi, see that lump of horse shit there? Well in Mongolian that's called *mernibas*, yes, and that there is *honibas*, and that one is *Darcie-bas*. Sorry,
I really needed to go."

Having learnt the name and how to tell the difference between about five types of poop, we cracked open the olives. Olives are strange things. When you grow up you can't understand why anyone would eat them because they taste worse than the No More Nail-Biting solution. Then one day, overnight, you like them and they are delicious. Well, olives don't exist in the Asian diet so they have never had time to decide what to make of them and their weird fucked-up taste. We had never even seen them in Asia before so I don't know why there was a single dusty can in a shop in the middle of nowhere in Mongolia. They'd probably been there for five decades. Maybe a Spaniard had traded them for some horse juice? Anyway we opened them and offered Sakal one.

His reaction was so funny we laughed to the point of not being able to breathe. He took the can and instead of taking out an olive like any normal person would do, he gulped down some juice, then, in absolute disgust, spat it everywhere whilst shaking and pulling the funniest faces imaginable all, whilst shouting profanities and trying to hit us. It took us thirty minutes for us to stop laughing. Each time he spat and shouted at us we'd roll around crying with laughter. It was so, so funny. He thought it was a wind-up and people didn't really eat them which is funny because that's how we feel in a country that where every meal comes out of a horse's tits.

After numerous hours in the car we eventually found our nomad family who had no idea we would be turning up especially in wrecked car. They were over the moon to see us, as were we to see them. We even enjoyed the alcoholic horse milk ritual with them. We noticed pretty bloody quickly that our yurt had gone. It just wasn't there anymore; there was just the flattened circle where it once was. They'd taken it to the winter location, so we didn't have anywhere to stay and they kindly offered the floor in their tiny yurt. I'm sure it was a huge compliment but this was without doubt the dirtiest place on Earth. It was tiny and did I mention filthy? There was food, cheese, animal blood and guts, a goat head (seriously), rubbish and just grossness on the filthy gross floor. Not to mention there were already five people staying there. We wanted to stay anywhere but the floor and insisted we sleep in the car. This for them was insulting. They insisted we sleep with them and we struggled to think of a way to get out of it without insulting them. After almost an hour of trying I used all my four brain cells and produced my asthma inhaler and waved it round talking about how we needed to stay in the car. The argument made absolutely no sense but waving the inhaler around did the trick and we would be sleeping in Sakal's wank pit which was smashed to smithereens. We were so relieved.

We'd bought the family the customary gift of alcohol. We'd heard they like whisky but it wasn't in their means to get it so when we pulled out two bottles of Bells whisky we had picked up in one of the shops, they were exceptionally pleased. Out came the single glass which Bodo topped up and began the ritual. Fifth in line was Natalie who knocked it back without a problem. Then it came to me but I insisted I couldn't drink and would never drink again ever and so the bullying started. Bizarrely, Natalie joined in the bullying again. I gave her the look of death and reminded her that her hair still had my vomit in it and stank from last time I drank but she was more concerned with the fact that 10 nomads were deeply offended at my lack of drinking so joined their side. I always hated whisky anyway. People are obsessed with it but they're all wrong because it tastes like shit. No it's not subjective or personal taste.

Whisky Face: Mmm, I'm getting a hint of peat and smoke. Can you taste it?
Me: Um no. It tastes like ass.
Whiskey Face: I'm also getting a hint of treacle and, mmm, yes a touch of charcoal.
Me: What the fuck are you on about? It tastes like the shit alcohol poison it is.

I lasted another four minutes of intense bullying before I gave up. I was instantly wasted as was everyone else. The night drew to a close with traditional folk singing and then my third recital of Baa Baa Black Sheep which I recited with such passion and thoughtfulness it actually sounded good. I even got a round of applause. We happily retreated to the car which was so luxurious compared to the previous week we fell asleep smiling. It was freezing cold, cramped and uncomfortable and smelled of petrol from the broken engine. It was extremely unsafe but we couldn't been any happier. I was so drunk however that I would have slept peacefully on a bed of nails, at the bottom of a lake, with mice. Actually no not the mice. Fuck mice.

*

11.09. Tuesday. Somewhere in Outer Mongolia.

I woke up and knew instantly. I forced myself to sleep in the hope it was a nightmare. It wasn't. I had peed the bed/car. It's unfortunately not that rare an occurrence in my life. It happened daily until an embarrassingly old age (23). Why am I writing this? Hey everyone I'm a known bed wetter… Anyway, it had never happened in someone else's car before. Now his car was not only smashed to bits but smelled like piss. I can only imagine him handing back the car to whoever actually owned it.

"Oh yeah sorry I smashed the car to pieces … ah yes … the smell … that girly boy bastard pissed in it. It's all his, her, its fault, he caused the crash too by being gay! Let's fucking get it and make it pay.

Natalie is normally understanding of my little problem because I usually only do it when I have nightmares so that means it not my fault, but drinking whisky and being comatose, well that is my fault and now she was covered in my piss and there was no shower. I felt so dirty and ashamed. I have no idea why I'm writing this. It's so embarrassing. The morning was spent trying to sort out the wet sleeping bags that we still desperately needed. There was nothing we could do.

They could never be washed because they were about 50 centimetres thick, they weighed about 12 kilos each and were fucking massive and far too big for any washing machine. We didn't use them as sleeping bags because it was too cold to not snuggle each other so we opened them into blankets which allowed us to snuggle, keep warm and for me to cover them both, and Natalie in pee. In the end we realised there were no options. It was raining so we couldn't leave them outside and so they'd have to fester in the car with closed windows. It was just horrendous.

I don't know whether the whisky was fake or bad but everyone was severely hung-over and was vomiting. It was like a scene out of the apocalypse. People everywhere vomiting and holding their heads in agony. They had given me a wolf skin and been so incredibly generous and hospitable and we had returned the favour by giving them alcohol poisoning.

We sat around the small yurt all comparing how hideous our hangovers were including Natalie who thankfully also felt like shit. Bodo was in a total mess. He had spent the night vomiting and looked green. His approach was hair of the dog so he hid a beer in the sleeve of his traditional dress. Jeffna however found out about it and so ensued a semi-serious play fight with him refusing to let go of it whilst she tried to prise it from his hands. It was pretty funny. It doesn't matter where you are in the world, whether you're in a yurt in Outer Mongolia or a hot shot in New York, the same argument is played out every day where the bloke wants to drink more and the wife is having none of it. As I mentioned earlier, he was a hulk of a man but the fighting was futile because he could never win against an angry woman.

Even though we could barely move with our hangovers it was decided that we'd help erect our old yurt on the new winter position so we hiked for an hour over a mountain to reach it. It took about an hour to build and was fascinating. It started with the central columns, the two wooden poles that hold the roof up. Once they are in position everyone helps to try and move the circular trellis wall to be a uniform circle around them, next the roof beams are placed on the roof and onto the top of the trellis. Then it's just a case of putting on the eight layers of fabrics that make up the walls. The fabrics are all wool based and natural. I don't reckon they have changed in millennia. Then the furniture is placed inside and some old tattered bits of rug placed crudely over the grass. It was hard physical work which I am naturally shit at. I am about as strong as an anaemic kitten that's fallen into a tub of glue and it didn't take them long to realise it. I genuinely do try! Natalie the short thin pretty blonde girl on the other hand is as strong as an ox and loves manual work so she was called to help with everything whilst I carried furniture, made coffee and cleaned. For them moving house was as normal as washing clothes or cleaning up:

"Oh just moving my house five kilometres away won't be long." For us it was out of this world and we felt honoured to have been part of it.

Building the yurt in the freezing cold wind and rain had chilled us to the core. Even with the fire and chimney erected and lit into an inferno, we couldn't get warm.

We were wearing everything we owned covered with our maroon tops which were disgustingly dirty. Nothing had been washed in more than four weeks; everything was covered in the shit and drool from five species of different animals, sweat, mud, BO and perfume — which only went to make our repulsive smell that much worse. We hadn't showered in so long we had both started to dream about showers. Our skin was sticky and gross and that was before Natalie decided to make us wipe ourselves down with a dirty wet sock, I had vomited in her hair, we bathed in an egg stinking pool of filth and I cleverly decided to cover us both in my pee. The only good thing about our state was that no self-respecting wolf would eat anything that smelled as bad as us. Well, at least that's what I said to Natalie to make her less angry about being covered in piss.

You know sometimes you do things that are really stupid and you know they're stupid and you'll regret them but you can't seem to stop yourself from doing them anyway? Well despite being dangerously cold and shivering I spotted my horse through the gap in the yurt and thought it would be a good idea to ride the thing to see if I could once again overcome my crazy phobia of them. Shivering cold I walked over and said hello before climbing aboard. The horse was lazy and refused to listen and instead spent most of the time eating grass. I didn't have the heart to assert my command over its desire to eat so looked like I was shitter than I actually was. As I sat there on a horse whilst it did what it wanted, Jeffna came running over and assumed that I wanted to help herd the cows and that's why I was on the horse. I couldn't refuse, so off I went to try and move the cows. Unfortunately for me the horse knew I was a bit of a wimp/absolute pussy and made the logical and correct assumption that it was in charge.

Me: Oh, are we going there, horse? Well I'd really appreciate it if we could go and get that cow instead. No? We're going to stand in the stream and shit in it? You do know this is our drinking water right? I bet you do, you filthy beast. Come on, come on, just move, I promise I'll give you a semi-mouldy bendy carrot I found in the car. No? Fine then be like that. I happen to know some French people that would find you very interesting ... to put in their mouths and eat. No, not listening? Well fuck you then. Natalie, Natalie help me. This stupid bastard won't listen to me.

Natalie: Darcie why are you just sat there? Why aren't you at least helping with the cows?

Me: I can't. It knows who's boss

Natalie: Well, make it know you're the boss

Me: Yeah how?

Natalie: With authority.

Me: It's a horse. I can't get off and explain the hierarchy of farm life. It knows I'm a pussy.

Natalie: Assert your authority on it.

Me: Stop saying that. What do you want me to do? Punch it into submission? Yeah, hold on. I'll just get off and punch it on its stupidly long nose to show it who's boss.

Natalie: Why are you so rubbish?

Me: I'm on a fucking horse, Natalie, a fucking horse. I fucking hate horses. You know I hate them, so how is this me being rubbish? This is me being great. I am a fucking champion for being up here. This is about as brave as I get.

Natalie: Well you don't look like a champion you look

like you're insulting them by just sitting on the horse as it eats grass and they're doing all the work. Why are you so weak? Even the dog thinks it's above you.

Me: Fuck you. You want me to start beating dogs into submission too? Or would you prefer I assert my dominance the way dogs do to each other? By dry humping them? Are you saying you want me to start humping people's dogs, Natalie?

Natalie: Jesus, what the fuck is wrong with your brain? You are mental. Here I'm going to help you.

She then grabbed the horse's rope and dragged it towards the cows. All whilst shouting at the cows in an insane voice which freaked the fuck out of the cows, the horse and me.

Me: Um, Natalie please don't make that noise it's terrifying and the horse is going to bolt.

Natalie: Shut up Darcie, you idiot. This is what you do to move the cows, they don't like it so they move.

Me: Yes, but it's not just the cows that don't like it. It's me and the horse. It's terrifying me and making me want to cry.

Natalie: You are such an idiot. I don't know why I married you.

Me: Well it wasn't for my horse bloody skills and bloody cow herding ability.

Horse: Yes, please stop making that noise it's scaring the shit out of me.

Okay so the horse didn't say that but it was definitely thinking it. The nomads made the cow moving noise too but Natalie's version was absolutely insane. I made her do it again to record it and I still use it as a ringtone. It's so demented. In the end we managed to herd a single cow and that's only down to Natalie's crazy noises and the fact the cow had special needs of the head. One of my favourite images from the whole trip is being sat terrified on a horse whilst Natalie pulled it along with the rope trying to move cows.

Apart from the piss-stinking sleeping bags we slept okay in the brand new yurt. It was actually a relatively decent night apart from the odd insult about the stench of pee that Natalie threw my way. Mongolians don't even use sleeping bags or duvets. They instead use, wait for it … carpet! They are obsessed with the stuff and happily put it on almost every surface. What should we put on the walls? Carpet. What should we use as blankets? Carpet. What should we place on our windscreens? Carpet. It's fucking everywhere and it's itchy and well, it's fucking carpet. It should be on the floor and nowhere else.

*

12.09. Wednesday. Somewhere in Outer Mongolia.

In the morning we both tried to make a fire and succeeded ... in filling the room with smoke again. So, slightly angry at our persistent failure at making fire I thought, right fuck this shit. I grabbed the box of tinder and the rubbish bag. I ignored Natalie's pleas to stop being an idiot and emptied the lot into the fire. Then I added the mounds of dried horse cheese we'd been given and were hiding in our bags. I sprayed the whole lot with hand sanitizer and lit it. It went up instantly like a firework. Apart from the fact I'd used their entire supply of tinder and all our hand sanitizer I felt like an honorary nomad. To top the triumph off, Bodo walked in and nodded in approval at our fire. We would have enjoyed the moment of approval more had we both been shitting it that he'd look inside the fire and see precious dried horse cheese burning away which would possibly the most insulting thing imaginable to the family and nomads in general. I reckon we'd have been executed and hung from a bridge — if they had bridges. Either way it'd be more polite to slap their grandparents in the tits than burn horse cheese. But it was undoubtedly better than telling them we found it vile and it made us gag. Thankfully horse cheese was good at burning - its only attribute.

Sakal had kept his distance from us for a few days. He was helping with the animals and odd jobs for the family. We were happy to avoid him because we were equally as sick of him, however we decided we had to get to the Internet so we could once again remind our families (not mine) that we were still alive so we went to find him to ask him to do the very job he was being paid for and drive us to town so we had phone and Internet signal. He huffed and puffed and we stood there with folded arms. We couldn't believe the cheek of the guy. So far we had driven into a tree, stayed in a beehive, two mouse infested fuck holes, a car, a wolf and bear infested forest in a fucking tent and now he didn't want to drive us in the car we'd already paid him for. He realised his options were either being pestered/bitch slapped to death by two angry women or driving us so, like a good little boy, he got in the car. We got to town with everyone asking him what the fuck had happened which he was most pleased about because drunkenly smashing a car and risking lives is hilarious in Mongolia. We didn't care, we had Internet and were happier (and probably dirtier) than pigs in shit.

We then went to the shop to buy some vodka for the family as parting gifts. Only things got very weird very quickly. In the shop, seemingly waiting for us, were lots of people we'd met around. I think we'd timed our visit with the shop's weekly delivery so everyone had gone to get their supply of sweets, vodka and pickles. The English-speaking woman and her husband were there along with lots of other faces we'd seen over the weeks. It was really nice. We were thrilled. We could now talk to Sakal through the woman. We wanted to say, please tell him he is a shithead and the worst driver known to man, but we thought it might not be so clever. We chatted about our travels and Sakal told an undoubtedly bullshit story about how his car got ruined. It was really nice. Then the vodka was opened.

The English speaker's husband opened it and gave us our shot in the shared single glass. With 20 faces turned to Natalie, she only managed to refuse four times before the bullying got to a level you couldn't say no to. She drank a tiny sip to the rowdy displeasure of the group who were all berating her to drink the rest. She obliged, to cheers. I didn't even try to say no. What was the point? I drank it, gagged, ran outside and was sick. I haven't drank since and never will. All I need to do is avoid Mongolia and nomads and it'll be easy. Sakal had about 10 large shots and was clearly drunk. His eyes were red and he was loud and annoying. We told him that he wasn't driving, I'd drive and that was that. He didn't argue.

We stayed in the shop for about an hour talking to an ever increasingly number of locals. Natalie had to explain our relationship and about me on three separate occasions and more people came to see the strange foreigners. The third time someone asked what kind of fuck-beasts were we? And one of the people who had already heard the explanation and who understood it better tried to explain it to them, then they in turn got helped by someone else. It was a special moment. I wish I knew what they actually said. Still they were nice about it and after they all laughed in our faces through a mixture of shock, embarrassment and disbelief they nodded approvingly as their brains tried to work out if they'd actually heard it right.

I think in that five minute conversation about Transgenderism and all things gay and lesbians, we influenced and educated enough people to make a real change. Huge changes in culture start from small beginnings. A lot of people were in that shop and they would all have gone home and told their family about the lesbos that weren't actually that bad and so the domino effect of opinion would start. We promised to return, we hugged everyone and left.

We all assumed we'd be driving home but no, Sakal instead directed us to another yurt. We were ordered into it where we were force-fed horse shit then more vodka was opened. We sat there as a cauldron of sheep guts and the sheep's head boiled on the fire. It looked fucking disgusting. We just refused the alcohol and blanked them, when the bullying started. We didn't know them and there were only three of them so we told them to fuck off in a polite a way as possible. Sakal at this point was paralytic and could barely stand up. We demanded to leave to which he replied with his fourth and fifth English words, "Five minutes" This would be his favourite sentence for the following hour.

Sakal: Five minutes, five minutes.
Me: No, you sheep shagging turd burglar, we're going.
Sakal: Five minutes.
Natalie: In five minutes it'll be your head and guts bubbling away in that cauldron, you prick.
Me: Um, Natalie shut up. I think he knows that word.
Natalie: What word? Prick? … Fuck he does as well. Just joking Sakal don't kill us you wank shaft.
Me: Jesus Christ.

Eventually we got in the wreck and set off. Natalie adamantly told him we wanted to go home to which he replied, "No ploblem." The drive would have been fun if it is wasn't for the super loud idiot singing in my ear as loud as he could, the car making some seriously fucked up noises, the wheels pointing in different directions, the fact we needed to top up the water in the engine every five minutes and the smell of burning plastic.

An hour later we came across another yurt, not bloody ours though. We were livid.

Me: No Sakal you take us back, right bloody now.
Sakal: No ploblem.
Me: I swear if I hear you say "no ploblem" one more time I'm going rip your arms off and beat you to death with them.
Sakal: Bodo dada.
Me: I don't give a fuck who lives here. Literally if the

fucking Queen is in there with a plate of fresh fruit, a shower and a bag of money I wouldn't fucking give a fuck. You take us back right now.
Natalie: Prick.
Me: Natalie, no. I don't want to die

I was too angry to talk. I'd had loud singing in my ear for an hour and the driving was intense, purely off-road, swerving burrows, rocks and cliffs. I wanted to cry but was too angry for that. Sakal looked at me and said, "Okay five minute Boda house, no ploblem" We went into the yurt and had the usual festering hideousness practically inserted into our mouths all whilst having to smile and act delighted. Then the family of four, including a woman who wouldn't stop farting, all came out, got onto a single motorbike and told us to follow them. Sakal's singing had gone to the next level and was making us both envisage killing him in cold blood. Sakal knew we were talking about him and didn't like it. We didn't care and thought his being angry would at least stop him from singing. No. He just got louder.

He then decided to take a rather keen interest in Natalie's boobs and was facing the back gawping at her which made us both exceptionally angry.

Natalie rather calmly told him, "Sakal stop staring at my tits you pervert, they're the same as your Mum's that you see every day."

Good job he didn't understand us because that might have got us killed. He then turned his attention to me and was asking questions that I assumed were bad whilst looking at my body with a disgusted look on his face. I slammed my hand on the dashboard making a loud noise and told him, enough now. He promptly shut up.

We followed the motorbike for an hour in the pitch dark whilst trying not to die. The conditions were not good. The wrecked car was starting to make some really weird noises and we couldn't see anything because the window was smashed into a billion pieces and had fogged up. It was easily one of the most stressful and dangerous moments of our lives. It was an absolute relief to turn up at our yurt. We went inside expecting to sit down and relax but here were about 12 people waiting there. The men were all sat on the floor at the back and the women on the beds round the sides. They had all been drinking and were happy to see us. We were then told to make of all things Spaghetti Bolognese and were handed two spaghetti packets a huge tin of tomato sauce and a lump of dead animal. Honesty, the weird shit that happened in Mongolia is endless.

We didn't even question the weirdness and instantly began chopping onions. We delegated the chopping of the meat to Sakal who was happily telling them how funny it was we were angry with him. We honestly wanted to kill him.

We made so much food so quickly, it was quite an achievement. We went from the stress of driving a wrecked car with a drunk dick to stressfully cooking for 15 anxious, hungry nomads. It was so odd. The meal turned out amazingly well which was a surprise. Especially because we'd cooked with meat which we don't eat because as vegetarians we don't eat meat because we're vegetarians. (Okay I promise to stop). We enjoyed watching them tuck in, have seconds and then want more. Even better than the meal was the fact we'd found the smallest watermelon known to man in town and were going to stuff our faces with it. But instead we chopped it up for them. I doubt handing them wads of money would have made them happier. They fucking loved it.

We had no concept of what day it was and had no idea that it was our last night before setting off back to the capital and civilisation. We would have savoured the yurt one last time, but we were too tired and passed out instantly.

Quotes of the last few days:

Me: Tomorrow we have a toilet.
Natalie: I know. I'm going to kiss it.
Me: I'm going to lick it out.
Natalie: That's gross.
Me: Same as licking you out.
Natalie: What the hell is wrong with you?
Me: A lot.
Natalie: I'm going to tell the toilet I love it and it's my best friend. Then I'm going to fuck it.
Me: And you said I was gross. How do you even fuck a toilet?
Natalie: Let me show you.
Me: What's wrong with you?
Natalie: A lot.

Me: I can't imagine anything worse than knickers made from badger fur.

Natalie: Where the fuck did that come from? What do you actually think about?
Me: I was just thinking.
Natalie: About badger knickers.
Me: Yes.
Natalie: I married a psychopath.

Natalie: I'm not buying *Always Ultra* anymore. They're just the same as own brand ones. There's
no difference.
Me: Yes there is, with *Always* you can wear a leotard and do backflips and rollerblade with puppies every day.

Me: Tired? Imagine Dopey's narcoleptic brother Coma-y. Well imagine he'd just had eight pints of Rohypnol, some sleeping pills and a lecture about paperclips by Ken Barlow and you're getting close to how tired I am.

*

13.09. Thursday. Somewhere in Outer Mongolia.

So our last day was upon us which was handy because we were absolutely done. We loaded up the wrecked car one last time and were handed about three kilos of horse milk products which we thanked them profusely for. We made our teary goodbyes and promised to return. We jumped in the car and set off. We spent 11 straight hours driving off-road until we hit a road, an actual road. I mean it was shit, had missing bits and potholes the size of cars but still it was a road and roads lead places. Four hours later we were in Ulaanbaatar and civilisation.

We checked into our hotel ran to the room and then the moment finally came where we had a shower. We couldn't wait for each other so both ripped off our festering clothes and got in. It was better than sex. Pure happiness and orgasmic feelings of joy and relief. We swooned making loud sexual noises and laughing uncontrollably with joy. The water was black with filth. Our hair took more effort. We used a full bottle of shampoo between us and a full bottle of conditioner. We had to leave it in for an hour then gently start to brush out the knots. We both lost that much hair we considered knitting it together to make some socks.

Feeling like we'd been re-born, we took our clothes to be washed. Fuck knows what they thought when we handed them a plastic bag with clothes so smelly and filthy they probably contained an entire ecosystem of bacterial filth. There's no way they didn't catch a disease from handling them. The filth that would have come off them must have broken the washing machine. You'd have to throw it away and get a new one.

*

Epilogue

I still have my maroon fluffy top and occasionally put it on to see Natalie's reaction. She normally screams at me not to come near her wearing it.

We spent five days in Ulaanbaatar which, to put it nicely, is a Soviet shitfest. No offence Ulaanbaatar but I have been to nicer toilets. Everyone was drunk. Well, all the men and they thought nothing of shouting at us. I feel very sorry for the majority of Mongolian woman who had the ability not be constantly drunk and have to deal with the smashed men being drunken idiots a lot of the time. Nothing of particular interest happened. We showered relentlessly just to feel clean. We ate food that wasn't instant noodles and didn't contain any poo. We drank water that didn't contain poo which was also nice. It was just a lovely poo-free existence. Natalie started saying "hello" to the toilet every day and told it she wouldn't leave it ever again. We bought more weird shit for Christmas presents including 15 pairs of camel wool socks. Everyone loves socks for Christmas, it's a well-known fact. Not really. They are shit gifts and anyone who thinks otherwise is wrong. Still camel wool is weird and unique at least, the fact that it's the worst substance known to man doesn't matter because they're cool, until you wear them.

Mongolia was a life-changing country for us. It's so very different from Western life. It was a bit like going back in time. Their lives are ridiculously extreme and hard and we are little snowflake bitches. The hardship they live with is just so extreme. And as for the poo... poo is everywhere, on the ground, on our clothes, in the bed, in the water on our faces. Then there's the living space and the bees, spiders, beetles, the fucking mice, the bears and wolves, the freezing cold, the food, the fucking horse milk, horse cheese, horse milk alcohol. Jesus just hearing the words horse milk alcohol - why would that shit exist? Why would it be sacred? It's vile beyond description and you're forced to drink it. I don't want to ever consume something that came out of a horse again. Holy bejesus.

The alcohol bullying, the fact everyone is drunk half the time. Just stop drinking vodka! It's 11am, seriously. The milking of a hundred cows by hand at five in the morning regardless of the weather which is always freezing. The milking of semi-wild horses which are inherently dangerous. The endless hard work, day in and day out, all year, every year. No holidays, no sick days. Nomads are the toughest people we have ever met. They're are amazing people and we learned so much from them. Everyone should go.

Just remember to these handy tips when staying with them:

1. Horses are absolute dicks.
2. All horse consumption is vile and you're going to have to pretend you enjoy stuffing the mouldy breast milk of a horse into your mouth.
3. Try not to vomit horse products out over the lovely accommodating family
4. At some point you're going to have to poop and 30 people will be watching.
5. Make sure when you climb a mountain to poop in peace, make sure it's not their sacred mountain where they bury their dead.

5. Not being a full-on alcoholic is frowned upon and you will be punished for it... with alcohol.
6. Enjoy yourself, it's life changing.....

*

Next…..

Right, so that's it for now. I am working on the next volume where we face the most amazing and absurd experiences you could wish for/dread. Follow our new adventures in India where we nearly got kidnapped and killed by a psychotic Taliban-loving taxi driver in Kashmir, nearly die on a speedboat in Laos, nearly die on in a tree house in a jungle in Laos, and see the beauty and insanity of Vietnam and Myanmar where we nearly die (not that I ever exaggerate of course!)

We stay in Cambodia in a hotel with a missing wall and roof and then to Morocco which was so traumatising I can't bring myself to start writing it. I then had a minor surgery and ended up with necrosis, nearly losing my nose and becoming disfigured and then Natalie's eyes take a turn for the worse and then something unbelievable happens. All in all, it'll make for one hell of a read.

So stay tuned or drop me a message to encourage me to get on and write it. We are now back in the UK and I am performing my stand up so come and see me make a tit of myself.

All you actually own is time so make sure you enjoy it.

Darcie Silver
xxx

Printed in Great Britain
by Amazon